PRAISE FOR
Finding Flowers in a little pile of sh*t

"Don Hanley's courageous and ruthlessly honest memoir offers the reader a blueprint for continually building and remodeling one's life.
A fascinating and inspiring narrative."

—Ellen Terich, Ph.D, psychotherapist, educator

"Everyone's life is a story waiting to be shared and Don Hanley has shared his in this brutally honest rendition of his story. He reveals his life challenges resulting in victories and defeats. joys and sorrows, fulfillment and emptiness. He discovers his true self and his worth as a true human being when he experiences being loved."

—Robert P. Merz, Ed.D, University Administrator in Division of Student Affairs and Graduate Faculty in the College of Education

"The author of *Finding Flowers (in a little pile of sh*t)* knows that I don't care much for the title. But the book is great! It is a heartfelt, passionate and insightful telling of the early years of his life. And what a life that has been. It exhausted me just keeping up with all Don went through, all the sorrows and struggles. Plus the triumphs. Fortunately his self-deprecating humor and his growing awareness of the complexities of the human condition kept me going, anxious to know what comes next. And now I also know why the title is important to him."

—John Costanzo, Ph.D, College Administrator, Rector, American College, Leuven, Belgium

"An invigorating account of a remarkably rich life, *Finding Flowers in a Little Pile of Sh*t* is gripping both in the life events it chronicles as well as in the refreshing world view it explores. From his birth in Nebraska and formative years in Kansas, California, and South Dakota, to his seminary experiences and beyond, Don Hanley's life journey is an adventure in belonging, connection, education, and meaning making. The memoir takes us, the readers, on a voyage of intellectual, emotional and spiritual growth where we uncover not only Don's experiences, but also how to live life not as casual visitors but as real participants.
Highly recommended!"

—Ghada Osman, Ph.D., LMFT, Faculty & Mental Health Clinical Supervisor, MiraCosta College, Professor Emerita, San Diego State University

Finding Flowers in a little pile of sh*t

ALSO BY DON HANLEY

Love by its First Name

Wrestling With God

A New World of Hope

How to Live with Yourself and Enjoy it

How to Live with Your Partner and Enjoy it

Finding
Flowers

in a little pile of sh*t

a memoir

Don Hanley

TOP READS PUBLISHING, LLC

Vista, California

ISBN: 978-1-970107-39-5 (paperback)
ISBN: 978-1-970107-40-1 (ebook)

Library of Congress Control Number: 2023901513

Finding Flowers in a little pile of sh*t is published by: Top Reads Publishing, LLC, USA

For information please direct emails to:
publisher@topreadspublishing.com

Cover design, book layout and typography: Teri Rider & Associates

Printed in the United States of America

Dedication

I dedicate this book to my parents and siblings, all deceased but did help me survive, and to my wife Anne and daughters Elen and Micaela who still help me to cherish the adventure of my life.

Family Tree

Mother

Margaret Taylor, 1896 - 1969

Father

Dennis Hanley, 1891 - 1947

Siblings and their children

Marie, born 1911, married Jim Abney
    children: Susan, Jim, Valerie

Glen, born 1917, married Elsie 1945
    children: Donald, Jerry

Bill, born 1921, married Helen
    children: Steve, Judy, Barbara, Janis, Nancy

Bob, born 1922, married Ann
    children: Bob, Vickie, Bruce

Agnes, born 1924

Jack, born 1926

Jim, born 1928, married Kay 1948
    children: Mary Kay, JD, Patrick

Bonnie, born 1931, married Jim White 1953
    children: Terry, Shelly, Kelly, Tony

Donald then Don, born 1933, married Anne 1970
    children: Elena Marie, Micaela Denise

Patty, born 1936, married Harold Grenoble 1971

Don is the only one living in 2023

Preface

"May you never live in interesting times," is an old Irish proverb. Well, I have lived for nearly ninety years in very interesting times. And I have spent a great deal of that time trying to figure myself out. And for the past year, I have been putting those thoughts on paper.

A friend once asked me, "Don, are you driving or are you driven?" So, I started examining my life, hoping to find what is driving my thoughts of all the people I have worked with as a psychotherapist, taught in graduate school and supervision, and that I have encouraged to love and be astonished by their own journeys in life. I realized I had never taken a good look at my own story.

I had dismissed a modern myth I heard many years ago: the story of a man who, as a boy, heard that there was a picture somewhere that could explain the meaning of life and of God. When the boy grew into a man, he began a search for that picture and traveled the entire world. He visited every art museum and gallery he could find on six continents. When he was in his eighties, he spent long hours exhaustively searching through a vast gallery in Rome. Late in the afternoon, feeling nearly spent, he returned to the library's entrance and sat on a beautiful antique bench. As he sat there, he looked across the foyer and saw an enchanting picture. He was mesmerized and beguiled by the work and walked up close to get a better look. Suddenly, it hit him—it was a mirror. The exquisite portrait of a tired old man was him! Behind the old man, in a hazy picture, were hundreds of people of all ages.

I realize that story is about every person. One of my mentors said that every person's life is worth a novel. I now would say many novels, and if we climb deeply into that mirror, we'll discover a meaningful story that will be a reflection of a more prosperous life, depending on how you have responded to the gifts you were born, given, and then decided to use for your own and others benefit.

At eighty-nine, I have completed a portion of my own written self-portrait. It starts in the Dust Bowl of the early 1930s in the Sand Hills of northwestern Nebraska. I was the ninth child of Dennis Hanley and Margaret Taylor. Two of the nine died only months before I was born. It was March 1933, the worst year of the Great Depression. Both Mom and Dad were in their own great depression and desperation about how to take care of nine children.

My story is also a bit of a portrait of my family. My parents' journey started in 1911—a twenty-year-old dirt farmer and his fifteen-year-old wife. Their routine Catholic faith gave them some hope that life had meaning and that they must adhere to a certain set of beliefs and rules and, if they did, they and their children would go to heaven. Theirs was a blind faith, as they did not have the educational background nor the time to examine the content of that faith. They were of the class of the working poor that took pride in just owning forty acres of land—until the drought and the economic depression hit in 1930.

I don't know what kind of consciousness I came into this world with, but I know that, very early in my life, I wondered about God and who He (or She) was and how He operated in the world. Maybe it started when I was six years old and in the first grade when my dad called me a "worthless little pile of shit." I had been sent home from school after wetting my pants. My first working title for this book was "Searching For Flowers in a Worthless Little Pile of Shit." In the early years, I don't think I found many flowers in my life. I wondered what kind of God would have a mean nun and mean priest serve Him. I have heard hundreds of similar stories from clients and students of different religions—or no religion—who have had similar stories and the same challenge of figuring out the meaning of life.

Join me on my journey, and you will notice that merely believing the traditional truths and myths of Catholic Christianity was not sufficient for me. I hope it is an interesting story you'll enjoy and maybe learn from—as I did from just remembering my past.

One

HOW OUR FAMILY BEGAN: THE HOMESTEADERS

This first chapter is a composite of different stories told to me by my mother, father, and sister, Marie. I believe it is essential in trying to understand my own life and maybe help you understand me, yourself, and others.

—⊗⊗⊗—

In late December 1911, my mom, Margaret—a short, thin, dark-haired teenager prematurely introduced to adult life—held my eldest newborn sister, Marie. I imagine she held her close as she entered the small door of her new home. It was a sod house recently finished by our young father, Dennis—still a muscular, twenty-year-old, red-haired adolescent himself. I'd like to think Mom saw baby Marie as the most marvelous being ever to come into her life. The only other positive thing that day was that Dennis had found a little coal to keep a fire going while he went to pick her and the baby up from his mother's house, five miles away. I don't know which was worse for her, the jostling of the old wagon or the bitter wind blowing over the hills. The fire was only embers, but the tiny one-room house was still somewhat warm.

The structure was built on a slight rise in the middle of the 320 acres of the homestead. Perhaps that day, she saw Dennis kneeling and putting a strange wood into the little pot-bellied stove. She didn't know that she would become very familiar with this peculiar fuel—dried cow dung.

Still holding her baby girl, she sat down on one of only two regular chairs near an old kitchen table, looked around the little dirt hut, and shuddered. Margaret had never seen a house made from sod bricks dug up from the prairie and held together by the deep native grass. She cried when she realized that the floor was dirt—it wasn't even a floor.

Margaret was born and raised in Chicago and had no idea that people lived in such houses anywhere on Earth. She had accompanied her dad to Nebraska after he lost his business and decided to become a farmer and start with a homestead—320 free acres if he agreed to improve the land. Now, this house was hers and her husband's "improved" homestead. On the bumpy ride to the house, she had glanced around and not seen a single tree, building, or person—only four scrawny cows, a barbed-wire fence, a small shelter for the horse, and miles and miles of barren, sparsely snow-covered hills.

Tears continued to fall down her cheeks and drip onto the wool blanket covering the baby as she sat there. Maybe she looked over at her husband and wondered how she could be a mother and the wife of this strange young man barely out of his teens at just fifteen years old. Dennis was thin but muscular and seemed strong enough to handle farm work. Sitting on the old chair, Margaret shuddered as she remembered the day when she was locked in a hotel room by this boy's two sisters, and then raped by him. She had only seen him once, with his family, and then there he was, pulling her clothes off. In those days, one had to marry if they became pregnant—despite the circumstances.

Dennis, seeing her crying, put down his water bucket and bent down, saying, "What's the matter, Maggie? Don't you like our new house? I'm really proud of it. I built it all by myself—even the door, windows, and the roof."

"Oh, Den, I know you've worked hard, but I've never seen such a house before, and I don't know how I'll keep the baby and everything clean," Margaret replied.

"Maggie, you're a full-grown, healthy woman, and we'll manage. You'll see; we'll manage."

Margaret wanted to scream: "I'm not a full-grown woman! I'm fifteen, five-foot-two, and ninety pounds, and I hate the name Maggie. My name's Margaret!" But she didn't utter a word. Her way was to suffer in silence.

⚮

REFLECTIONS: I don't know how many years they lived in the sod house, and no one talked much about it. Both Mom and Marie were genuine heroes. Somehow Mom survived and lived to be seventy-three, and Marie lived to eighty-one. As do most parents, mine did their best, which was not very good. I now believe that we, as a species, have an evolution of consciousness in which we become more and more aware of what is possible. For example, no woman should be forced to marry someone who raped her, and no one should have to begin life in such dire poverty. Just like no race should be able to displace—and sometimes kill—another through eminent domain. When my parents homesteaded in Nebraska, there was never any talk about the Indigenous people they had displaced. In my lifetime, I have experienced the need for women's liberation and the realization that poverty should never be a death sentence.

Two

JUST ANOTHER MOUTH TO FEED

I wish I could write a second chapter about how Mom and Dad lived the next twenty-two years. All I know is that they had two more girls and five boys after Marie and before I was born. I so wish I knew some of the stories of those years, but I think that time was so hard and sad that no one wanted to talk about it. Hopefully, the day will come when everyone—not just in my family—will be proud of themselves for surviving such trials.

———— ✦ ————

This is my birth story as told by my sister, Marie—the baby mentioned in the first chapter. I was born in Alliance, Nebraska, in a hospital where she worked as a nurses' aide. She is twenty-two years older and closer to Mom's age than mine. After Dad and our siblings went to Kansas, she stayed with Mom. Dad was going to Kansas to be a tenant farmer—one who lives on a farm and works the farm for the owner and, in return, gets a place to live and a portion of the income from the sale of crops.

Marie, a slight, pretty, and strong young woman, was driving a cousin's car in the middle of a dust storm, part of the Dust Bowl, in 1933. She dropped our very sick and exhausted mom off at the small Catholic hospital in Alliance. Mom was expecting me to be born any minute. Marie then took our dad, four brothers, and baby sister to the train station. A dry, chilly wind was blowing dirt everywhere, and it was hard to breathe. She gave Dad an awkward side-hug and kissed each of our siblings on the cheek. Marie felt like a mother to all of them. She was six years old when Mom gave birth to Glen, who was now fifteen, and she remembered changing Glen's diapers when they lived in that horrible little sod house. Then she was Mom's main helper when Bill, now twelve, and Bob, now eleven, were born. Mom nearly died when Jack was born two years after Bob. He lived only a few weeks. Then there was Aggie, who she hoped would be her helper, but she died in Denver when she was eight, after we lost the farm. Mom never got over her death. Jimmy was born when Aggie was two. Bonnie Jean followed the next year.

As Marie climbed into the car, she waved to her sad-looking family. Dad, carrying Bonnie, the baby of twenty months, waved with one hand peeking out from under a baby blanket. She could tell that Dad was also barking at Glen to pick up the two largest suitcases as Bill and Bob each carried two medium-sized ones. That was all of our worldly possessions except for the clothes Mom and Marie were wearing and had packed away in a couple of small suitcases. Five-year-old Jimmy held onto Dad's coat as they trudged toward the train.

Marie recalls how Dad looked so tired and sad—as he had for months, even years, ever since they moved away from the farm in 1930. It was like all the life went out of Dad that day. All he had known in his life was farming. So, he and a fellow evicted farmer pooled their meager savings, bought a truck, and attempted to make a living for two families hauling goods between Alliance and Denver, Colorado. They didn't even make enough for one family. Then Mom's uncle near Kansas City, Kansas, offered him the tenant farm position.

The wind seemed to have picked up, and the dust was terrible. Marie was relieved to get into the hospital, where all the windows and doors had rags tucked into every opening. Sister Louise ushered her into the hospital room, where Mom was sleeping restlessly, then the two went back out into the hall to talk.

Marie caught her up on what led our mother to her current state of exhaustion: Bonnie Jean's birth in Denver two years earlier and Aggie dying of diphtheria in Denver around that same time— an illness that almost took our mother, too. The sister already knew about our brother Jack, who had died when he was only six weeks old—there in the same hospital.

Sister insisted Marie go to the cafeteria and get something to eat. Knowing that she would have little or no money, she gave her a note to give the cashier. When Marie got back to Mom's room, she was still sleeping, and she fell asleep in the chair beside her.

It was dark and still dusty when Sister Louise touched Marie on the shoulder. Delivery was nearing, and the doctor was on his way. As a former nurse's aide at the hospital, Marie was familiar with the regimen. She helped put Mom on a gurney, and they wheeled her into the delivery room. The room was a little cleaner but still smelled of dust, and the wind howled outside the windows. Mom's labor was weak, and, for the first time, her many previous births helped me, the new baby, come out. Mom said his name would be Donald Francis Hanley.

Dr. Kennedy said, "Well, Maggie, I can't say congratulations. Only here's another mouth to feed." He then got to work to save Mom's life. It took him and the nurses three hours. She came through it all, thank God.

———⊸⊷⊶———

REFLECTIONS: Now, eighty-nine years later, I believe in some way, as a newborn infant, I knew Mom was in great pain and near death because of me. I was told that Marie asked the doctor if Mom was going to die because they were having a hard time stopping the internal bleeding. For years, I wondered why I thought that to be close to a girl or woman was to hurt her. I wonder if my traumatic birth had something to do with that? Many other psychologists and I believe babies are born with higher consciousness than previously thought. The flowers in this story blossom forth through the strength and courage of Mom and Marie. I hope you will see why I call them heroes.

Three

I'M ANOTHER WORTHLESS LITTLE PILE OF SHIT

—⊶∞⊷—

Memories of the first five years of my life are few and scattered, but I clearly remember my first-grade experience at St. Patrick's school in Paola, Kansas.

I was lined up with three other first graders who had their seventh birthday near the end of first grade. We were behind the second graders, who were going to march over to the church for our first confession. As seven-year-olds, we were presumed to have the use of reason. So, I guess that when we were six, we could sin all we wanted, and they were only venial sins. But now, some sins would be mortal sins that could send us to hell—if we died with them staining our souls. I pictured my soul as a blob of pure white with shit smeared on it. Anyway, I had to march out of the school building, past the priest's two-story brick house, and to the church. As I passed the house between the school and the church, I thought about how one person, the priest, lived in that nice, big, two-story house and that sometimes ten, and always at least eight of us, lived in our old, almost falling down house. The priest had a cook and a housekeeper. Mom didn't have a housekeeper to help her take care of the house or a cook for a bunch of people. It didn't seem fair.

All of us students knelt down near the confessional boxes to examine our conscience. I stared up at the massive picture of God the Father above the altar. He had a long white beard, and he was writing in a book on his lap. He looked ferocious and mean—like he meant business. I once asked Sister Mary why he seemed so angry, and she said, "Oh, he's not angry. He's sad because of all our sins." I still thought he looked mean and angry. So, I thought I better get busy examining my conscience.

I thought of the second week of the first grade. I had not gone to kindergarten because it cost ten dollars a month, and we could not afford it. Every day I had to work hard not to have to go to the restroom during class, but I would ask Sister Mary for permission when I couldn't hold it any longer. But this time, she said I could wait until recess. I said, "Sister, I can't wait!" She ignored me. Pretty soon, I couldn't hold it any longer, and I felt the warm pee on my leg, on my pants, and then it dripped on the floor. I saw several students turn and sneer at me and stifle a giggle. I felt awful.

Then I saw Sister whisper something to my sister Bonnie, a third-grader in the same room. Bonnie scowled at me and left the room. She returned with our brother Jim, a sixth-grader in an upstairs room. With a scrunched-up face and through gritted teeth, Jim growled, "Get up, you little weasel. I gotta take you home." He grabbed my arm, jerked me out of the desk, and dragged me to the door. When we got outside, and while he was still painfully twisting my arm, he nearly screamed, "This better be the last fucking time, you little snot-nose, or next time, I'll beat the shit outta you!"

For several blocks, I couldn't keep up with him, and every time I fell back, Jim would yell, "Hurry the hell up," and jerk and twist my arm. When we got within sight of our old, run-down house, he said, "Now, see there, stupid? That's our house. Do you think you're smart enough to find it?" Just then, Pal, our collie-shepherd dog, ran up with his tail wagging. He ignored Jim and came up and licked my face. Jim said, "Pal will show you the way, stupid."

I left Pal on the back porch and went into the kitchen. Patty, my three-year-old sister, ran and climbed into Mom's lap like she owned it—which she did. Mom, seeing my wet pants, muttered, "Oh, son, I don't know what we're going to do with you." Mom always seemed to look tired and worried. Just then, Dad came out of the bathroom and seeing me, reached out and backhanded me and yelled, "You're nothing but a worthless little pile of shit!" He knocked me down and I crawled under the table before his foot could get to me. He kicked the rung of a chair instead and yelled again, "Stupid little shit." Suddenly, Dad started making choking sounds, then fell down and squirmed all over the floor. Mom yelled for my brothers to come and help. I think it was Bill who ran to Dad first. Glen got a flat stick and put it in Dad's mouth so he wouldn't bite his tongue. They held onto him, and someone said, "Another grand mal seizure." I didn't know what that was, and I had never seen Dad act like that before, but I was sure I had caused it because I wet my pants. I was bad.

As I continued examining my conscience, I remembered Sister Mary had said if we didn't intend to do something, it wasn't a sin, so I guess wetting my pants wasn't a sin. I thought I should confess that I got angry with my sisters and brothers lots of times.

There was also three whole months I had missed school because all of us kids had measles, mumps, whooping cough, and scarlet fever, and we had to stay in the house the entire time, which was pretty bad, but of course, that wasn't my fault. Sister said I should have an exact number about my anger, so I decided to say that I got angry with my sisters sixteen times and my brothers seventeen times—that would be lots, I thought. I glanced back up at the picture of the angry God and thought of the *really* baddest thing I'd ever done.

It was the previous summer before school started. My brother Jim ordered Bonnie and me to go up in the attic with him and a few other kids. We took all of our clothes off and ran around the attic, laughing and touching each other on the bottom and all over. I hated to do anything Jim ordered me to do, but I was really having fun. He told me to kiss Sally between her legs, which was super fun. When I stopped kissing, Sally would giggle and say, "Do it again," and I would. I found out that was bad because Sally and her brother told their mom, and the next day, on our way to school, both kids threw rocks at us and yelled that we were sinners and would go to hell. After that, I felt sure that I was a sinner, and I was ashamed of myself. We took turns watching the door, so I should have known it was not right—better confess that too.

Finally, it was my turn to go into that dark box next to the priest's box. I was shaking with fear when I pushed the blood-red curtain aside and went in and knelt down. I said, "B-b-bless me, F-Father, for I have si-si-sinned. This is my first confession. I got angry at my sisters sixteen times and my brothers seventeen times. And I played naked in the attic."

In an angry, gruff voice, Father said, "What do you mean, my child, you 'played naked?'"

I thought he shouldn't say "my child" because I wasn't his child, but one should never talk back to a priest, so I just said, "We took off all of our clothes and ran around the attic and touched each other."

"Where did you touch each other, boy?"

"In the attic, Father."

Father almost screamed as he roared back, "Where on the body did you touch each other?" I hoped nobody in the church could hear him.

"On our bottoms and down there, between our legs, Father."

"You know, son, that is a terrible sin and makes God very sad and angry and could send you to hell? You know what hell is, don't you, son?"

"Ye-ye-yes, Fa-Fa-Father. It is a place where we burn up over and over and over, forever." Tears by the thousands were running down my face. I knew what burning felt like because I had touched a fire on the stove once and it hurt like mad. After the way he reacted to what I said about playing naked, I couldn't dare tell him about kissing Sally between her legs.

"Now, for your penance, say ten Hail Marys and ten Our Fathers, and now say your Act of Contrition."

I sniffled through the Act of Contrition and stumbled out of the confessional. I was shaking and crying as I knelt down and looked up at the angry God above the altar. Now, I was not only a stupid and worthless little pile of shit; I was a terrible sinner who could burn in hell forever.

Four

LOSING MY CLOSEST FRIEND: 1941

Just as I was getting ready to go for a walk with Pal, a police car drove up to our house with Dad in the back seat. I didn't know what the police would be doing with Dad, but it scared me. I ran back into the house and hid behind the kitchen table. Peering out between the rungs of the chairs, I saw a chubby policeman holding my dad's arm and leading him into the back door. Dad looked terrible. His face was all scrunched up, and I think he was crying. His pants were wet like mine were when I was sent home from school. I wondered if he felt he was just as worthless as me. I wiped some tears from my face.

The policeman said to Mom, "Mrs. Hanley, you're going to have to do something about your husband. The store owners don't want him in their stores. I think you know that he's had one of his fits in almost all the downtown stores. He scares the hell out of people." Dad just looked at the floor and didn't say a word.

Mom said, "Thank you, Officer Kline. I'll see what I can do." Mom led Dad back to their bedroom—the only one on the ground floor. Mom must have called my sister Marie because the next day, a Saturday, she and her husband, Jim Abney, came to the house from Wichita, where they had moved.

Remembering the day when they got married last summer, I thought Marie was so beautiful in her white wedding dress. Even my brother Jim looked angelic in his altar boy's red cassock and white surplice. I heard someone say that the father of the bride was supposed to walk down the aisle with the bride and give her away to her husband, but Dad couldn't do that because he might have one of his attacks. Dad seemed to be the only one in the church who wasn't enjoying the wedding. It was the first really nice thing to happen in the family. I hadn't had a nice day for a long time— every day seemed like a bad day, especially since I was told I would have to repeat the first grade.

The only nice days were when I left the house with Pal and walked barefoot all over town and the countryside. Mom said I flunked first grade because I missed so much school due to all the sickness and not for wetting my pants; it was not because I was dumb. Maybe, but it also could be because I was worthless like Dad said—and like he was, too.

Marie said, "Mom, we've checked around about what to do about Dad, and several doctors said the only thing we can do is put him in a state mental hospital. There is one in Osawatomie—only about twenty miles from here. I'm sure Dad won't like it, but I think he'll go. What do you think?"

Mom looked down at the floor and, in a weak voice, said, "I guess that's what we'll have to do." So, Marie and Jim made arrangements and took Dad to the Kansas State Hospital the following week. They had to take Mom with them because she had to sign the papers committing him. The way they talked about committing him sounded like they were taking him to jail. Bonnie said it was an insane asylum, which was worse than jail. I slapped her, and she slapped me back.

When they brought Mom back home, I heard Marie tell Mom, "Mom, if Bill and Glen don't start sending you some money to pay rent and buy groceries, then Jim and I will just pack you all up and deliver you to them in California and dump you on their doorstep." It sounded like we were a load of trash. She went on, "Jim and I can't continue giving you so much each month. All we're asking is for them to send $30 a month. That isn't so much. After all, Glen was giving you that much for three years when he was working for the Civilian Conservation Corps."

I hated being a burden on Jim and Marie or anybody. Every week, my brother Jim and I pulled our rusty red wagon to the Paola County warehouse and picked up food commodities that were set out for the poor. We hated the trip back home and avoided blocks that had folks we knew because we didn't want anyone to see us take home our poor people's food. Maybe going to California wouldn't be so bad. I'd even be away from Sister Mary and the grouchy old priest.

A few Saturdays later, Marie drove Mom and us four youngest kids—Jim, Bonnie, Patty, and me—to Osawatomie to say goodbye to Dad. My brother Bob was in the Army, and Glen and Bill had found jobs in California. Other patients had visitors too. It was a nice day in June, and clusters of folks sat around in circles talking. We didn't stay long because no one seemed to have anything to talk about except that we would miss Dad. I wouldn't miss him, and I wondered if any of the others would either. As we left, I looked out of the car's back window and saw Dad standing alone on the sidewalk in gray hospital pajamas and a bathrobe. He gave a weak half-wave, and there was no smile as we drove away.

The next day I went with Marie to take a load of clothes, blankets, and other stuff to Lenny's house. Lenny was the Black lady who helped Mom once a week. She had brought her son, Johnny, with her. We played together when we lived outside of town until I was five. In town, he couldn't come to play anymore because the neighbors didn't want their children to play with any black kids, whom they called the "n" word. Johnny was better than any of them in the neighborhood, and I thought all the parents were stupid. Lenny's family lived in a house near the railroad tracks that was even poorer than the old house we rented for five dollars a month. I learned Johnny was going into the third grade. I felt ashamed all over again that I was only going into the second grade.

The night before we left Paola, I had heard Jim Abney tell Mom that their 1939 Ford had little room in the trunk, so we needed to take only what was absolutely necessary. He said that he and Marie would sit in front with one kid, and Mom and three of the kids would sit in the back seat. I said, "Where will Pal be?"

"We'll have to leave him here, Donald," Marie said as if everyone knew this.

I had never given a thought to the idea that Pal, who I considered my dog, was not going to California with us. I yelled, "He's gotta go with us! He's part of the family. He's going with us—that is for sure."

My brother Jim said, "Don't be stupid, stupid. Look at this little car. There's barely enough room for all of us as it is. We'll be like sardines in a can. So don't be stupid."

"Well, then I won't go either." Jim said that would suit him just fine. Without saying another word, I decided to take Pal for a walk. Pal came faithfully when I called, and we headed down the street. No one paid any attention because Pal and I often took walks around town ever since school let out in May. An hour or so later, I got hungry, but I wouldn't turn around and go back home. I walked toward a pond at the edge of town so Pal could get some water, and we sat down near the shore. The sun went down, and I laid down beside Pal and fell asleep.

I don't know how late it was, but it was dark when I heard my brother Jim yell, "Well, there you are, stupid!" He called to Marie, who was in the car back on the road, and she came running.

"Donald, honey, we've been looking all over for you. You know we're going to leave for California in the morning, and we all need to get some sleep before we go."

"I ain't goin'." I got up and just stood there, planted like a tree.

Jim grabbed at me, and I hit him in the face and made his nose bleed. He yelled, "You little bastard," and he hit me so hard, my nose bled too. I fell down.

Marie pushed Jim away, knelt down, and put a handkerchief to my nose. "Donald, our mother is really worried about you. Please come with us." Because I was so cold, I grabbed Pal's collar and went with her to the car. She put Pal and me in the front seat.

When we got home, I wouldn't go into the house, so Mom came out with some food for Pal and me. She tried to talk me into cooperating. I felt sorry for her, but I wouldn't budge and still wouldn't go back into the house. She said, "Well, we'll see in the morning. Come in when you are ready for sleep."

I couldn't imagine living anywhere without Pal. I thought of him waiting on the brick wall halfway between school and home, no matter when I came home from school. He was always there—morning or afternoon. Thinking Pal was the only one in the family who cared about me at all, I fell asleep on the lawn with my arms around this big, wonderful dog; he kept me sort of warm. The next morning, Marie and Jim Abney came out to get me. They had already taken Pal somewhere. While I was groggily looking around, they picked me up, held me tight, dragged me into the house, and put clean clothes on me. I kept asking where Pal was, but no one answered.

I kept looking for Pal, and everyone was getting into the car. Marie said, "Get in the car," patted the side of the front seat near the window, "and we'll go find Pal." I climbed in, and we drove out onto the street. Then I saw Pal: he was tied up to a porch railing down the street, looking at the car and me. I tried to get out of the car, but the door was locked. Marie said, "Pal is going to live on a farm where he can run free."

I kept looking back at Pal, barking and lunging on the rope. I was crying and kept looking back even after we turned the corner, and I could no longer see him. After a while, I quit crying and started paying attention to where we were going. I did my best to forget Pal, but something died inside me that day.

Five

GLOOMY GUS'S CAVE

—— ❧ ——

"Oh, My Lord. Oh, My Lord, look at that ocean. It is terrifying," Mom exclaimed, seeing the Pacific Ocean for the first time. I thought it was amazing and magnificent as we drove over a rise in Manhattan Beach, California. It was late Sunday afternoon on a beautiful June day. We had left Kansas early Saturday morning, and Jim and Marie took turns driving through the night. We could not stop in a motel because of the cost. I didn't get much sleep because I wanted to see everything, even when it got dark.

Jim shouted, "It's fantastic! I can't wait to jump into those beautiful waves."

I said, "I can't see Japan. Why can't we see Japan?"

"It's on the other side of the world, stupid," Jim yelled back.

We found Glen and Bill's small apartment, and it had an ocean view. Jim, Bonnie, and I dug out our bathing suits and ran the two blocks to the beach. Mom had told Bill and Glen that we'd be too scared to get into the ocean, but just in case, Glen got in his car and followed us. Jim took to the waves like a duck to water. Glen later told Mom that Bonnie and I waded in up to our waists, jumped up and down, laughed, and were having a grand old time. Then a huge wave hit us, knocked us down under the water, and threw us clear up on the sand. I remember swallowing what seemed like a gallon of seawater. I wouldn't go back in the water. From that day on, Jim loved the beach and waves, and I was afraid of them.

After three weeks of everyone but Mom sleeping on the floor, Glen found a new little house in Redondo Beach. It was three miles from the ocean, and the area was known as the North Redondo sticks. There were vacant lots behind us, across the street from us, and on each side of the house, and only four houses on both sides of the long semi-rural street. There was no dirt anywhere, nor any kind of real topsoil—it was all sand. The only vegetation was in the yard of a Japanese family near us and what Glen called highway ice plant. I never learned why they called it that; it never snowed or froze in California. The house was too far away for us to go to the Catholic school, and Mom said that we couldn't afford to pay bus fare to go to church for catechism classes on Saturdays, which suited me just fine.

The elementary school for Bonnie, Patty, and me was about a mile away, and we could walk there. Jim could also walk to the junior high school. Patty turned six in late June, but Mom decided she should start school in kindergarten. Unlike Kansas, kindergarten was free in California. There were two bad things about California: the real big one—no Pal, and a minor one—I had to share a bed and a room with Jim. The second one wasn't too bad because he was gone to the ocean most of the time, even at night.

We were in the new house only a few weeks when Mom came outside and asked where Patty was. Mom had looked everywhere in the small house and garage. We began looking all around outside the house and among the eucalyptus trees that lined the backyard, but there was no Patty to be found. Mom told Bonnie to go west and me to go east down the street. I walked about two blocks and found Patty crying and sitting in the middle of a big patch of ice plant on the side of the road. She stopped crying and reached up to me with both arms. I pulled her up, and we climbed out of the tangled ice plant. Patty said, "I got lost. I couldn't find my way back home. I'm glad you found me, Donald."

For the first time, I realized Mom left Patty alone in the yard back in Paola because Pal was always with her. He would herd her back toward the house when she headed for the street. Sometimes she'd hit at the collie-shepherd and yell at him, but he wouldn't get out of the way. Again, I cried because Pal wasn't with us. After that, Mom asked Bonnie and me to take Patty for walks so she could get to know the neighborhood. I don't think we ever let her go outside without one of us. Mom also took Patty for an eye exam before school started and found out she needed glasses. Mom had often told us that Patty had been a blue baby, which means that she did not get enough blood to her brain when she was born, so she was a slow learner. Bonnie and I tried to stop calling her stupid when she couldn't see or learn things as easily as we could. Jim never stopped calling all of us stupid.

By the time school started in September, we had begun what became our favorite routine—at least for Bonnie, Patty, and me. Every Sunday, Mom and the three of us would catch the bus and go to Redondo Beach. Jim didn't want to go anywhere or do anything with the four of us, so we ignored him. We'd go to Mass, down to the Redondo Beach pier, get hamburgers and malts, and then go to the afternoon movie. I didn't even mind going to church because there was no picture of a mean-looking God above the altar. The Sunday outing was better than anything we had done in Kansas.

Mom used the Sunday treat to bribe us to be good all week—at home and school. She would say, "If I ever hear one word about you misbehaving at school, there will be no beach and movie for any of you on Sunday." School was fine—I had a pretty young teacher who let me go to the bathroom whenever I needed to and didn't scold me for anything, so I was okay. Patty even liked kindergarten, and Bonnie made a bunch of friends in the fifth grade. I took it for granted that Bonnie, Patty, and I were a trio that always went together with Mom. I don't remember ever wondering what they thought or felt about anything.

Some Sundays, Glen would take us to Mass in Redondo and then take Mom shopping. It was one of those Sundays, December 7, 1941. We were in Glen's car heading to church when we heard on the car radio that the Japanese airplanes had bombed Pearl Harbor. "Oh my God!" Glen yelled, pulling the car over to the side of the road. I never saw him so shook up, and Mom cried out mournfully.

I didn't know what it was really all about. Why would the Japanese attack us? One of our closest neighbor families was Japanese. They were very nice, quiet people and had the cleanest and greenest place in the neighborhood. Their yard was the only one that was pretty with flowers. Unlike everyone else, they grew lots and lots of plants—from trees to all kinds of vegetables and stuff. Mom said they were city farmers because they sold some of what they grew. I was sure they didn't hate us. A few months later, we saw soldiers with guns order the whole family to climb into the back of an army truck. We never saw them again, and their gardens just dried up.

The war did not affect us very much. We just had to cover all of our windows and doors with black paper and not let any light show outside whenever it was dark. We were told that the Japanese ships out in the ocean might see where all the people were. At first, I wondered why our government didn't just call on Superman and Batman and all those so-called superheroes to beat up the Japanese. I'm glad I mentioned that only to one of the neighborhood kids who thought I was joking because those guys only exist in comic books. I chuckled and said, "Yeah, I know that." If I had said that to Bonnie or Jim, I would never have lived it down. All of us kids were asked to collect cans and rubber for the war effort—to build planes and ships and guns. Some stuff was rationed like sugar, coffee, and some other things. The radio kept playing a super stupid song that said, "Praise the Lord and pass the ammunition"—as if God made guns and bullets and wanted us to kill people. Jim said I was stupid to condemn that song. That was one thing I was sure I was not stupid for.

Bob was still in the army. He went into an officers' training program, and he was called a ninety-day-wonder because he was made a second lieutenant in only three months. Most lieutenants went to college for four years. Mom said he did that because he was smart. I was pretty sure that I was too stupid to ever be an army officer. Bill and Glen worked in defense plants, so they weren't drafted into the military at first.

When I was nine and during our second Christmas in California, Glen took us to see Bob at Fort Ord, near Monterey. All the soldiers called it Fort Pneumonia By The Sea. It was cold and rainy, but we were all glad to see Bob, who looked good in his new officer's uniform. Mom said he looked so handsome and put his picture in the living room where everyone could see it.

"What's with Gloomy Gus?" Glen asked Mom one day. I was sure he didn't know I could hear him.

"Who do you mean?"

"Donald. He never smiles or laughs. What's the matter with him? He looks so sad all the time."

Did I look sad? I wondered about it and wanted to know if it was true, but I couldn't ask Bonnie or Jim because they'd say, "Yeah, you look sad and gloomy, *and* stupid and ugly." I'm sure I looked gloomy after hearing Glen say that and because I still really felt sad about Pal. Thinking it over made me realize I was still mad at myself for flunking the first grade and being ashamed of myself for what the priests said were sins. I had a lot of bad thoughts—like thinking Jim was a bully and hating that girl back in Paola who looked like Shirley Temple and called us Hanley kids "poor white trash." And I even hated Shirley Temple because she looked like that girl. I often thought about wanting to see pretty girls naked and tons of other sinful, evil, and bad thoughts. Did other kids have stupid, sinful thoughts like I did?

Mom said, "I think he still misses Pal a lot." Glen asked if it would help if we got a dog, but Mom said that we couldn't afford to build a fence, and she didn't want a dog in the house. Anyway, there was only one dog in the world that I wanted.

Around that time, I did two of the stupidest things I've done in my entire life. The first one happened when I was playing with four neighborhood boys, and we saw a very well-dressed boy get off the bus a block away. He, as Mom would say, looked the perfect little gentleman. None of us neighborhood kids ever looked like perfect little gentlemen. One guy said, "Hey, Donald, you're about his size; why don't you go over and knock his block off?"

"Why would I do that? He hasn't done anything to me or anyone else I know? That would be stupid." I was genuinely puzzled. The biggest kid in our group said, "Because he looks so damned stuck up, that's why!" He got me when he said I must be a chicken. Another guy picked up a small piece of wood, put it on my shoulder, and said, "Just walk up to the smarty pants and hit him in the face. Don't be a fraidy cat."

I didn't want to be a chicken or a fraidy cat—two names Jim often called me—so I put the stick firmly on my shoulder. Feeling totally stupid and shaking, I walked out in front of the dressed-up student. "Hey, we don't like you walkin' through our neighborhood," I said. "I dare you to knock this stick off my shoulder."

He looked me in the eye like I was nuts, put down his bookbag, and hit me right in the face. My nose spurted out what felt like a pint of blood, and it hurt like hell. The little gentleman looked at me, slowly reached down, picked up his books, and walked away, like this happened every day. Talk about feeling stupid! I put my arm over my nose, letting my shirt sleeve absorb the blood, and ran home to Mommy. The little gentleman never got off the bus near our street again. I still felt stupid.

The second, totally stupid thing happened one time when my sister Bonnie and her friend Nancy were cooking something in the kitchen, and I was playing with her little brother, Eddy. Nancy reminded me of Sally, whom I had played naked with in Paola. I wanted to see Nancy naked. I told Eddy about our taking off all our clothes and playing in the attic. He thought it sounded like a lot of fun. I didn't know how to ask them to take off all their clothes and get naked, so I marched into the kitchen and yelled, "Do you girls want to fuck?"

It was like I threw a hand grenade into the room. I didn't know that fuck was a worse word than naked. Nancy dropped a plate, broke it, and cried, "I'm gonna tell our mom!" Bonnie screamed that she was going to tell our mom, too. Nancy grabbed Eddy's hand and dragged him out the front door. We never saw them again except from a distance. As soon as Mom got home, Bonnie told her about my terrible, sinful crime, and Mom grabbed my hand and jerked me into the bathroom. She yelled, "Donald, where'd you hear a word like that? From your little hoodlum friends?"

"No, from the boys back in Paola who couldn't play with Lenny's son Johnny."

"Well, I want you to be a real gentleman and not be trashy. This is what you deserve, young man." She picked up a bar of soap and tried to put it in my mouth. I clamped my teeth together so quickly I bit one of Mom's fingers real hard, and it bled.

Bonnie was watching all this and yelled, "Now see what you've done, Donald. You've made Mom bleed, and now she's crying. I hope you're ashamed of yourself!"

There was one thing I did while we lived in California that I believe I can be proud of, and that is going on the bus by myself to visit Bill and Helen, who were married and had a baby and lived in Alhambra. I had just turned ten. Glen or somebody thought it would be good for me to get away from everybody at home, and Bill suggested I visit him and Helen and their new baby boy, Steve. Yeah, I was an uncle—twice because Marie and Jim had a baby girl named Suzie back in Kansas, but I didn't feel like an uncle. Uncles are supposed to be old, aren't they?

Bill sent the money for bus fare and the directions on how to get to Alhambra and their apartment. I was scared, but I was going to show everybody that I could do it—that I was not stupid. Solely focused on watching every street sign we came to, I couldn't see what all the towns looked like—I was not going to miss my stop for anything. It took me three transfers, four buses, and almost three hours to get to Alhambra. Lucky for me, Bill was waiting on the corner when I arrived. He gave me a big hug. "Donald, my man, you made it! Good for you," he said.

When we got to the apartment, I met Helen for the first time. She held baby Steve so I could see him. He was only a few weeks old and looked all wrinkled up and pinkish. Helen smiled down at him. I thought she was very pretty. I felt proud of myself because I didn't get lost getting there. And I was glad that I didn't have to take the bus back home. Bill and Helen said they would take me home so Mom and the others could see Steve. Even Jim complimented me for making the bus trip alone. Soon after that, Bill was drafted into the Navy, and Helen and the baby moved to San Diego to be near him while he trained to be a sailor.

My sister Patty had a wonderful singing voice, and Mom found a free singing teacher in Hollywood who could coach her. Bonnie complained that she should get some special lessons too. Mom found a dancing class for her at the same time and place. I was happy to stay home by myself every Saturday from eight in the morning until five in the afternoon. All I was asked to do was clean up around the yard and the garage. Then I could do anything I wanted—as long as I didn't do anything wrong.

That same year, I told Bonnie that I would go with her and her friends trick or treating at Halloween.

The second house we went to, a grouchy old man came to the door and yelled, "You little beggars, get the hell off my porch." That was enough for me. I couldn't think of a worse insult than being called a beggar. I went back home and never went trick or treating the rest of my life.

It was right after Christmas when I decided to gather up all the pop bottles that had been sitting around the garage for months. I took them to the convenience store and got a little over a dollar for them. I felt wealthy and generous, so I bought candy and pop for all my buddies in the neighborhood. When Mom and the girls got home, I told them what a grand time I had with my friends. Mom started scolding me for wasting all that money on trashy stuff for my hoodlum friends when we had to skimp and save every week to buy groceries. For the first time I can remember, I defended myself: "Every Saturday you and the girls go off to Hollywood, and I stay here by myself. And one time, one time, I take the old, empty bottles to the store and buy pop and candy for my friends. I don't think it's fair."

To my delight, Mom replied, "You're right, Son. I wasn't being fair. I was wrong. And I didn't thank you for cleaning up the garage so nicely. Will you forgive me?" Wow! I shook her hand and gave her a sideways hug. I think that was the closest I ever felt toward Mom.

Soon after my birthday, March 28th, 1944, Mom got a letter from Dad that they had released him from the Kansas State Hospital, and he no longer had any seizures. He had been working as a carpenter in Casper, Wyoming, where his sister, Edna, lived. He had been buying lumber at the Rohlf Lumber Company, and Mr. Rohlf asked him if he would like to take over their line lumber yard in South Dakota. One of the positive things about the offer,

Dad said, was that the yard had a rent-free house near the yard, so Dad wanted the family to join him.

Mom had been struggling for three years to keep us all fed and clothed on what little Glen could provide, along with a pittance occasionally from Bill, Bob, and Marie. Mom had worked at a Lerner clothing store for a while, but it didn't pay much, and she could only work during school hours. Jim was in and out of the house all the time and didn't want to move away from the ocean. Everyone said the surfboard he spent weeks making was a work of art. He was as attached to surfing, the ocean, and California as I had been to Pal in Paola. Mom needed him to come with us. When he finally agreed to go, he gained some respect from me.

How Dad had hurt me was now a distant memory. Remembering how sad he looked that day the policeman brought him home and the day when we all left him in that hospital helped me not to be too afraid to be with him again. I could say goodbye to California. So, in late May 1944, we caught the Continental Trailways bus and headed for South Dakota.

Six

ANOTHER BEGINNING: 1944

As we climbed onto our third bus in Cheyenne, Wyoming, I saw the changeable sign above the windshield, BLACK HILLS. I asked no one in particular, "Where's the Black Hills, and why do they call it that?"

Jim answered, "Because the hills have so many pine trees, they look black from a distance. And Edgemont is on the edge of the hills, and that's where we're going."

Bonnie added, "And there are no beaches in the Black Hills." I thought Jim would hit her.

Sitting next to Jim on the bus, I worked up enough courage to ask, "Uh, Jim, when we get to our new place, would you please not call me stupid?"

He put a hand on my knee and a snarky smile on his face, "Yeah, little brother, as long as you don't do or say anything stupid."

I took that as a no and didn't say another word. We went through a few small towns and thousands of barren hills. Wyoming was a dreary place. Two hours after leaving Cheyenne, I heard Mom tell Bonnie and Patty, sitting in front of us, "Before we went to Kansas, our farm was just about an hour's drive from here—in Nebraska." She pointed east and added, "Your brother, Bill, was born near a tiny town called Van Tassel, Wyoming. We lived on a farm in Nebraska near the Wyoming border. Van Tassel was the nearest town, so his birth was registered there."

Bonnie asked, "So, Mom, does this seem kinda like a homecoming?"

"I never thought of it that way, but I guess it is. Oh, how I hated the winters—so cold, and it seemed like we were always freezing. I'm sure South Dakota is just as bad or worse."

From behind, Jim told them, "I looked up Edgemont on the map, and it's only about twenty miles from Nebraska and ten miles from Wyoming—out in the middle of nowhere, just like what we're looking at right now."

Our bus stopped in the middle of this nowhere at Mule Creek Junction. The five of us got off the bus and were told to climb into what looked like an old school bus painted the Trailways colors. We were the only ones on the bus as we headed east to South Dakota. Within a few miles, we saw a sign in colorful letters, Welcome to South Dakota, and soon we were in Edgemont. The town and streets reminded me of the towns in western movies—only with cars instead of horses and buggies.

Mom looked terribly shaken as the bus driver said, "Ma'am, your tickets say Hot Springs. This is Edgemont, and this is where I take a break, so you can stay on the bus for a while or get off and back on in twenty minutes." He stepped off the bus.

Mom said, "Oh my, I don't know what to do! Your Dad said that he'd pick us up in Hot Springs. I guess he didn't know the bus would stop in Edgemont first. If we all get off here, and there's no one to meet him in Hot Springs, he'll be furious. Oh, my Lord." She was visibly shaking. After a few more minutes, she decided Bonnie, Patty, and she would go on to Hot Springs, and Jim and I should stay here and get acquainted with the town.

Jim and I stored most of our luggage on the side of a building and set off to explore our new town. We hadn't gone a half-block when he said, "What a hellhole. We've come 1,400 miles to this pile of shit! God!"

I couldn't tell Jim, but I kind of liked it—it was more my size and not spread all over the place like Los Angeles. It was hot and dusty, but I didn't care. It was one block back to the north-south main street, and it took only a few minutes to explore the business district. We learned it had five saloons, five churches, and about 1,800 people. The Burlington Railroad's roundhouse engine repair yard was the big employer. There was so much dirt blowing around because the government was building roads in and around an ammunition dump south of town, and gravel trucks were coming through town all day.

We found Edgemont Builders Supply, Dad's lumberyard. It was locked up. We guessed it was so small that it had only one employee, our dad. It was across the street from the city park—a dusty block long patch of weeds with two old World War I cannons aimed at the lumberyard and a small lake with an island in the middle of it. On the other side of the pond was an immense pile of cinders from train engines. There was a rickety wooden bridge to the island and its picnic tables. It needed mowing, and there was a lot of trash lying around. No one was in the park.

We peered through the windows of the lumberyard office and hardware store. We sat down on the concrete step in front and waited. A few minutes later, a small flatbed truck drove up and parked in front of the other small building on the front side of the lumberyard. Dad was driving, and Mom, Bonnie, and Patty were scrunched in on the only seat. I wondered if he planned to tie Jim and me down on the truck bed if we had been with them.

Dad got out of the truck as we walked over. He didn't hug either of us, nor did he offer to shake our hands; he just said, "Well, Jim, Donald, glad you two had sense enough not to stay on that damn bus. Can't figure out why your mother would travel 1,400 miles and then add another thirty useless miles to the trip."

Mom was standing there with the girls as Dad went on condemning her for being stupid. Mom acted like she didn't hear him. "Well, did you boys get to see the town?"

We told her about our discoveries. Dad said, "Okay, cut out the jabberin' and let's put this stuff in the house."

It didn't look much like a house, not even a dinky one. It was about a third as big as the little house we rented in Redondo. There was a double bed to the left of the door and two more double beds close by with two old, shabby chests of drawers. They took up about two-thirds of the so-called house. Beyond the beds were a round kitchen table, a kitchen cabinet, a kerosene cook stove, six miss-matched chairs, and an icebox. We had a similar icebox in Paola, and an ice-man brought ice about every three days. There was a small bathroom behind the stove with a sink and a toilet, but no tub or shower. All four of us kids looked over at Mom. She shook her head and looked like she was about to cry.

Dad didn't notice Mom's looks and said, "Well, you all make yourselves at home. Settle in. I better get over to the lumberyard for an hour or so before I lock her up for the weekend."

Mom sat down on one of the beds and cried. "I'm so sorry, children. I didn't think it would be this bad. How can we live like this?"

Again, Jim surprised me. "Mom, we saw an old house on the other end of this block with an Apartment for Rent sign on the front. I don't know how big it is or how much the rent is, but we could check it out."

Mom suddenly brightened up. "Oh, my, that sounds like something we should look into. Let's go take a look right now." So, all five of us walked down the block and knocked on the one front door that seemed to be occupied. There were letters on the window, Dr. Otis Beringer, D.O. It appeared to be an office, so Mom opened the door, waved for us to wait for her, and went in.

In only a few minutes, she came out, followed by a gray-haired fellow. Mom introduced the four of us, but the doctor didn't even notice we were there. He unlocked the other front door, and we all trooped in. There was a rather spacious living room furnished with a well-worn couch, two old, overstuffed chairs, and end tables. Next was a dining room with a China cabinet, a table, and six chairs. Behind that room was a kitchen with a smaller table and chairs, a kerosene stove, and an icebox.

The apartment also included a screened-in, unfurnished back porch. Between the kitchen and dining room were stairs leading to the bedrooms. We all climbed the stairs and found one large bedroom and two smaller ones—all furnished with a bed and chest of drawers. This apartment was about six times as large as the lumber yard bungalow. The whole place smelled a bit moldy, but that seemed to be a very small problem as far as Mom was concerned.

The doctor said the rent would be twenty-five dollars a month, plus water, electricity, and fuel for the cooking and heating stoves.

Immediately, Mom unclasped her purse. "We'll take it." She pulled out her small roll of dollars, handed the man twenty-five dollars, and said, "June first is Tuesday, so this is for June. May we move in today instead of waiting until Tuesday?" I never heard Mom sound so strong and business-like.

"All right by me. The owner lives in Cheyenne, and I'm sure he won't care. You all look like you're honest folks, so I expect you'll take care of things. And, by the way, where's the mister?"

"He's the manager of the lumberyard down the street. His name is Dennis Hanley, and I'm Mrs. Margaret Hanley. We have been living in California and are just now moving back."

"Well, welcome to Edgemont. If you need anything, let me know. Ya know where I am."

Mom had a pleasant smile on her face as we marched back to the yard. We began picking up our boxes and suitcases when Dad came over from the store. "What the hell is all this?" he yelled.

Mom walked over to him and said, "Den, I know you've worked hard to make this little bungalow a living place, but this just can't work. Look at the children. Jim is all grown up, and Bonnie and Donald are not far behind. We found a nice old place just down the—"

"Now, wait a damn minute. I don't have the money to pay rent on any damn place just down the street or any other damn place. What the hell are you thinking, Maggie? The only thing that makes this job worth taking was having a free house for us!" He was yelling, and I was afraid that he might hit Mom.

Thank God he didn't. I hoped he wouldn't have one of those seizures.

Jim had put his suitcases down and was balling and unballing his fists. I reached out and touched his hand. He looked down at me, and I shook my head slightly, hoping he had got my message.

Mom said, "Now you kids go ahead and take things over to the apartment. Your dad and I need to talk."

When we were far enough away so we couldn't be heard, Jim said, "If that son of a bitch hurts Mom, I'll kill him, I swear." We silently trudged on to the old house. Jim and I took the back bedroom, and Bonnie and Patty took the middle one. We were all unpacked and downstairs when Mom and Dad came into the house. We kept quiet. I never learned what they talked about after we left the lumberyard, but Dad looked unhappily grim.

Dad had a box of groceries, and Mom had a box of dishes. Mom said, "All of you, except Patty, please go back to the bungalow and bring back all the pots, pans, silverware, and dishes. Then we'll eat dinner." They both started silently putting things away.

The next morning, Sunday, we all walked to St. James—the parish church. It was a pretty brick church, and it was almost full of people of all ages. That afternoon, Bonnie and I went to see *Casablanca* in the dinky little theatre that held about forty people. Jim had already seen it, so he just went for a walk. Before the main film, we saw a newsreel showing us 1,000 American bombers dropping bombs on Berlin for the first time, and the audience clapped. I wondered how my brother Bob was doing and whether he would come home when he finished fighting Hitler. It was all very sad and worrisome. It kind of ruined the movie for me. I told Bonnie how I felt, and she said, "Aw, it's only a movie." I asked if she meant the newsreel, and she said, "Sure," I just shook my head.

Dinner was nearly silent. I think everyone was afraid or angry or both. Dad asked us if we wanted to play cards after. Bonnie and I said okay, and Jim decided to go for another walk. Patty perched on Mom's lap while we played pinochle.

And so, we began a silent life in Edgemont.

Seven

WORKING TO AVOID RELATING

———— ✦ ————

To everyone's surprise, on the Tuesday after Memorial Day, Jim, at age sixteen, got a job driving one of the gravel trucks. I learned South Dakota did not issue driver's licenses, but I never learned how or when Jim learned to drive. Jim had red hair like Dad and was nearly as tall. When he was serious, he looked older than he was. When he was home and Dad wasn't, he acted like a big shot, ordering Bonnie and me around and demanding we get him a drink or something, like he was the king of the castle. Whenever Dad was home, he left. I went over to the lumberyard and helped out as best I could. Being eleven, I was limited to sweeping out the store, the sidewalk, and other minor things. I paid attention to everything Dad did—waiting on customers, weighing nails, sacking grain and chicken feed, and everything I could. Dad said that the company needed to sell grain and other livestock feed and supplies because the town was too small to support two lumber-only yards.

Our brother Bob had learned to fly and was now with the Army Air Corps in England. On June 6th, the American army and navy made a massive attack on the Germans, who were then in France. Bob would be flying a little Piper Cub airplane and telling the infantry where to aim their artillery. We prayed every day that he would be safe. When I saw the newsreel of the Normandy invasion, I was glad Bob was in an airplane rather than going ashore with all those guns coming at him.

Of course, the war was horrible, but something horrible happened in Edgemont the following week. Two nuns arrived to teach catechism to us poor Catholic kids who were not able to go to a Catholic school. Mom insisted that Bonnie, Patty, and I go to their classes. The two sisters divided us into two groups—those who had been confirmed and those who were not. I had been confirmed back in Paola, so they put me in the older group with Bonnie. We were ordered to go up to what had been the choir loft in the old wooden church that had been turned into the parish hall. The older and grouchier-looking nun was the already-confirmed students' teacher.

After writing down all of our names, Sister Loretta looked at me before any of the others. I immediately froze. I guess I was the youngest one in this older group, and Sister asked, "Donald Hanley, are you sure you were confirmed?"

"Yes, Sister, I was confirmed when I was seven in Paola, Kansas," I answered hesitantly.

"Okay, then, tell me, who are the three persons of the Blessed Trinity?"

"I dunno." I'm pretty sure I sounded kinda snotty, but I was actually scared to death.

"And who is Jesus Christ?"

"I dunno."

"You mean to tell me you were confirmed, but you don't know the answer to these very basic questions?"

"Yeah, I was confirmed, but I didn't learn any of that dumb stuff."

Sister scowled down at me, turned scarlet, and looked ready to explode. "Well, young man, right now, you go down to the lower class and learn all this *stuff* again." When I didn't move, she yelled, "I mean right now—move."

I glanced at Bonnie, who was shaking her head as I went down the stairs. I didn't join the younger group. Instead, I went out the door and ran to the lumberyard. Dad might order me to go back to the dumb class, but someone would have to tie me down if he did. I prayed Dad would understand. When I got to the lumberyard, Dad was helping a customer, so I waited until he was finished and then told him what happened. Of course, I omitted calling basic doctrine "dumb stuff." To my surprise and relief, Dad said, "Well, then you can help me around here. How's that?"

I wanted to hug him, but I didn't, of course. Dad, I decided, had a bit of love in him.

Bonnie told Mom about how I had embarrassed her, but Mom never said a word to me. I began working harder at learning everything I could about the lumber business.

Jim's truck driving job ended after only ten days, as the ammunition dump had all the gravel they needed. Jim gave Mom some money to pay the July rent. I'm sure she needed it. Dad surprised me by asking Jim to drive the truck to Rapid City to pick up some millwork—new windows and doors and stuff. He said I could go with him so I could see the Black Hills.

When we got about halfway to Rapid City, we saw a highway sign that said Needles Highway and Mt. Rushmore. Jim said, "I bet that's interesting. Let's take that route." We had gone only about fifty yards and saw a second sign, No Trucks Allowed. Jim muttered, "I'm sure that means big trucks." We kept on going. The road was very winding, and we made a bunch of funny pig-tail turns up a hill and then came to a narrow tunnel in front of us. The tunnel framed Mt. Rushmore. It was amazing, fantastic, and wonderful. Jim slowed down so we could take it in. The tunnel was so narrow we scraped the paint off the side of the truck bed, but Jim just kept on going. There was a parking area on the other side, and Jim pulled the small truck into a parking space. There was a telescope on a post, and for a dime, we could get a closer look at the faces on the mountain. Jim had a dime, and we took turns getting a better view. Jim read from a plaque next to the telescope that said the four faces were of Presidents Washington, Lincoln, Jefferson, and Teddy Roosevelt. It also gave some dimensions, like Washington's nose was twenty feet long. That's four or five times taller than me, I thought. There were two more framing tunnels, and after the final one, Jim said, "Wow, wasn't that something! Someday, we'll have to take another trip and drive up close to that mountain. We damaged the truck a little, but it was worth it."

That was the best time I ever had with Jim, and I felt good about him for the first time. I think. Dad, of course, noticed the truck bed's scratched paint and asked about it. Jim said, "Yeah, some jerk at the warehouse had some damn iron thing hanging out of his truck. He was parked next to us, and when he pulled out, he scratched the hell out of our truck." I think Dad believed him.

The goodwill between Jim and Dad flew away the following week. I went to the warehouse at the back of the yard to give Dad a message. They were cleaning out the place. I could tell there was some kind of tension between them as they were standing on the loading dock yelling at each other. I heard Dad tell Jim to sweep up the rat shit on one side of the building. Jim said, "Let small fry here do it. I want to go back to the house."

Dad replied, "No, I want Donald to go back up to the office, so get the broom and get to work."

"And I don't want to shovel shit, so shove the broom up your ass." He no more than got the words out of his mouth when Dad hit him so hard he knocked him off the dock and onto the ground. I ran over to Jim, and he pushed me away, looked up at Dad, and yelled, "You can go to hell, you son of a bitch!"

I handed Dad the written message and went back to the office. The last time I saw Jim, he was walking with a small cardboard suitcase and heading to the highway. Mom said he was planning to hitch-hike to Wichita, Kansas, find work or join the navy or something. She looked so sad.

As Mom would say, you could cut the tension with a knife around the house for several days after Jim left. A few weeks later, Mom got a letter from Marie saying that Jim had lied about his age and joined the navy. He was in Jacksonville, Florida.

A week later, I was raking leaves in the duplex's backyard when I heard Mom scream. I dropped the rake and ran into the house. Mom was in the dining room, bent over, holding tight to a heavy drape, crying. She screamed, "Den, stop, please stop!" as Dad hit her on the back and shoulders with his fists. I grabbed one of his arms, and he threw me across the room like I was a pesky fly. Anger boiled up inside of me; I wanted to kill him, but he was twice as big as me, so I jumped up and ran out the front door. I ran the two blocks to the town marshal's office and yelled at the old fat man to come help us. The portly guy jumped up as best he could and began to run-walk after me as I ran back home. I had to stop several times so he could catch up with me. By the time we got to the house, Dad was standing out in the front yard, looking down at the ground. The marshal said, "Sir, tell me what's going on here."

I didn't wait to hear what Dad said; I just ran into the house. Mom was sitting on the couch crying, and Bonnie was sitting on one side of her, holding Mom's hand and crying. Patty was on her lap, crying and trying to wipe Mom's tears away with a handkerchief. I sat down beside her and put my arm around her. "I'm so sorry, Mom, I'm so sorry." I felt so bad for her, and I cried, too.

That day, I didn't go back over to the lumberyard, and Dad didn't come back to the duplex. Later, Bonnie told me she heard Mom and Dad arguing about money and how they were going to pay the rent if we stayed in the duplex past July. Mom had insisted that we could not move into the bungalow.

The next day, Bonnie, Patty, and I escorted Mom to the train station. Mom was going to take the train to Wichita and be with Marie. As soon as Mom told us she was going to Kansas, Patty insisted that she would have to go with her. Mom kept insisting that Bonnie would take good care of her and help her in every way. She promised she would stay only a few months and then be back and that Dad had promised he would not hurt any of us. Bonnie and I had to hold on to Patty real tight to keep her from climbing on the train. All three of us were crying when Mom waved to us from the train. Patty was inconsolable for days.

The war went on, and we were told that Bob was safe in France. It did not seem to affect life in South Dakota. The days were hot, sunny, and dusty, but our lives and future were cloudy. Around this time, I started getting headaches nearly every day, and Dad let me have aspirins from his full bottle. Dad often had headaches too, but he never talked about them.

Eight

MAYBE I'M NOT TOTALLY STUPID AND WORTHLESS

—⚬⚬⚬—

Before the end of July, we moved back into the bungalow. Dad had only removed one old double bed, meaning I had to share a bed with him. He couldn't be worse than Jim, I thought. Patty continued to cry a lot and walked around like a sad zombie, saying, "I wish Mom would hurry up and come back." Bonnie had made a couple of friends at the summer religion class and was nice enough to take Patty with her wherever she went. Dad was usually quiet, but Bonnie and I learned that when he asked us to do something, we better do it without question or waiting one minute. He was very patient with Patty. I found out that I was better at reading Dad's moods than Bonnie was. Within minutes, in the morning, I could tell whether I could joke around with Dad or if I needed to be very cautious around him. Bonnie never figured that out and was often at odds with him about something.

I admired her courage but thought my conflict avoidance was a better strategy.

Jim had left a reminder of his time with us before he left. One day, when Dad was delivering some lumber to a customer, Jim had taken a handful of feed corn out of the bin and planted them in front of the store. Every kernel sprouted, and by August, the cornstalks were taller than me. By September, they were as high as the roof of the building—about ten feet. Even the Edgemont Tribune, the weekly paper, took a picture of them. I sent a copy to Jim in Jacksonville.

We began school the day after Labor Day. Mom had written to tell us to enroll Patty in the second grade. Bonnie was going into eighth, and I was headed into fifth. My teacher was Mrs. Reed, a large, friendly woman who learned everyone's name on the first day. There were about thirty students—half boys and half girls. There were four of us new students—two girls and one other new boy, Ted Torres. I liked Ted immediately, partially because he was thirteen—two years older than me—but about two inches shorter. His family had come from Mexico, and Ted had begun school the previous year—starting in the third grade. Even so, he was very smart and fit right in. Like me, he was quiet and shy. We walked home together that first day and nearly every day after that.

At lunchtime, Bonnie, Patty, and I walked home. Dad locked up the store and prepared lunch for us. One of the best parts of each school day was the time after lunch when Mrs. Reed would read to us. The book that semester was *The Royal Road to Romance* by Richard Halliburton. Mr. Halliburton, we were told, was a world explorer and adventurer. In this book, he was traveling to all Seven Wonders of the World—starting with the Great Wall of China. It amazed me that he could get along so well in China and not know a word of the language. Would I ever be that intelligent and courageous? I wondered. It made me want to read more books like that. I would often stop at the town library on the way home from school and check out books by Zane Grey, Jack London, and others.

Dad said that I needed to be back at the lumberyard within fifteen minutes after school was out. The two school buildings were on the west side of town, about a mile away, so I couldn't piddle around. Dad was okay with my stopping at the library as long as I told him in advance. I was still studying everything I could about the lumber and feed store business. Bonnie seemed to be making friends in the eighth grade, and we both held Patty's hands as we walked her to school most mornings. I think all three of us looked like Gloomy Guses.

Mom sent letters almost every week and told us she was being treated well by Marie and her husband, Jim. They appreciated her being available to take care of three-year-old Suzie. Mom also kept us informed about Bob, Bill, and Jim. Bob was still in France, flying the little airplane and directing artillery fire. Bill was finished with navy boot camp but was still in San Diego, and he and Helen had a second baby they named Judy. Jim was still in Jacksonville, Florida.

As soon as it got below freezing several days in a row, Dad brought home a quarter of a hog and hung it up in a small, well-insulated closet he had built into a corner of one of the lumberyard warehouses. He said that it would save us lots of money and provide for all the protein we'd need. I was glad that the head and the lower part of the legs were cut off. Bonnie took one look at it and almost vomited on the spot. She was sure she would never eat a bite of anything that came from that thing. Later, after Dad had cut it up to look like bacon, ham, ribs, and roasts, she forgot what she had said. That winter, we had an awful lot of fried food. Nearly everything was cooked in pork fat.

Between Thanksgiving and Christmas, Dad was ordered to take our 1940 Chevy truck to Casper and get another truck. Dad wanted us to meet his sister, Edna, so he squeezed the three of us into the truck with him, and we went to Wyoming, about six hours away. Aunt Edna lived on the fourth floor of a downtown apartment building and was very nice to us, even treated us to a nice dinner in the swanky restaurant where she worked. Dad was expecting to get a smaller and nicer truck, but he got a 1935 Dodge pickup with a heavy steel rack on each side. I agreed with Bonnie that the little truck looked hideous—like a giant beetle with six iron legs. It was a rattletrap. The Chevy had a heater, so we were okay on the way to Casper, but the Dodge's heater didn't work, and we nearly froze to death on the way home.

While Dad was putting the truck away, I went with the girls to the bungalow to start the wood-burning stove. Bonnie said, "I suppose Dad, the big goof, thought the trip would be nice for us. Yeah, nice, like a trip to hell."

Dad had replaced the kerosene cookstove with a wood stove. He had also begun selling wood to others for their stoves. He had the big wood piled next to the yard because it wasn't officially part of the lumberyard business—it was a side business, so we would have more income. My job was to load the truck when needed and chop wood every day for our own stove.

We also sold Christmas trees at the lumberyard and took the last scrawny one that no one wanted and put it in the bungalow. Patty's second-grade class made most of the ornaments we had, and they were definitely better than not having any at all. Mom mailed presents for all of us—a doll for Patty, books for Bonnie and me, but nothing for Dad. Dad gave each of us some clothing for Christmas; I got a new shirt. The most important present was a long-distance phone call to Mom in Wichita. Dad said it cost four dollars for a three-minute call and one dollar for each minute over three, so Bonnie and I should just say a few words and let Patty have two minutes. We were all huddled around the desk at the lumberyard because the bungalow didn't have a phone. I had gone over earlier and made a fire in the office stove. Dad had to take the phone away from Patty, and, of course, she cried piteously.

In late January, we were all back in school. On a Monday morning, Mrs. Reed answered our classroom door and called, "Donald, please come here." I was afraid for no reason other than just being called. "Donald, this is Mr. Nelson, and he needs you to go with him, so please get your coat and all, and go with him, okay?"

Mr. Nelson was a well-dressed man; he wore a dress overcoat and tie and held a hat. "Donald, I have your dad down in the ambulance. He fell and hurt his leg badly and needs you to come with us." Then I was really afraid.

Mr. Nelson opened the passenger door for me, and I climbed in, knelt on the seat, and looked over the back. Dad was lying under a blanket in the back of the mortuary hearse that was being used as an ambulance. Dad said, "We'll take you back to the lumberyard, and you can call Mr. Rohlf in Casper and ask him to send someone to Edgemont to manage the yard until I get back from the hospital in Hot Springs. Okay?" I nodded, and they dropped me off at the yard.

I called Casper and asked for Mr. Rohlf. When we had gone to Casper, I hadn't met him, so I didn't know what he looked like. After I told him what happened, he said, "There's a bad snowstorm, a real hell of a blizzard going on between here and Edgemont, so it'll be several days before I can get someone over there. Do you think you can keep the store open until he gets there?"

I didn't wait a minute; I just said, "Oh, sure." He didn't know I was eleven years old, I'm sure, but I really thought that I could do everything I needed to do. Watching Dad closely about nearly everything was going to pay off—waiting on customers, answering the phone, making sales tickets, depositing the money and checks, and everything except making deliveries. They could wait, or I could call the drayman, as Dad called the fellow with a truck. I put some more wood in the stove and unlocked the gate.

When I went to the bank to make a deposit each day that week, the teller would say, "Thank you, Mr. Hanley. We'll see you tomorrow." The other three bank people looked like they were about to laugh—and probably did after I left. I didn't care if they laughed or not. I felt like I could do important things and be somebody for the first time in my life.

Bonnie seemed more relaxed with Dad not being around. She wasn't a very good cook, but she managed to fix something for us every day. Patty smiled and even sang some songs for us as we went to school. The snow kept the fellow from Casper away until the following Sunday. I wished he would have stayed away even longer. Anyway, I had already stayed home from school for a week and then added a Monday, so I could tell the Casper fellow where everything was. He was a rather stuffy guy, and I never did learn his first name. He stayed until Wednesday when Dad got back from the hospital in Hot Springs. Dad was on crutches, but he insisted that I go back to school.

When I got back to school, I learned that on Friday, everyone in the class would receive a blank map of the United States with only the outline of the 48 states. We had to fill in the name of the state and the state capital. I really liked geography and had studied the map for weeks, so I was pretty sure I filled in every space correctly. Mrs. Reed said that no one could go out for recess until they had completed the map correctly. Over the weekend, another big blizzard hit Edgemont and closed the schools for three days. On Thursday morning, I learned I was the only one who had completed the entire map correctly, so I was the only one who could go out for recess. Big deal, the snow was a foot high. The entire sixth grade went out for recess, and I didn't know any of them, so I stood in the doorway and watched them make snowmen and throw snowballs. But I was beginning to believe that I wasn't totally stupid—maybe this little pile of shit was actually fertilizer.

Our grade school had two plays each year—one at Christmas and one in the spring. The upper four grades had one play, and the lower four grades had the other. That year, the upper grades put on *The Legend of Sleepy Hollow.* Everyone in school was encouraged to make a poster to advertise the play. There was a contest for the best posters: the top prize was a dollar, the second prize was seventy-five cents, and the third was fifty cents. I copied the front of the playbook that depicted Ichabod Crane on a horse wearing a pumpkin on his head. I won first prize and my poster, with a nice blue ribbon, was put in the window of the biggest grocery store.

Also, in March, Father Groel, the pastor of St. James, walked clear across town to the lumberyard and asked me to be his altar boy. He saw me attend weekday Mass with Dad a few times, and he didn't have a regular server except on Sundays. The whole idea made me very nervous, but I thought it was a real honor. "I, uh, would like to do it, Father, but I don't know any Latin prayers, and I don't know how to be an altar boy."

Father Groel arranged for me to meet with a high school boy who would teach me. He went over the prayers with me and helped me pronounce each word. Thankfully, I didn't have to memorize them; I just read from a card on the steps of the altar. I went through them many times. A week later, I nervously put on a cassock and surplice, then led Father Groel out to the altar, knelt, and mumbled through the Latin responses.

Many churches have a small bell that the altar boy rings for important times in the Mass when people are supposed to kneel or stand. St. James had a little box with three chimes on top and a little drumstick. I wasn't sure when to ring the chimes, so I hit them almost every time Father moved. Some people in the church chuckled. I was sure that Father would ball me out when Mass ended. The priest followed me out of the sanctuary into the sacristy. He smiled and said, "Well, Donald, you made it through your first Mass. I think you need to study a little more on when to hit the chimes, but you did fine. Thank you for your help." He was far more patient and kind than any adult I was ever around.

Although the fifth grade was a good year for me, it wasn't good for America. President Franklin Delano Roosevelt died on April 4th, 1945. He was the only president I had known because he took office the same month I was born. Both Mom and Dad adored him. Mom often said how FDR had saved our lives with programs like the Civilian Conservation Corps (CCC). Glen worked for the CCC for years which helped us pay for groceries.

In March, Dad decided to add a bedroom to the bungalow, hoping that Mom would like it, and we could all continue to live there when she returned in June. After school and on weekends, I helped Dad with the construction. I learned a lot about building, and at the same time, I had one of the worst experiences of my life. The bungalow's ceiling was not insulated, so Dad decided to fix that. The crawl space in the attic was small, and Dad said I was just the right size to drag the slabs of Rockwool insulation into the attic and place each piece between the ceiling joists. It was a warm, sunny spring day when I did this. Rockwool must be the itchiest stuff in the world. Dad told me not to scratch it and that I should take a shower right after I finished. Each Saturday, we paid twenty-five cents to take a shower at the bathhouse near us. I took a very long time trying to get rid of the Rockwool, but it still itched for two weeks.

Because of the cost, Dad used the most twisted and knotty lumber in the yard—stuff that we couldn't sell. Using that kind of material made the work go slower. Instead of regular wood siding, we put tarpaper on the sides and left it like that because we ran out of money.

Bonnie, and especially Patty, were impatiently waiting for Mom to return. We went to the movies about once a week, and that was a very welcome outing for all of us—especially for Bonnie. Dad only went twice the entire year. It cost twenty-five cents for him, but only a dime for us kids.

The new room was all painted and waiting for Mom to get home. We all sat around the radio in the bungalow and listened to President Truman announce that the German army had surrendered to the Allied forces and the war was over in Europe. After Dad left the room, Bonnie said, "I hope the war is over between Mom and Dad when she gets here." I had never thought of it as a war, but I hoped Mom would be back for good.

Nine

A FAMILY DIVIDED

———∞———

In mid-June 1945, while Dad locked up the lumber yard, Bonnie, Patty, and I went to the train station to get Mom. I don't think I ever saw Patty so happy and excited. Mom looked really nice as she stepped off the train. First, she bent down, picked up Patty, and then reached out and pulled Bonnie and me close to her. We were all happy.

Back at the bungalow, Dad and Mom gave each other a brief hug, and Dad led Mom into the bathroom and the door leading to the new room. We could still smell the paint. All three of us crowded into the bathroom behind them. We were very interested in how Mom would react to the new room.

Mom was definitely not delighted. She carefully looked at the room with its two small windows and blue Celotex walls, frowned, and said, "Oh, Den, I can see that you and Donald have worked hard to create a nice room for us. Thank you." She let her sentence trail off, then added, "We'll see how it goes."

I could see that Dad was disappointed in her reaction, but he didn't say anything. He went back to the cookstove and tended to the pork roast he had fixed for dinner. I looked at Bonnie, and we both shrugged. Patty took Mom's hand, led her back into the kitchen, and climbed into her lap.

Mom seemed to struggle through the next few days, and then one day, Bonnie came over to the lumberyard and told me that Mom wanted me to come over to the bungalow. After we all sat down at the table, Mom said, "Well, children, after your father and I had an argument this morning, and he hit me, I went to see Father Groel. The priest said that it is okay for me to leave your dad. I may get a divorce for financial reasons—so your dad will legally have to pay child support and alimony. He also said that in the eyes of God, we would still be married, and neither of us could marry again. Of course, I do not plan to marry anyone again, ever. With the priest's help, I've arranged for a fellow to take us all over to Hot Springs to live. I have packed all of your things, and we'll be leaving in about twenty minutes. You may go over to the store and say goodbye to your dad if you wish."

Slowly and reluctantly, I walked over to the store. Dad was sitting behind the desk, looking like he was lost in some barren land. In a way, I guess he was. He whispered, "I guess you know what Mom's plans are, huh?"

Dad looked up at me, then looked at his hands folded on top of the desk. "I asked her to let you stay with me, but she said you belonged with them. I hope you kids will come visit me." He stood up and opened his arms, and I hugged him. I was crying so hard my tears made his shirt wet, and when I looked up, he was crying too.

Gingerly, I unwrapped myself from his arms, went to the door, and looked back. "Bye, Dad." We both were still crying. Neither

Bonnie nor Patty wanted to say goodbye to Dad. A four-door Ford sedan was parked in front of the bungalow, and I climbed into the back with Bonnie and Patty. Bonnie looked questioningly at me like she couldn't figure out why I had been crying. She and Patty didn't share any of my sadness for leaving Dad alone.

Hot Springs was about four times as big as Edgemont and definitely prettier. We moved into the old Hot Springs Hotel. It was clean and well kept. It had been a rather luxurious place back when many people came to Hot Springs for the springs' healing powers. We had one room that was much larger than the bungalow, but we had to go down the hall to the bathroom.

The best part was that it had a hot spring swimming pool that was half indoors and half outdoors. Maybe I could learn to swim. I sure as hell didn't have anything else to do. The next day, I jumped into the pool and did my best to move my arms and legs like I saw Jim do and knew that I had a lot to learn. There was no one around to ridicule or tease me, so I kept at it that day until I could awkwardly swim across the pool without touching the bottom. I swam to the outdoor part of the pool, where I could not touch the bottom without dunking my head. I managed to swim across that larger part too.

About the time I was getting comfortable being alone in the pool, I saw three guys about my age get into the pool and swim toward me. Rather snottily, the lead one asked, "Who the hell are you?"

"I live here, and I have the right to be in this pool. Who are you?" I replied more calmly than I felt.

"We'll see about that. This is our pool, and we belong here too," the snot retorted and lunged toward me. I quickly swam backward until I was in the corner of the pool. I put my arms on the two sides of the pool and stuck my legs out in front of me. As soon as the snot and one of his friends got close, I kicked both legs out and kicked them both in the face. Their noses started to bleed buckets, and they backed off and all jumped out of the pool.

I got out of the pool and ran up to our room. I told Mom what had happened, and just as I finished talking, another tenant on our floor came to the door and told Mom she was wanted on the phone. The woman said, "It sounds like a very angry lady who's lookin' to speak to the mother of a boy who was in the pool. I know your Donald spends a lot of time in the pool, so I think she wants you."

I followed Mom down the hall to the phone and heard Mom say, "Hello, this is Margaret Hanley. Who is this?"

"Never mind who I am. I want you to know that your son attacked and wounded my boy and his friend, and I want you to know that he needs to be punished." She was talking so loudly I could hear her six feet away.

"Are you and your family residents of this hotel?" Mom asked politely.

"No, we're not, but my children often use the pool—with permission, of course. And my boy and his friends just wanted to take a little swim, and your son attacked both of them and made their noses bleed. You should do something about it!"

"Well, ma'am, my son just told *me* that three boys attacked him in the pool, and he kicked them when they went after him. My son does not lie, so I am proud of how he defended himself. I will see that he is properly rewarded. Goodbye." Mom slammed the phone back into the holder. I gave her a hug around her waist. I liked this new Mom.

The following day, I stayed in the outdoor pool for three hours. I didn't have brains enough to know that I could get sunburned even though I was in the water the whole time. The sunburn was the worst one I ever had in my life. Mom called it a third-degree burn. Even with all kinds of lotions and salves Mom found, I was in agony for three days.

Mom found a job at a ladies' hat shop. That helped with our expenses and with Mom's spirits. Soon we moved into a small, one-bedroom apartment across the street from the Sisters' Hospital. The apartment complex was built on the side of a hill, and our apartment was on the top row. The back wall smelled like dirt, like it was the side of the hill itself. At least we didn't have to go down the hall to the bathroom; we only had to share it with the apartment next door.

Bonnie, then fourteen, got a part-time job as a nurse's aide, and that same week she asked the nun in charge of the janitors if she needed any part-time help. If so, she had a twelve-year-old brother who was a very good worker. Sister Angela told her to send her brother over to meet with her. My track record with nuns wasn't great, but the next morning, I fearfully walked over to see her. Sister Angela was quite old and serious but did not seem mean-spirited like the one in that catechism class. She looked me up and down like she was observing a plant of some kind. "You're pretty young, but I have a job for you to do right now. Let's see what you can do. Follow me."

We went up to the fourth floor and across a walkway to a beautiful garden built into the side of the hill behind the hospital. The garden was in a kind of small valley in the hill, about the size of a football field. On the north side was an open cave with a pretty statue of the Blessed Mother. To the right was a patch of weeds and old flowers that had died. Sister said, "I want you to clear out all the weeds and then plant these flowers in rows.

Make the rows a foot apart. Show me what a foot is." I held my hands about a foot apart, and she said, "Good. The tools you'll need are over there." She pointed to my right. "I'll be back in about two hours."

I looked at the plot of ground. It was about fifty feet wide and twenty feet deep. Dad said that whenever you have a job to do, do it like it was your place and do it the best you can. So, I took a hoe and began digging up all the weeds and dead plants and putting them into nearby trash barrels. Then I took a shovel, spaded up the entire area, and raked it clean and smooth. I was planting the second row of flowers when Sister Angela came back. She looked at the plot and put her hand to her chin. "I see that you have an eye and energy for work. How would you like to work for me about twelve hours a week until school starts? We can pay you twenty-five cents an hour."

For the next three weeks, I helped the janitor, but liked best working with Sister Angela in the grotto. Between Bonnie, Mom, Dad's court-ordered support, and me, we were doing pretty well financially.

The second week we got a letter from Dad inviting us to visit him in Edgemont. I was the only one interested, and I took the bus on a Friday afternoon and helped Dad at the lumberyard on Saturday. We played cards each evening. On Sunday, I joined three other boys serving Mass. I felt like I belonged in Edgemont. Dad was kind and pleasant to be around. On Sunday, I took the bus back to Hot Springs.

In late July, I told Mom that I wanted to go back to Edgemont and live with Dad. When she asked me why, I said, "You have Bonnie and Patty, and he doesn't have anyone. I think he needs me, and I like to work with him, and I like school there."

"It's nice of you, Son, to want to help your dad, but the judge said I have custody. And, honestly, I'm afraid that he might hurt you. Aren't you afraid of him?"

"Maybe a little, but he's usually okay with me. He's never really hurt me as much as he did Jim."

We went back and forth for a few days, and I think I wore her down. She believed that I'd stay only a few weeks and then be back. It felt good to make an important decision like that for myself.

The hardest part for me was telling Sister Angela that I had to quit working at the hospital. She was very kind and told me she appreciated my fine work. That really felt good. I left her quickly because I didn't want her to see me crying. Sister Angela did a lot to change my opinion about nuns.

The next morning, when Mom and Bonnie were at work, Patty walked me down to the bus station. She said she'd really miss me. I told her I'd miss her too and would visit every couple of weeks.

I climbed on the bus and sat on the side where Patty was standing. She was crying when I looked at her. I was too, but I hid my tears from her.

Ten

THE END OF THE WAR AND FINDING AN IMPOSSIBLE DREAM

I got off the bus a couple blocks from the lumberyard and trudged the rest of the way with my two small suitcases. Dad gave me a brief hug and led me over to the bungalow. He let me have the room addition. I felt privileged and proud to be an occupant of the room I had helped build. Dad went to Mass every morning at 6:30, and, although he never asked me to, I went with him and served Mass for Father Groel. The routine felt very comfortable.

Another routine we developed was listening to the news on the radio each evening after dinner. On August 6, 1945, we learned that the United States Army Air Corps dropped what they called an atomic bomb on Hiroshima, a large city in Japan, and it killed over 100,000 Japanese people—mostly civilians. Then three days later, they dropped another bomb on Nagasaki and killed 74,000 more people. The announcer said that it saved many thousands of American lives because, since the Japanese surrendered, we wouldn't need to invade Japan. The following Saturday, I saw pictures on the newsreel of this huge mushroom-shaped cloud. I wondered if the generals thought of dropping the bombs in Tokyo bay or maybe on Mount Fuji to show the Japanese government how powerful the bomb was without killing so many people. I said this to Dad, and he wondered too, but we never heard anyone else mention this idea.

World War II was officially declared over on August 15, 1945. We soon learned that Bob, Bill, and Jim would all be leaving the military and returning home. Neither Bill nor Jim ever had to go overseas and fight in the war, and Dad was glad of that. When I saw Mom the following weekend, she was elated that her three boys were coming home safe.

I visited Mom and the girls three times before school started in September. Each Sunday, Bonnie and I went to Mass in the old sandstone church in Hot Springs. Mom hardly ever went with us. She never felt up to it, she said. Bonnie said that our sister Marie once told her that one time, when Mom could not get me to stop crying, a priest yelled at Mom, "Lady, take that squalling brat out of the church right now!" After that, Mom didn't like going to church. Neither of us ever asked Mom whether that was true. I remember thinking that priest was stupid and mean. Usually, on those Sundays, Bonnie and I would go to Evans Plunge, an indoor hot spring swimming pool that was quite large—about five times as big as the one at the Hot Springs Hotel.

I felt quite happy to go back to school and start the sixth grade. Our teacher was Miss Kirby, who was younger than Mrs. Reed but not any prettier. All but one or two of the students were the same as in the fifth grade. I was glad that Miss Kirby would continue to read to us right after lunch. The book for the first semester was *Call of the Wild* by Jack London. One recreational habit I began in fifth grade was reading novels, and I read every evening before going to sleep—a habit I've kept up all of my life.

On the first week of school, on the way home, Ted Torres, Jeff Daniels, and I were walking behind four girls from our class. Jeff loudly said, "Donald, let's walk like girls." He began to prissily swing his hips in a silly way, and I mimicked him. This went on for about half a block, and the girls frowned at us.

One girl, JoAnn Williams, turned around and said, "Donald, why aren't you smart like you were last year?" She gave me a snarky smile and turned around. I'm sure no one in the world would ever know how much that meant to me. This girl, one of the smartest ones in the class who always got on the honor roll every six weeks, thought I was smart! Wow. I'd show her and the other smart-alecky girls that I was just as smart as they were. I couldn't remember whether I had been on the honor roll in the fifth grade, but right there and then, I decided I would do my best to be on the honor roll in sixth grade.

On Thanksgiving and Christmas, I went to Hot Springs and spent three days with Mom and the girls. They had moved into a one-bedroom apartment in the Braun Hotel. It only had a hot plate for cooking, so we ate at a small diner across the street from the hotel. The owner and cook, a very nice, generous, older woman, made a delicious turkey dinner for the four of us. There were no other customers, and we were sure that she did all this just for us. And, perhaps, also for herself as she sat down at the table with us. Mom said this was very Christmassy of her.

Almost every Friday or Saturday night when I didn't go to Hot Springs, I would go to a movie by myself at our little Edgemont theatre. Dad rarely went to the movies. Right after Christmas vacation, *The Keys of the Kingdom* was on, and I went to see it. I liked Gregory Peck and Father Chisholm, the missionary priest he played in the film. The snow was falling as I came out of the theatre. Standing there on the sidewalk, looking up at the sky and the falling snow, I said aloud, "I am going to be a priest."

Like that priest, I could build a school, a convent, and a church and help the people get food and medical care. I could do all that, but I didn't know if I was smart enough. However, some people, like Mrs. Reed and JoAnn Williams, thought I was smart. So, if I studied really hard, maybe I could become smart enough. My other big worry, and this was a huge one—was I good enough? I thought I could be more kind, thoughtful, and less complaining in my thoughts and words. I knew I would have a hell of a time trying to stop thinking about naked girls. Standing there in the snow, I thought that I'd be good enough if I could do at least ten nice, pure, and thoughtful things every day.

That night, when I knelt by my bed to say my prayers, I counted the positive things I had done that day: I had decided to become a priest. Just before starting my prayers, I stopped my negative thoughts about saying my prayers in a bedroom with no heat. Even though it was only bacon, fried potatoes, and bread, I told Dad that dinner was very good. I chopped wood without being told. I made Dad's bed as well as my own. I went to Mass that morning. I stopped myself from playing with my pecker in an impure way. I completed all of my assigned homework. I played cribbage with Dad, although I wanted to read my Zane Grey book. I did the dishes. Then I thought back and counted all the good things I did, and yep, there were ten. Good job, Donald! Uh-oh—was complimenting myself a sin of pride? Working to do at least ten good things every day became absolutely necessary, and I recounted them every night. I told nobody about this new habit of mine.

I wanted to tell someone about my desire to become a priest, so I wrote a letter to Jim. He was still in the Navy, so if he laughed at the idea, I wouldn't have to hear it. I also told Bonnie and asked her not to tell Mom or Patty. Bonnie didn't laugh at me but said, "Aw, come on, Donald, get real. No one in our family has ever even gone to college, and Jim hasn't even graduated from high school. We Hanleys don't do things like that. We're farmers, store managers, mechanics, carpenters, and workers—not professionals, for God's sake."

She said this all so nicely. I just responded, "Well, I don't think we just have to be what other Hanleys have always been. I will become a priest, and I'll show everyone." About two weeks later, Jim sent me back a letter. It began, "Dear Padre: In case you don't know, Padre is a Spanish word for Father. Anyway, I say, good for you, little brother. I hope you do become a priest and save all your heathen brothers. You got the stuff, fella." He told me about becoming a chief petty officer, which meant that now his shit didn't stink. That remark didn't surprise me, but his positive words about my idea of becoming a priest did. So, I did a positive thing and thanked him for the letter.

We had a lot of snow that winter, and one day Dad saw me looking out of the store window at the boys pulling their sleds. They were going to the sledding hill three blocks away. Dad said, "Son, we can't afford to buy a sled for you, but I could make one for you. Would you like me to do that?" I nodded, and he got to work. Within a few hours, he built a nice-looking sled and painted it white. The next day, I went to the hill. I watched as the other kids ran, lied down on their sled, and went lickety-split down the hill and clear into the next block. I ran and jumped on my sled and slowly went about fifteen feet into the snowbank on the side of the road. Thinking it was my fault, I tried again; the sled went a few feet further and stopped. The wooden runners were just not slick enough. At least none of the other guys laughed at me and my poor sled.

Dad found a roll of chrome-plated metal used to cover the seams in linoleum flooring and nailed it onto the sled runners. I gave that a try, and it helped the sled nearly go to the bottom of the hill. The store-bought sleds had the ability to be guided, so they stayed on the course; my poor sled kept getting off track. It was no fun. I gave up, thanked Dad for all his effort, and told him I understood that he needed to send Mom and the girls all the money that he could.

During that school year, a black-and-white dog began hanging around the lumberyard, and Dad put food and water out for him. We didn't know his name, and we just called him "the dog." Dad said he was part border collie. I liked him and petted him a lot, but not too much because I told myself that would betray Pal, wherever he was.

When the weather turned warmer, we began having another visitor. A four-year-old named Salty, son of the couple who ran the Marshall-Wells store next door, started wandering over to the lumberyard. I'd take his hand and lead him back. The third time, I said to his mother, "We could watch him and bring him back to you when we get busy if you'd like." The pretty young mother thought that would be nice, so Salty began spending time with us. He was cute and smart and had the most wonderful laugh. He and the dog became best buddies.

Another notable incident happened in the sixth grade. A skinny kid named Stanley Dudley, about my size, joined our class. The first week he was in our class, when we were walking home from school, for no reason I could think of, he came up behind me and pushed me down. I got up, and he hit me in the chest. I hit him back, and he grabbed me, and we wrestled to the ground. We were rolling around on the grass when Mrs. Margaret Litzen, the school principal, drove up.

She yelled, "You two, get in this car right now!" I knew her because she owned the Texaco service station across the street, north of the lumberyard, and she worked there most Saturdays. She was the kind of person who, as Bob would say, "Would take no shit off nobody." We climbed into the car, and she took us to her classroom. She taught seventh grade in addition to being the principal and running a service station. "Now, you two will sit there until I tell you that you can go home, and if I ever see you fight again, there will be *real* consequences. Do you understand me?" I nodded.

As far as I was concerned, it was unfinished business. Dad allowed me to take Sunday afternoons off for playing around, so I went over to where Stanley lived. I wasn't sure why I wanted to finish the fighting business, but I think it was because I wanted everyone to like me, and he pushed me. I wanted to know why. His place was shockingly bad. I had always thought the old motor court was abandoned. It was six one-room cabins in a U shape, and every one needed paint. Only two seemed to be occupied. They made even our small bungalow look good. I knocked on the first one, and a shabbily dressed woman with a cigarette hanging from her mouth came to the door and grumpily asked, "Whaddya want?"

"Is Stanley here?" The woman looked about the right age.

She turned around and yelled, "Stanley, get your skinny ass over here! There's a kid here wants to see ya." I looked around her at the little one-room cabin, and it was a mess—old clothes all over the floor, beer bottles and dirty dishes everywhere. There wasn't a bathroom. I felt sorry for Stanley and lost all interest in resuming our fight.

Stanley came to the door and said, "Hi Donald, what do you want?"

"I want to talk to you about the other day. Can you come outside?" His mom didn't seem to have any interest in us. Stanley stepped outside and closed the door. "Why did you pick a fight the other day?"

"I don't know why I pushed you. I just hated being in your crummy school, and you were there. You want to play some basketball?" I said I did, and he went back into the cabin and got a ball. We played horse until dinner time. Stanley and his mom moved away a few weeks later. I'm glad I went to see Stanley that day.

I didn't win the poster contest that year, but I won first place in a landscape painting contest at the school art fair. And I did get on the honor roll for the entire year. Bonnie said, "Donald, you're becoming a serious stick-in-the-mud and pain in the ass. You're no fun to be around anymore."

I quickly replied, "So what? Teachers and other adults like me." Secretly, I worried she might be right and that was why I never got invited to any birthday parties and other kinds of events like that.

Also, I wondered if I was becoming too serious because of needing to do ten positive things every day. Nearly every time I did or said anything, I asked myself if it was good or bad.

Eleven

NOW FOUR HANLEY HOUSEHOLDS IN SOUTH DAKOTA

—⟨∞⟩—

In May, we got a letter saying that both Bob and Glen were coming to South Dakota to see about starting a body and fender shop in Hot Springs. I was looking forward to seeing them and especially hearing about Bob's time in Europe. They both had gotten married and had baby boys—and wives, of course. Just thirteen, and already I was an uncle five times.

I was also nervous about their coming to South Dakota. Dad and I had established a comfortable routine, and I was sure that their arrival would bring a lot of tension and change into our lives. Just thinking about it gave me a headache. Ever since we moved to Edgemont, I had a lot of headaches until I settled in with just Dad. I usually took one aspirin, but sometimes I took two or three if the headache was bad.

The second week of June 1946, a tan 1939 Chrysler New Yorker pulled up in front of the lumberyard. Two men, whom I hardly recognized, got out. It was Glen and Bob. They both looked years older than when I saw them last. With dark wavy hair and a big smile, Bob hurried over and gave me a big hug and said, "Boy, little brother, you're really grown up." Glen, equally handsome, I thought, was slower and more serious, but did give me a hug. "Hi, guy." I had forgotten that he had a Clark Gable mustache. It looked good on him. Dad slowly followed me out of the store and stood back as I hugged both of my brothers.

I said, "Where're the babies and their mothers?"

They ignored my question and slowly went over toward Dad. Dad held out his hand and said softly, "Hello, boys. It's good to see you both. And, Bob, I'm sure glad you made it back safely. It must have been hell."

"Yeah, Dad, it was. And how have you been?" All three of them talked like they had never met before, or had met, but only briefly, and did not like one another.

"I guess I could say I've had a bit of hell myself, but not dangerous like yours. Why don't we go over to the house, and I'll fix some coffee or something?"

Bob said, "I noticed your town has several saloons. How about going down to one and getting a beer? Donald, I heard you were pretty good at running things around here now. You wouldn't mind taking care of the store while we're gone, would you?"

Of course, I said, "Sure, I can do that." But I really wanted to see and hear more about them and their lives.

Dad hesitated, and I'm sure it was because he didn't want to spend the money, but he said, "Sure. Let's do that. After all, you boys have earned a beer or two." I had never seen Dad drink anything stronger than coffee, but they walked a block to the Stockman's Bar. After about an hour, they came back smiling and joking. Bob patted me on the back. "Dad says you know more about the lumber business than he does. How about that?" There's no way Dad said any such thing, but I felt sure he bragged about me a bit like I had heard him do with Mr. Benton, and that thought made me feel good.

They came into the store, looked around, and then walked into the yard. They said they told Mom that they would see her before dinner, and, surprisingly, they both gave Dad a hug.

After only a week, they had found an elderly man who wanted to sell a Sinclair gas station and a bulk plant. They gave up the idea of the body and fender shop, and Glen sold his Chrysler for enough to make a down payment on the business. Later I learned that a bulk plant was a place, usually near a railroad, where they have big tanks that hold thousands of gallons of gasoline and diesel fuel and have a tank truck to haul the gas around to filling stations and homes that have oil-burning furnaces. They immediately named their company *Hanley Brothers Oil Company*. Glen called Elsie, his wife in Oklahoma, and Bob called Ann, his wife in Arkansas, and asked them to take the train or bus to South Dakota.

Two weeks later, Tom Benton, a trucker and friend of Dad's, came into the store with a copy of the Hot Springs weekly newspaper. He held the paper out for Dad and pointed to an article on the front page. "Hey, Dennis, are these two guys your sons?"

I was standing behind the counter near the nail bins and was close enough to read the headlines on the paper. Dad took a glance and said, "Yep, they are my grown sons. One is just back from serving in Germany, and the other one from building planes in California. They're settling down in the Springs." He sounded like he was really proud of them, even though he never talked about them.

"Nice article about the boys, but it doesn't mention you two." He nodded towards me and handed the paper to Dad. That evening, I saw Dad reading the paper and then writing something on it. He dropped the paper onto his bed, glanced toward me, went into the bathroom, and closed the door. I think I saw a tear or two fall down his face. I picked up the paper, and next to the part about how the Hanley brothers were the sons of Margaret Hanley, a resident of Hot Springs, Dad had written on the margin, "And their dad died in Edgemont in 1945." Then it was me that did some crying.

Two weeks later, Bob brought his wife, Ann, and son, Bob Jr., with Elsie and Glen's son, Donnie, over to meet Dad and me. Glen stayed in Hot Springs to take care of the gas station, which was doing a "land office business." I never did figure out what that meant, other than that the station was busy, but figured Bob brought the wives and babies because he was friendlier with Dad than Glen was. What had happened between Glen and Dad, I often wondered. Both Ann and Elsie were beautiful and had nice figures. I couldn't take my eyes off of Elsie. She was not only beautiful but also voluptuous and moved like a movie star. She hugged Dad like she had known him all her life, "I'm pleased to meet the handsome man who is father to my husband." Her voice had a bit of a southern drawl, and she actually made Dad blush. Elsie had strawberry blond hair, nice breasts, and dressed in a way that was quite sexy.

I appreciated that they had named their first child after me. Donny was still a baby, and Bob Jr. was a little over a year old and could toddle around the store and knock stuff off shelves. Dad was even more awkward around the attractive women and babies than I was—and that was really awkward. Ann was much more reserved than Elsie, and when she talked, there was no doubt that she was from the South. It was a pleasant and melodious accent, but she said very little. The visit would have been a real bust without Elsie. She even asked Dad if I could go back to Hot Springs with them because the next day was Friday, and she had learned that I was due to visit Mom and the girls the coming weekend. Dad thought about it for a minute and then said, "He was planning to go there on Saturday afternoon, but I guess I can get along without him tomorrow, our busiest day. Well, son, you've worked pretty hard this week, so you can go with them." Ann and Bobby got in the front seat of the '38 Ford, and I nervously got in the back seat with Elsie and Donny. Elsie smelled good, too, and that made me even more nervous. I think she liked me, but I had never sat near any woman who was so gorgeous.

When we got to Hot Springs, Bob dropped Elsie and Donny off at their rental house. It was one of three flat-roofed apartments that would someday be the basements of houses built on top of them. For now, it was a typical two-bedroom house and furnished quite nicely. Then Bob took Ann and Bobby to their place, which was a two-bedroom apartment in a triplex built from a remodeled old army barracks. There were four barracks triplexes in the complex they called Vet's Housing. Neither of the two dwellings was in any way luxurious, but neither of the women seemed to mind the simple residences. I guessed they were probably from working-class families.

Bob and I went on to the Sinclair station. Glen was servicing two cars in the attractive, modern-looking building. I stayed at the station while Bob climbed into an old Ford gasoline truck to deliver a load of diesel to a construction company. Glen had on a green shirt with a Sinclair dinosaur logo on it. He finished up taking care of a couple of cars, and then when the next car came in, I washed the windshield, filled the gas tank, checked the oil, and collected the cash from the customer. Selling lumber and hardware suited me better than gasoline—I didn't have to wash anybody's windshield or get under their car's oily hood.

I called Mom to tell her I was in Hot Springs and would be spending the night with them. "Oh, honey, Bonnie's friend is here, and she's going to spend the night. You know we only have the couch for an extra bed." Mom was such a worry-wart, and I hated that.

I put my hand over the phone and asked Glen if I could stay with him. "Sure," he said, "No problem." My only worry was seeing Elsie again and possibly having impure thoughts. In confession, the priest would ask me if I entertained those impure thoughts—did I keep them running around in my head? I didn't want to be a sinner, so I'd say, "Uh, no, Father." Maybe then I'd have to confess that I lied. My pecker wanted to push its way out of my pants, which bothered me. What if someone noticed?

Lucky for me and my dumb morals, Elsie kept busy with the baby and making dinner. This gave me a chance to know Glen a bit better. He was around more when we lived in California, so I knew him more than Bob or Bill. In the morning, he went into the bathroom, took a bunch of vitamins, and came out kind of shaking and dancing and singing, "Okay, bring on the world, I'm ready." What a great way to start the day, I thought. Grinning, I glanced at Elsie, and she smiled and shook her head. On Saturday, I helped Glen out, and he dropped me off at the hotel where Mom and the girls lived.

I visited Hot Springs nearly every other weekend and Labor Day weekend when school started. Bob proudly announced that Ann was expecting their second baby in a few months. Because of her morning sickness, I stayed with Glen and Elsie when I came over on Friday afternoons.

There was a small Sinclair station in Edgemont, and Bob tried to arrange deliveries on Fridays, so I could ride back to Hot Springs with him. I got to know him better on those trips. He didn't enjoy talking about the war in Europe but told me about a few incidents. He laughed when he talked about how the American soldiers would drive on the right side of the road when driving in a convoy in England. The Brits, as he called them, drove on the wrong side of the road and would shake their fists at the Americans. On the bad side, he said one of the worst things he had to do was to direct artillery fire at a bunch of Germans who were in a beautiful Catholic church's bell tower in France. He received a Purple Heart after he was wounded in France. He said that he didn't deserve it because he just got his head cut open when he was rushing to get into his plane. The doctor and his commanding officer insisted he get the medal. He was only twenty-three when he went to England. I felt very proud of him.

While we were going to Hot Springs one day, I worked up the courage to nervously ask, "Uh, Bob, do you have to do that nasty, sinful thing with Ann when you're married?"

He smiled and chuckled a little. "You mean make love?" I nodded, and he said, "Yes, Donald, but it isn't a nasty and sinful act when you're married. It is a wonderful thing to do. It is the way a couple shows their love to one another, and it is a lot of fun. Of course, making love is how the woman becomes pregnant. The husband gives the woman his seed, and she puts it with her ovum, and sometimes they come together in a way that makes a baby. It is one of the best things in the world. Does that answer your question?"

"Yes, thank you very much." The way he said it, like it was man-to-man, made me feel very good.

It also helped me to feel more normal about having sexy thoughts, even though I couldn't do anything like that now. Then I thought, If I become a priest, oh, my God, I'll never be able to make love with a woman!

To distract myself, I started singing, "She'll be coming around the mountain when she comes." Bob joined in, "She'll be driving six white horses when she comes."

My older brothers opened up a new world for me. However, my confusion continued—if sex is so joyful and good, why is it sinful before we're married? Does a person just pull a switch that makes bad and sinful things into good? I worried my impure thoughts would stop me from becoming a priest, but tried to bury them with work, reading, and studying.

Twelve

SEVENTH GRADE AND ALL As

—⊗⊗⊗—

Every year, our class would lose a few students and gain a few students. In the fall of the seventh grade, we got four new students, including LeRoy and Janis Hudson. LeRoy was a little older than me, about my size, and lived on my way to school. We hit it off immediately, and I got to know him and his family pretty well, especially his mom, who always seemed to have freshly baked cookies around. I called her Mrs. Hudson at first, but she encouraged me to call her "Frenchie" like everyone else except her kids did.

I set a goal for myself to make straight As that year, so I studied hard. Even though Mrs. Litzen had to put me in detention the year before, she seemed to like me and my hard work. Every Friday, we had a spelling bee—boys against girls. And just like in the sixth grade, I would be the last guy standing and would have to beat five or six girls. It was a good and bad experience. The good was that I was proud that I was the best speller among the boys, and the bad was that I didn't like standing there by myself and almost always losing to the last one or two girls. The few times I ended up the winner, the other guys would clap for me, and I really liked that.

Bonnie didn't like high school in Hot Springs and took the train to California to live with Bill and Helen's family. She had a very bad case of acne and felt depressed most of the time but put on a good front and acted like she was actually okay. She never wrote to me while she was there, and I wondered if she thought I was a traitor to her, Mom, and Patty. I kept up the routine of visiting with Mom, Patty, and Bob's and Glen's families when I went to Hot Springs nearly every other weekend.

One of the new students in my class, Debbie Stern, really got to me. We had several quite attractive girls in our class, but Debbie was in a class of her own. She was a younger Elsie—beautiful, a classy dresser, and, well, sexy. She sat several seats behind me in a different row, and I often turned around to look at her, and, damn, nearly every time, she would wink at me. Every time I felt my face burn, and I'm sure I turned as red as a beet.

Bonnie came back from California in early December and seemed angry most of the time. I think something bad happened in California, but she never said what it was, only that it wasn't the Catholic high school she went to there. Both Ann and Elsie were happy to have her as a babysitter for their little boys, and she enjoyed being with them.

Thanksgiving and Christmas were nicer with Bob, Glen, and their families around. Bob and Ann hosted Thanksgiving, and Ann prepared a splendid feast. She was a wonderful cook. Elsie almost matched her with the Christmas dinner, and I enjoyed seeing a big, beautiful Christmas tree at their house. There seemed to be a little tension between the two wives, but they didn't let it keep them from being gracious hostesses. It was so nice to have real family gatherings again like we had before the war. I wanted to know how Bob and Glen spent the holidays during the war, but they didn't want to talk about it. I often thought of Dad being alone on the holidays, and I felt sorry for him. He never mentioned it, though.

After Christmas, we returned to school facing final exams. I didn't mind the tests because I had been studying hard since September. When the report cards came out, it surprised me to find that I had received As in all my subjects except penmanship. That was a B. Dad looked at the card and smiled, then asked, "What's the B doing in here?" I thought he was really serious and vowed to correct that.

Another new thing I did in the seventh grade was to attend teenage dances in the school gymnasium. The dances were the project of one of the prettiest girl's dads. He was the school's maintenance man and thought that we teens needed the dances. On Saturday evenings, when I didn't go to Hot Springs, I would go to the dance, and I was usually the first to walk across the floor and ask one of the girls to dance. It disappointed me that Debbie Stern never came to the dances.

In the spring semester, it was the fifth to eighth-grade students' turn to put on the spring play. Someone chose an operetta called *The White Gypsy*. Ms. Libby, the eighth-grade teacher, was the play's director, and they chose Debbie Stern to play the white gypsy princess. An eighth-grade boy played the gypsy prince, and about two weeks before the performance, he fell and broke his leg. He could walk, but he couldn't dance, and the dance was, according to Miss Libby, one of the most important scenes in the play. They re-wrote part of the play so a disabled prince could still be in the play, but they needed another gypsy fellow to dance with Debbie. They chose me! Of course, I was nervous as hell every time we practiced. I am sure I danced like a wooden soldier rather than a carefree gypsy, but Glen, Elsie, and Dad said I did fine. A tepid fine was far from fantastic, but it was way better than calling me the klutz that I was.

The big event was this: Dad bought a beautiful, luxurious 1939 V-12 Lincoln Zephyr for us. We both had admired it for years and thought it was a fantastic automobile. My immediate thought was, how could Dad afford it because he often said we needed to scrimp and save so he could send child support and alimony to Mom? I had mixed feelings about the car, but I enjoyed taking rides around the countryside with Dad. Though we didn't talk about big things, we sang together, and that's when I felt closest to him.

I got all As for the second semester of seventh grade—even in penmanship! Still, I didn't feel good enough, and I felt confused about both girls and my family. Dad and I still went to Mass every morning at 6:30, and I served. Dad stayed in the back row but never went to Communion except on Sundays after going to Confession. I didn't go to Communion either, and I knew why—because of masturbation. I never learned why Dad didn't go to Communion.

Thirteen

FLOATING, THEN TRAGEDY

—— ◦◦◦ ——

Riding in the Lincoln was like riding on a cloud. I never asked Dad how he paid the $1,500 for the car, but he told me that the previous owner had bought the Chevy dealership in Edgemont, so he had to sell it. Anyway, we had the best time driving all over the countryside together. I saw Mt. Rushmore again and the famous town of Deadwood, and lots of places around the Black Hills. I learned that Dad liked to sing, and he had a great voice. He taught me dozens of old folk songs like *You Are My Sunshine, Home on the Range,* and *I'm Looking Over a Four Leaf Clover.* I really enjoyed these quality times with my dad, and they're some of my fondest memories.

We took an entire four-day weekend off over the Fourth of July holiday. On Friday, we headed south to where Mom and Dad had homesteaded after they married in 1911. Dad's nephew and my first cousin, Octave Hanley, lived on a ranch near Harrison, Nebraska.

Harrison was about twenty miles north of Dad's homestead, and to my surprise, it was only about an hour and a half drive from Edgemont. Octave and his wife, Opal, had three daughters and two sons. They invited us to stay with them.

That first evening, the Fourth of July, we went to Crawford, the town where Mom and Dad got married and joined in a community picnic and pot-luck dinner to see the fireworks. The fireworks were just about the same as Edgemont's, but the abundance of good food was a real treat. Edgemont never had that.

On Saturday, I said something about never having ridden a horse. Opal volunteered a girl cousin to give me a lesson. Her name was Maggie. She was a little younger than me and a tomboyish smart-aleck. I never figured out how we were related, but she was staying with the family that summer. I hadn't realized that Dad had one brother, James, Octave's dad, who died years earlier, and six sisters, so she could have been from several families. They only had two riding horses, and they saddled up one for me to ride. Maggie rode bareback on the other. I was a bit afraid because I had never even been around a horse before, but I was excited too. With help, I climbed up on the horse and took ahold of the reins—one in each hand. Maggie yelled, "You hold both reins in one hand, dummy!" She sneered at me and trotted off. My horse trotted off after her, and I held onto the saddle horn for dear life.

Maggie stopped after about a hundred yards and waited for me to catch up. She watched me, laughed, and said, "You ride a horse like a sack of potatoes." I wanted to tell her she was a lousy teacher, but I didn't. I just said, "Could we just let the horses walk for a bit?" She shrugged and nodded, and we walked the horses for about a mile and then turned back. After she helped me get off the horse, she jumped back on her horse and took off like a light.

It was obvious she was a skilled rider, but she had taken all the fun out of my first horseback ride.

As far as I was concerned, the highlight of the trip was seeing the sod house that Mom and Dad lived in for a few years right after they married. Octave took us there in his old Ford pickup because he was afraid the Lincoln would get stuck on the old cow path leading up to it. We drove for several miles on a gravel road, then on a two-track path for about a mile before we came to the old, dilapidated building. In awe of this window into my family's past, I climbed out of the truck and slowly walked over to the little house, gently pushed open the handmade door, and went in. I was just a little over five feet tall, and I had to duck a little to go in. Only two small windows admitted a sparse amount of light and a few old, rusty implements leaning against the walls. There was also some light coming through holes in the thatch roof. It smelled of dirt and dust.

Stepping outside, there were nothing but barbwire fences and low rolling hills—no houses, no barns, no trees. As I walked around, Dad was still standing where I left him. I asked him where the water pump and the outhouse had been, and he walked down a slight incline to the place of the well and pump and then to the toilet site. It was baffling, thinking about how they had managed to live six or so years in such a barren place. "It must have been a real hard time surviving the winters and summers here— especially for Mom and the baby."

"Yeah, I was just thinking about that. I was out and about most of the time, fixing fences and helping my mother and three sisters at their places. Don't think I gave a thought to how your mom was doing. I think it plumb wore her out. My dad died when I was your age, and I guess I never learned how to be a good dad and husband." He shook his head, and I thought he might cry, so I looked away.

All three of us were quiet and solemn on our way back to the ranch house. Having dinner with Octave and Opal's raucous bunch picked up our spirits. I don't think we would have sung the old songs on the way home if we had left from the sod house.

Eighth grade started without the beautiful Debbie Stern, and I was sad and glad at the same time. She definitely distracted me from thinking about the priesthood. I told Mom and Dad about how I was thinking about becoming a priest. Mom said, "That's nice, Son." Like I had said I would buy her some flowers when I went to the store. Dad was a little better; he said, "It's going to take a lot of work, Son."

Mom told her sister, Aunt Agnes, and she subscribed to a little magazine called *Jesuit Missions*. In it were many stories about Jesuit priests everywhere in the world: South America, Africa, Asia— especially India, and Indian reservations in the U.S. Dad made me read the Catholic weekly newspaper, *My Sunday Visitor*, and it had many stories about different religious orders. There were several articles about Bishop Walsh, who was put in prison in China by the Communist government there. The stories of Bishop Walsh intrigued me. He reminded me of the priest in *Keys of the Kingdom*.

One time, the bishop from Rapid City came to Edgemont, and I served Mass for him. I had never served Mass for any priest other than Father Groel, so when it came time to pour wine into the priest's chalice, I poured a little bit, as I did for Father Groel, and the bishop stood there and moved the chalice up and down a little like I was supposed to do something. He finally took my hand and poured about five times as much wine into the chalice as Father Groel always wanted. He never scolded me, but I was sure that I had really goofed. Even Father Groel treated the bishop as someone special. I wanted to be someone special, but I never told anyone that not only would I like to be a priest, but that I'd like to be a bishop. That would be a sin of pride, I was sure. But anyway, I was attracted to the Maryknoll Fathers because Bishop Walsh, the heroic priest in China, was a member.

Because I had proven something to myself by getting all As in the seventh grade, I thought I didn't need to shoot for that again. So, I concentrated on completing my assigned work as quickly as possible, and then I would go to the encyclopedias to look up countries and their religions and practices.

One day in early November, I came home for lunch to find the lumberyard store and the yard gate all locked up. I ran over to the bungalow. It was unlocked, and I rushed in. There was Dad, lying in his bed with his eyes closed. His chest was moving a little up and down. I yelled, "Dad, are you sick?" He didn't respond at all, didn't even open his eyes. Again, I yelled, "Dad, Dad, what's the matter?" Still no response. So, I ran back over to the store and fumbled with the lock, and after I finally got it open, I ran to the telephone. Glen answered, and I told him about Dad.

I felt completely confused and lost seeing Dad unconscious. Little did I know that this would become another turning point in my life.

Fourteen

DEATH WATCH

—⊗⊗⊗—

Glen said it sounded like we should take Dad to the hospital in Hot Springs. After I locked the store back up and returned to the bungalow, I pulled a chair up near Dad's bed and waited for a few minutes. As I sat by the bed, I ate a sandwich I had quickly fixed myself. About ten minutes later, my brother Jim came through the door. I didn't even know he was back in South Dakota. Bob followed, and it amazed me that Jim was even taller than Bob.

Bob felt Dad's pulse by putting fingers on his wrist. "His pulse is very weak. Has he said anything since you've come home?"

"Nope. He's not even opened his eyes once."

Dad was still dressed for work and had only a light blanket over him.

"Jim, let's pick him up and put him in the Lincoln's back seat," Bob said. "Donald, you can get in the back seat with him while Jim drives. Give me the keys, and I'll call Casper and have them send someone over to run the lumberyard. I'll drive the Ford back to Hot Springs and see you at Sisters' Hospital, okay?"

I picked up the keys from the dresser's top drawer and unlocked the car. As gently as they could, they put Dad in the back seat. I climbed in after him and put his head on my lap. When we got out on the highway, Jim said, "Now this is a proper car!" I could tell he was far more interested in the car than he was in Dad. There were many curves on the highway, but there was an eight-mile straight stretch, and we whizzed down it. I looked over the front seat at the speedometer—it read a hundred miles an hour. Usually, people took forty minutes to drive between towns, but Jim made it in twenty. We pulled into the ambulance entrance at the hospital, and Jim ran in and got two white-coated orderlies to come out with a gurney. A nurse came with them, and they eased Dad onto the gurney and into the emergency room.

One sister ushered me to a waiting area, and Jim left to park the car. Bob arrived about twenty minutes later. A doctor came out to talk to us after his preliminary examination. "Your father is very ill, as you know. When did he lose consciousness?"

"I don't know. I left for school about a quarter to nine, and he was all dressed and had opened the lumberyard. When I came home for lunch at noon, he was still dressed and lying down and unconscious on his bed at our house. Do you know what's the matter with Dad, doctor?" I stuttered and started crying. I was ashamed of myself for crying in front of these grown men, especially my brothers.

"We don't know yet. He is having trouble breathing. I'm sure you know that, and now we have him on a ventilator. His pulse is slow, and his blood pressure is low. He is definitely in danger." It irritated me that the doctor kept looking at Bob because he was older. "Do you live with him?"

"No, I do," I said.

Then he started addressing me with his questions. "Has your dad been sick?"

"No."

"Was he in good health the last few years and months?"

"Yes, as far as I know. He came to this hospital three years ago because he fell and broke his leg pretty badly. But not since then."

"Well, we'll take him to a room now and watch him closely. We'll let you know how he is doing. Let the nurse know how and where we can reach you."

A nurse came in, and Bob gave her his phone number and the number of the service station. I said, "I'm gonna be right here in the hospital—in Dad's room." I stared at her in a way that I hoped dared her to tell me I couldn't stay here. She shrugged and walked away. Jim had already taken the Lincoln back to the station, and Bob waited with me until we saw Dad being wheeled out of the emergency room. I said, "I'll call you when something happens, okay?" He nodded and patted me on the shoulder, then left. I followed the gurney up to the second floor.

They gently moved Dad onto the hospital bed, hooked up the oxygen mask, and inserted an IV tube into his left arm. I pulled up a chair and took his right hand. A few minutes later, a nun who was also a nurse came in and greeted me kindly before showing me how to check Dad's pulse by putting my fingers on his wrist. I had to fiddle around with it several times before I learned how to do it, but the sister was patient with me. Dad continued to breathe lightly, and nurses came and went as I sat there. I only left the chair when I had to go pee.

I was famished when it came time for dinner, but I didn't say anything to anyone. A nice nun named Sister Theresa came in and asked me if I would like to have dinner. When I nodded, she had a tray brought to the room. It was kind of tasteless, but it took away my hunger. I don't think I ever sat in one place so long. Around nine o'clock, a nurse asked me, "Donald, is someone coming to take you home tonight?"

"No, I'm gonna stay here tonight."

"That's not allowed." She said this as kindly as she could, but I could tell she was determined to get rid of me. I shook my head, and she said, "Well, we'll see."

Sister Theresa came back a few minutes later. She had her friendly smile with her, and I appreciated that. "Donald, the floor nurse, Miss Tracy, informed me you plan to stay in that chair tonight. Is that correct?"

"Yes, Sister."

"Ordinarily, that is not allowed. Do you and your father live together—just the two of you?" I nodded. "Well, that chair will become very uncomfortable. How would it be if I have a cot sent up for you for when you get sleepy?"

An army-type cot was sent for me to sleep on.

Dad's pulse was the same the next morning, and he did not wake up. The orderlies came and put Dad on a gurney to get X-rays and other tests. I stayed in the room. Around noon, they brought him back, and a doctor came in and told me that all they knew was that Dad had a severe bowel impaction. I didn't know exactly what that meant, but I didn't say anything and show how stupid I was. Maybe Bob or Glen would be able to explain it to me.

A little later, Sister Angela, the nun I had worked for here in the hospital, came to Dad's room. I was very happy to see her. She remembered me, and I shook her hand, and she put her other hand over mine. That felt very comforting. She told me she had never found a young man who was as able as I had been to help her. That made me feel so good.

Bonnie and Patty had moved with Mom to the Braun Hotel, only two blocks away, and they came by after school to see me and see how Dad was doing. Mom never came by, and I wondered how she could have lived with Dad for over thirty years and then couldn't walk two blocks to visit him when he was sick. The girls didn't stay long, nor did Elsie and Glen a little later.

There was a tall window behind and to the side of Dad's bed, and a blind covered the bottom third. From where I sat near Dad's bed, I could see two beautiful ponderosa pine trees and the sky. I loved to see the trees dance with the wind. As I sat there, I had a lot of time to think in between taking Dad's pulse. My mind went back and forth over the two and a half years that we lived together. Most of the time, he was pretty nice to me. I liked how he taught me so many things and rarely was impatient with me. I did not like the slogan he often used, "Listen here, Son, you do something right, that's the way it should be done. You do something wrong, I'll tell you about it. So don't go around expecting compliments all the time." He then would point a finger at me and add, "You got that?" He first said that after I thanked him for a rare compliment. Though I could usually tell when he was pleased, even if he didn't say anything.

The only time he hit me was last spring when a small circus came to town, and a classmate and I stopped by. One of the circus men saw us admiring the two old elephants they had. He asked if we would like to feed the elephants if he gave us tickets to that evening's show. We both said yes and fed the elephants. It took about half an hour. When I got to the lumberyard, Dad didn't say anything, but I could tell he was angry because I was late. At dinner that evening, I looked at the clock and noticed that I only had a few minutes to get to the circus show. I said, "I better hurry. The circus comes on in ten minutes."

Dad calmly said, "You are not going to the circus tonight."

"But I have a free ticket for feeding the elephants."

"But you did not tell me you'd be late, so you are not going to the circus."

"I am, too. I earned the ticket. Nobody's gonna tell me what to do!"

Big mistake. Dad jumped out of his chair and hit me so hard I flew out of my chair. He came around the table, and, fortunately for me, his bed was only three feet away, and I quickly crawled under it. He had pulled back his leg, and he missed me but hit the iron railing under the mattress.

"You miserable little shit! Don't you ever talk back to me like that!" he yelled.

I stayed under the bed until I was absolutely sure it was safe to get up. I never talked back to Dad again. I didn't want to be another Jim.

However, I wasn't totally obedient. As early as the fifth grade, Dad bought a khaki hat for me to wear. It was just like the one he wore every day at the lumberyard. It was shaped like a policeman's or army officer's hat—a black bill, round band, and round, khaki cloth top larger than the band. On Dad, it looked okay, but ridiculous on a boy. Dad insisted I wear it everywhere—even to school. I wore it about a block until I was sure I was out of sight and then put it in the paper sack where I kept my books. If Dad had ever learned of my deception, he never mentioned it, and I was sure he would have.

There were other negative things during our time together, like having to sleep in a room with no heat when it was below freezing outside. In those mornings, I'd grab my clothes and run to be near the stove before putting them on. The one good thing was that Dad had bought tons of blankets for Mom and the girls before we had arrived, so I was not in danger of freezing to death.

The other thing I wish Dad had changed was my schedule. I could play with others only on Sunday afternoons after I had read *Our Sunday Visitor* newspaper. Most Sundays, I would go over to the Torres family and play football or basketball, but I never had enough time to get good at either—or any other sport. After LeRoy Hudson and his family moved to town, I enjoyed going to their house too, but that and the dances were all my social time.

I liked living and working with Dad. I had an important place in his life—most of the time. Even though I had spent more of my fourteen years of life with Mom, I felt closer to Dad. It was probably because Dad involved me in his life, whereas Mom endured life and tolerated me because she was my mom. And I took her for granted in a similar manner. Glen once said that Mom just never got over the death of our sister Aggie, who died when she was eight years old. That was the reason she was so depressed all the time. She never did anything I could be involved in like I did with Dad. Dad needed me to be his companion, as well as his helper and co-worker. That was more involving, I believed, which was why I felt closer to Dad.

I spent most of every day sitting beside Dad's bed with my fingers on his left wrist. Sister Theresa visited daily, and Bonnie stopped by for a brief visit most days, but Patty never returned after that one visit. Jim never came back for a visit, and I guessed he never forgave Dad for knocking him off the dock that time. Bob and Glen seemed to alternate visits every other day. One day, Bob came in and caught me smiling. "Hey, little brother, what's you got to smile about?"

I looked up and said, "I was thinking of the time I came home, and Dad was hiding behind the nail counter. He was usually in the store, but sometimes in the yard. Anyway, that day, I was looking around for him, and suddenly Dad jumped up and yelled, 'BOO!' He scared the shit out of me, but I never saw Dad laugh so hard. I remember thinking that I would like to have seen more of that from Dad."

"Yeah, he was always a very serious guy. I think Glen got the worst treatment from Dad. Dad was always pretty kind to Marie, but not Glen. He was hard on Bill and me, but we're only a year apart, so we had each other while Glen was off by himself most of the time. I think we—except Marie—were more than a little afraid of him." We talked a bit longer, and he tousled me on the head and said, "Donald, I think he loves you a lot, you know?"

I nodded.

After four or five days, I was sitting in my usual place beside the bed, and Dad's pulse stopped. I moved my fingers, thinking that I had not felt for the pulse correctly, but no matter how I put my fingers, I could not feel Dad's pulse! I pushed and pushed the nurse's call button and screamed, "HELP!"

Fifteen

FEELING TOTALLY ALONE IN THE WORLD

—◦◦◦—

A nurse rushed in and heard me scream, "Don't leave me, Dad. Don't leave me, Dad." I don't know how many times I yelled this, but between utterances, I sobbed and sobbed before my utterances finally faded. The nurse put a stethoscope on Dad's chest and said, "I'm so sorry, Donald, but your father has died."

Just then, Sister Theresa came into the room and put a hand on my shoulder. "I'm afraid, Donald, that God has taken him to heaven. I'm so sorry,"

I put my head on Dad's hand and continued to sob. Sister Theresa must have called Bob or Glen at some point, but I was still bent over the bed with my head on Dad's hand, crying, when they came into the room. They each put a hand on my shoulders, which helped a little, but I still couldn't stop crying. This time, I didn't care who saw me crying. Someone, I think a nurse, pulled up the sheet and covered Dad's face. I dragged it back off and gazed at him. I couldn't allow myself to say, "Goodbye, Dad." Just thinking that made me cry more. I don't remember who took me home, but I remember thanking Sister Theresa for her kindness.

The two living beings I had been closest to were Pal and Dad. Now I had neither. We had never talked about death or anyone dying, so I was more than a little lost. Death, like sex, was something you just didn't talk about. Why did God let Dad die? Or did God kill Dad? Dad was fifty-six years old—not *real* old, so why did he die? I wondered if Dad made it to heaven. He often did his best to be a loving person and show his love for God, but he was also evil when he hit Mom and us kids. These and hundreds of questions ran around in my head about life, death, and God.

Later that day, Bob or Glen asked me if Dad had ever said anything about where he wanted to be buried. I said, "He once mentioned he might like to be buried next to his parents near Verdon, Nebraska. His sister, Gertie, is a nurse in Falls City. She'll know," I said.

One of them called her and made arrangements for Dad's burial service there after the funeral in Edgemont. Bonnie and I went with them to pick out a coffin for Dad. I told them it should be the least expensive one they had because Dad said he wanted to be buried in a pine box, and I was sure he wasn't joking. He would think it was stupid to get him an expensive coffin after he spent his whole life being poor. I was proud of that part but ashamed of the way Bonnie and I clowned around in the showroom where they displayed the coffin—acting like we were going to climb into the fancy ones and dancing around like we didn't have a care in the world. I felt like I didn't give a shit what anyone thought about anything. Bob scolded us, but the funeral director said that children often acted that way after a parent's death. For once in my life, I didn't care if someone thought I was acting like a child. I felt ashamed later, though.

Bob took me to a store, and I got my first suit. The one I had worn for my First Communion was a hand-me-down from all four brothers. My funeral suit was, of course, the cheapest one in the store and still cost over twenty dollars. I told Bob I'd pay him back.

Jim Abney—Marie's husband, Bob, Glen, Jim, and I were the pallbearers. When we solemnly marched through the church doors, I was amazed to see that the church was full of people, some I didn't know at all. After accompanying the casket up near the sanctuary, we went to the pews we were assigned. Bob with Ann, Glen with Elsie, and Jim Abney with Marie sat behind Mom. Bonnie, Patty, Jim, and I sat next to Mom near the aisle.

When Father Groel gave the eulogy and talked about what a good man Dad was, Mom and everyone but me cried like babies. I looked down our pew and then back and saw that Bob, Glen, and their wives were all crying too. At first, I felt sad. Then I realized that, except for the early days of our arrival in South Dakota, Mom, Bonnie, Jim, and Patty acted like they hated Dad. And Glen and Bob seldom visited him and acted like he was a stranger. I sat there with clenched fists and thought of the day Dad wrote in the newspaper's margin that he died in 1945. They seldom or never visited him in over two years, and now they were sitting there crying. It made me mad.

At the end of Mass and the final blessings, we pallbearers followed the priest and the altar boys down the aisle. After we left Father Groel and the casket in the church's vestibule, we went outside to greet people as they came out. A well-dressed, distinguished-looking man about Dad's age came over to us and looked down at me. "Are you Donald Hanley?"

"Yes, Sir." I was surprised that this man might want to talk to me.

"Well, Donald, I'm Sam Rohlf. We've talked on the phone, but I believe this is the first time we've met. Now, how old are you, Son?" He said this respectfully, like I was a grown man.

"I'm fourteen, Sir. Why would you like to know that?" I hope I sounded respectful.

"So, over three years ago, I asked you if you could keep the lumberyard open while your dad was in the hospital. Remember that?"

"Oh, yes, Sir, I sure do."

"You were only eleven years old, correct? Do you remember how you answered me that day when I asked you if you could keep the yard open for a few days?"

"I think I said 'Okay' or something."

"I remember clearly that you said, 'Oh sure,' like you kept the store open all the time. And I remember your dad was really proud of you and your work. I'm impressed and honored to meet you. I wish it was under better circumstances." He reached out and shook my hand and then put his other hand over mine. That felt fantastic. Mr. Rohlf then turned to my brothers and told them the story of the snowstorm and my minding the store when I was eleven years old and in the fifth grade. They all—even Jim—seemed to be impressed. I felt bad that I had been mad at them.

Father Groel told us he would open the casket for us if we cared to give Dad a final viewing.

All five of us brothers went back up the stairs for the viewing. None of the women or girls wanted to follow us. After everyone left, we loaded the casket into the hearse and followed it to the train station. I wanted to yell at the railroad guy who called to his helper in the baggage car, "The corpse is here?" like it was just any old piece of crap. I wanted to yell, "That's my dad, not a corpse!" But I didn't.

We went into the church hall for a reception. I tired of people giving me hugs and sympathetic pats—especially on the head. The women of St. James prepared a very nice lunch for everyone, and after a while, our family went over to Hot Springs and had our own family gathering. It was the last time all eight of us siblings were together for seventeen years.

Marie, her husband Jim, Glen, and I drove the Lincoln to Falls City, Nebraska, the next day. We stayed overnight in a hotel there and had dinner with Aunt Gertie and two of her children. The next morning, we went to the country cemetery. A priest and the cemetery caretaker were waiting for us. It was a cloudy, chilly, windy day, and the priest wore a purple stole over his overcoat as he greeted the four of us.

I stood between Marie and Glen, and the priest stood at the other end of the freshly dug grave. He read the Latin prayers, followed by a very short eulogy. I was glad that he didn't say anything about Dad because he didn't know him at all.

The priest nodded to the caretaker, who picked up his shovel and pushed it into the pile of dirt next to the grave. As if in slow motion, I watched him lift the shovel full of dirt and throw it on the casket. Suddenly, I had an overwhelming urge to jump into the grave so I could be buried with Dad. I never told anyone about that urge—or that I silently said to Dad and myself, "If I don't belong with you, I don't belong with anyone anywhere."

These words haunted me for years. It turned into a core belief of mine. It was like I remained a stranger no matter where I went until much later in life.

Sixteen

LIVING ALONE

―⁂―

After Glen and I dropped Marie and Jim off in Wichita, we immediately turned back toward South Dakota. As we drove into Edgemont, I was amazed at how truly ugly the town was, and I felt like it had been years since I had been here. The old duplex we had lived in for two months when Mom and us kids had first arrived four years ago now looked like an old, run-down shack rather than a refuge from the little bungalow next to the lumberyard. Worst of all, even the lumberyard looked dismal—as dismal as I felt.

I was surprised to learn that Bob and Jim had arranged for Jim to be the Edgemont Builders Supply manager. The only condition Mr. Rohlf put on the plan was that I would teach Jim how to run it. They had talked with him before he had gone back to Casper the day after the funeral. Bob had called when we were in Falls City and asked if I wanted to continue working at the lumberyard.

He didn't say anything about Jim being my boss. My fear of Jim's bossiness was relieved after I talked with Mr. Rohlf myself. My interaction with Jim via mail was cordial, so I felt fairly sure we could get along.

After we locked up the yard that first evening, Jim surprised me by cooking a delicious dinner of spaghetti and meatballs, something Dad and I never had. I don't know where Jim learned to cook, but I was glad that he did because I didn't like to cook at all. I would do the dishes but not cook—except make cold sandwiches if I had to. There was another surprise that evening when Jim said he was okay with my staying in the new bedroom. That night, I threw my old khaki hat in the corner of my room and left it to collect dust.

Then, on my first day back in school, I got another surprise. Four guys met me at the school door, and one shouted, "Guess what? You've been selected to play Scrooge in the Christmas play!" They sounded so excited that you'd think they were telling me I had been named the starting quarterback for the Notre Dame football team. Another fellow added, "You're probably the only guy in the class smart enough to learn all the lines."

"Are you sure of this?" They all nodded. I felt flattered and honored but didn't feel like doing anything much at all—even going to school, which was something I usually enjoyed. "Thanks, I guess." I trudged up the stairs to our classroom, and Miss Libby met me at the door. One of the guys had gone ahead of me and informed her they had told me about playing Scrooge.

She smiled and said, "So, Donald, what do you think? When we first thought of you for the part, I worried it might be too much so soon after your father's death, but then we talked about it and thought it might be a fun experience and help you get over your dad dying."

I had not smiled at all while she was talking, and I was silent for a minute and then said, "Can I think about it for a while? Maybe tell you for sure tomorrow?" I told her how I had to train Jim at the lumberyard.

Miss Libby, a woman about five feet, nine inches tall, straightened to look even taller and then looked at the ceiling. I hoped she was not asking God how to handle this smart-alecky kid. She seemed a bit shocked about what I said about managing the lumberyard. "Will you be needing your brother's permission to be in the play?"

Even the idea that Jim would have any control over me made me upset, so I practically screamed, "Oh, God, no!" I should have apologized, but I didn't. "He'll sorta be my boss, but I'll also sorta be his boss, too. I'll just ask him if he can get along by himself so I can do it, that's all." That might have sounded smart-alecky, but I thought it was okay. She nodded and said I could let her know tomorrow.

When I got to the lumberyard at 3:45 p.m., I told him about the part in the play. He said, "I saw that play one time. Scrooge's the main part of the whole damn thing. You'll be great at it. If I have a question about something, I'll just ask you about it later."

We began play practice the week before Thanksgiving. It was mostly a male cast as the main characters were Scrooge, Tiny Tim, and Marley and his ghosts. The guy chosen to play Marley and his ghost of the present was Eugene Helsel, also in the eighth grade. He was six feet tall and gangly. He was a slow learner—kinda like my sister Patty—but looked perfect for the part. I learned that first week that I'd have to prompt him on all his lines in practice. He had the second most lines in the play, and most of them were with me. Miss Libby and I both hoped he would be able to remember his lines when we put on the play for an audience. Just in case

Eugene could not remember his lines, I practiced prompting him with a hand or paper hiding my mouth.

The day before Thanksgiving, Miss Libby asked each of us to share what we were thankful for. I looked around the room as each student said things like, "I'm thankful that all of my family will be home for Thanksgiving," or "I'm grateful that we have plenty of food to eat when many in our world do not." I liked that one but didn't want to be a copycat, and to be honest, I wasn't in a very thankful mood, so I said, "I can't think of anything."

Miss Libby said, "Aw, come on, Donald, I'm sure you can think of something."

I just sat there, wishing she'd just shut up. After some moments of silence, LeRoy Hudson said, "Hey Hanley, you're thankful for being Irish, aren't you?"

"Yeah, I'll go with that," I growled, and Miss Libby went to someone else.

Jim and I closed the lumberyard early that Wednesday and went to Hot Springs. As usual, Ann put on a very delicious dinner. I was down in the dumps and glad to go back to Edgemont and be at the lumberyard on Friday and Saturday. Jim went back to Hot Springs Saturday afternoon, and I ate dinner with LeRoy Hudson's family. Between Thanksgiving and Christmas, I spent a lot of time at the Hudsons' and liked it best when the kids were all out of the house and I could visit with their mom, Frenchie. The Hudson's weren't Catholic, but Frenchie was as kind and patient as Sisters Angela and Theresa. Those two nuns took away a lot of the negative feelings I had about nuns from Sister Mary in Paola and Sister Grumpy in Edgemont's summer catechism.

The Friday before Christmas vacation, we put on *A Christmas Carol.* Sure enough, I had to prompt Eugene. I hated to admit it, but Jim was the only member of my family to attend. It was only twenty-eight miles to Hot Springs, and it wasn't snowing or anything. I guessed my playing the lead in the play wasn't very important to them. I received many compliments but thought most of them were said to me because they felt sorry for me.

To my great surprise, I received the best Christmas present of my life. Even more surprising, it was from my brother Jim: a brand new bicycle. He brought it home from Hot Springs before Christmas and said, "Go ahead, try it out." I was glad it was snowing because I didn't want to admit, even to him, that I didn't know how to ride a bicycle.

"After Christmas I'll try it out, when it won't get all snowy and wet," I said, ashamed to admit that I did not know how to ride a bike at fourteen. Of course, I had never had one before. I thought every kid in the United States knew how to ride a bike before they were eight years old. The following Sunday, I kept the gate locked and practiced riding the bike around the yard. Every time I fell, I looked around to see if anyone saw me. As far as I could tell, no one did. I managed to go from the front gate to the back warehouse, but I wasn't ready to venture out into the street for another week.

The following week, I found Frenchie at home alone. I confided in her that I got the bike for Christmas and just learned how to ride it.

She seemed to sense that I was ashamed of that fact. "That is the first bicycle you've ever owned, right?" I nodded, and she continued with her warm, pleasant smile. "I think it is wonderful that you've finally got a bicycle to ride. From what I've learned about your life so far, you haven't been living in the lap of luxury, but here you are, the brightest student in your class and the most polite young man I think I've ever known."

I asked her why she thought that, and she told me both LeRoy and Janis told her so.

"You shouldn't ever be ashamed of yourself because you work so hard to be a good student, worker, and person," she said. "Now, don't say anything; just let my words sink in. Okay?"

Frenchie put up a hand to stop me from saying any more. It felt good hearing her say so many nice things about me. I wished Mom would say things like that. Then I thought of Dad and cried and wished he would have said things like that too. I also wondered if he thought such things.

Frenchie saw my tears and put a hand on my knee. She said, "I really believe all of what I just told you, and I also think you have not heard enough about how you are truly a very fine person. I'm sure your dad is looking down from heaven and liking what he sees in you. So, stand up here and give me a hug." I did, and it made me feel quite a bit better.

After I mastered the bike, one day, I was feeling my oats and cruising rapidly up the street in the direction of the school. I was intrigued by how fast I was going and how fast my feet were moving on the pedals. Then I glanced down at my feet and ran into the back of a parked car, flew over the handlebars, and hit the car's trunk with my face. I made a small dent in the trunk and broke off one of my top front teeth. Blood gushed from my nose, and I had to put my upper lip over my broken tooth because it hurt so badly. The next day I had to go to the dentist. He said that I needed to have the tooth capped or I would lose it. It would cost over a hundred dollars. I told him I could not afford that, and he said that all he could do was file down the sharp edges, but the tooth would be sensitive to hot and cold food and drinks. I ended up habitually putting my upper lip over the tooth, thus creating a crooked smile that I've kept all of my life.

A few weeks after Christmas, I learned another new skill—driving the old Dodge truck. After I learned how to ride the bike and had Sundays free, LeRoy and I took the lumberyard's old pickup out for a ride. LeRoy knew a little more than I did, but we both had a hard time learning to shift. We'd manage to herky-jerkily get the old junker to a side street and then practice so we could go a few blocks without killing the engine. We picked a street where we were fairly sure no one knew us well enough to call LeRoy's parents. I never told Jim, but he found out about it one weekend when we drove a few miles out of town, which used up a gallon or two of gasoline.

"You know the lumberyard pays for the gasoline, so keep track of how much you use and pay it back, okay? And if you wreck that piece of shit, I'll kick your ass." He started to leave and then added, "I got one up on you, little brother—I started experimenting with driving in California, where it was against the law. I could have gotten my ass in jail, but they've got so many farm kids here in South Dakota that they don't require a license. So, anyway, be careful." I would have liked to hear more about his experimenting.

In March, Bodie, a friend of Jim's from the navy, joined us and helped Jim build a new shelter for cabinet-grade molding and lumber. Jim found a cot for Bodie so he could sleep in the bungalow, and they began a side business of installing aluminum roofing on houses and barns. Several times that spring, Jim asked me to stay home from school on Monday or Friday to keep the lumberyard open.

My time living with Jim was a test of my ability to live alone because Jim spent more time with his girlfriend in Hot Springs than with me when the lumberyard was closed. And that fit my feeling of not belonging anywhere or with anyone. I went back to being a gloomy Gus, detached observer. Before my talk with Frenchie Hudson, I don't think I was aware of how much I yearned for someone to notice me and say kind things to me. She was a flower in my life. Still, I believe I tried to jump over adolescence and devote my energies to being a good worker and student.

Jim paid me well for working when he was away. And Bonnie, Patty, and I all got $15 a month from Dad's Social Security account. Because he and Mom were divorced, she could not receive any of his benefits, which didn't seem fair to me. Besides what Jim paid me for filling in, the company paid me $15 a month—the maximum I could get paid and still receive an SS check. With those monies combined, I could give Mom some each month.

In May, my school had a nice celebration for the graduating eighth graders: a dance. We needed to invite the seventh graders to have enough students to really have a party. I invited Janis Hudson for a date, and she was kind enough to accept. I felt like a dork, but I don't think Janis minded my stumbling around. School ended on the Friday before Memorial Day, and I was thrilled to say goodbye to the eighth grade. It was even worse than the first grade, the first time around.

Business had been slow during the spring and continued to be slow during June and July. I wondered if having two kids—as some people called Jim and me—running the lumberyard was the reason. Anyway, Rohlf sold the Edgemont yard to a small Nebraska chain called Foster Lumber Company, and I was suddenly out of a job in mid-August. A young man took over and said he did not need anyone to work with him. He and his wife moved into the bungalow.

Seventeen

THE FAMILY QUARTET REUNITED

———⊙⊱⊰⊙———

Bob and Glen found an old, small house in Edgemont that they could purchase for $2,000. So, they bought it for Mom, Bonnie, Patty, and me. I think they sold the Lincoln for enough to pay Dad's funeral expenses and part of the cost of the little house. It wasn't much of a house, but the mortgage payment was less than what Mom was paying for the two rooms at that old hotel in Hot Springs.

The back part of the house had settled into the ground, but the front part hadn't. We joked that if you fell down in the living room, you'd roll into the kitchen before you could get up. It had two small bedrooms, and I had to share one of them with Mom, but I had my own bed. And believe you me, I never told anyone I had to share a room with my mom. The house had a working bathroom, and for the first time in years, they didn't have to go down the hall to use the bathroom, and I didn't have to pay a quarter each week for a shower. Bonnie wasn't terribly happy with Hot Springs High School and had threatened to hitch-hike to Wichita, so she was willing to try Edgemont High School. She still had a severe case of acne and hated how she looked. Mom and Patty seemed to just go along with whatever others in the family told them to do, including where to live. Years later, I learned that Bob and Glen had found the old hotel in Hot Springs for us. Patty always hated all the stairs she had to climb at the Hot Springs school, so she was glad to be back in Edgemont. She also seemed glad to be in the fifth grade, but she struggled just to get Cs and Ds in every subject. Mom and the girls seemed okay with Edgemont, as long as Dad wasn't there. Bonnie liked Edgemont High School the best of the three schools she had attended and ended up with the third-highest grade point average in her class.

Jim had been dating Kay Brenner, a beautiful nurse who worked at the Lutheran Hospital in Hot Springs. That was why he left Edgemont early every Saturday and most weekday evenings. I never figured out how all four of my older brothers managed to find beautiful and intelligent women. Jim and Kay were planning a wedding in Kay's hometown in eastern South Dakota. Jim got a carpentry job at the construction company building a dam on the Cheyenne River, south of Hot Springs. He went to work the same week we left the lumberyard.

It didn't take me long to learn that there were no jobs available for a high school freshman in Edgemont. Being unemployed, I tried out for the football team. Edgemont High only had eighty-three students, but still played eleven-man tackle football. Nearly every one of the forty boys tried out for the team. All the newcomers were given a football uniform on a sweltering day the week before Labor Day. We did a bunch of calisthenics, ran around the track, and then gathered on one end of the football field. I was exhausted as we all listened to coach Al Thomas's pep talk, and he then ordered us to duck walk the length of the field. I squatted down and started the awkward movement, slowly and painfully moving my way down the field. Within a few seconds, I was ten feet behind the next closest fellow. Coach Thomas, acting the Air Force major he had been, came up behind me, booted me in the ass, and muttered, "What's the matter, Hanley, ya outta shape?"

I muttered back, "Yeah, I guess." He kept tapping me on the butt, and finally, without a word, I stood up and walked off the field back to the gym's locker room. I hated being humiliated by anyone, and I also hated being a quitter. My hatred for humiliation won out, and I left the uniform folded on the bench in the locker room.

Mr. Thomas also taught the two-hour woodworking class and the general science class that all freshmen were required to take. I was afraid that he would hold it against me because I had quit the team. After school started and the football team left to play a game in Wyoming, he told the remaining wood shop students, "While I'm gone, Hanley here is in charge. He knows more about carpentry than any of you misfits will ever know. He'll let me know if any of you screw up or don't show up." They all looked at me. I shrugged and playfully tried to look like General MacArthur. I didn't know how Mr. Thomas knew of my woodworking skills, but his words helped me relax around him.

Besides woodworking, we had three other classes: science, English, and algebra. Twenty-two of our thirty-one eighth-grade classmates enrolled in the high school freshmen class. We all had the same required classes except the girls, who had home economics while the boys had wood shop. Ted Torres and I thought it was a pretty light load. On the way home during the third week of school, I said, "Ted, do you know that a guy in last year's senior class finished high school in three years?"

His eyes lit up, "Oh, no! I didn't know that. We could take five credits for two years and six for one year and be done. Who do we need to talk to about this?"

I thought that Ted still had more fear of authority figures than I did, so I said, "I think the principal, Mr. Jackson, will know. Want me to talk to him about it?" He gave me an enthusiastic yes. The next day I hesitantly made an appointment with Jackson's secretary.

That same afternoon, I went into Mr. Jackson's office, and he stood up and shook my hand. "Hello, Donald Hanley. Welcome to high school," he said. "I've heard a lot about you, and now I get to meet you."

Amazed that he had heard about me, I asked what he'd heard.

He could probably tell that I was shaking in my boots. (I literally did wear boots—like cowboy boots, but not as fancy.) They were always black, like oilmen wore. Jim wore them for work all the time, and I followed him on that.

"Both Carolyn Libby and Margaret Litzen said you were the smartest and hardest worker of any student they have had here in Edgemont," he said. "And, you know, Miss Litzen doesn't give out praises very often. So, Donald, what may I do for you?"

I wanted to say, *First, get me down off the ceiling.* But I said, "My friend Ted Torres, and I were thinking of the student who graduated last year after three years of high school. Ted is a good student too, and we think we can do it, but we need to know the procedure."

"Why are you in such a hurry, Donald?"

"Well, Mr. Jackson, I, uh, I plan to become a Catholic priest and, uh, my dad died last year, and all four of my brothers have helped our Mom and us three younger kids, so, I think I need to help Mom too and, well . . ." Damned if I didn't start crying. I had no idea why and blubbered, "I'm sorry, sir, I don't know why I'm being a baby."

Jackson reached in a drawer and pulled out a box of Kleenex, gently pushed them over to me, and said, "Donald, in no way do I think of you as a baby, so please let that go. From what I know, it has been less than a year since your father died, and then you were running a lumberyard with your brother. That, young sir, is a lot for one person to experience in such a short time. Now, please take a deep breath and tell me when you decided you want to become a priest."

Tears were still running down my face. "Thank you, sir. I've been thinking about it for about three years. I guess I want to hurry it up a little. Anyway, what would we need to do to get an extra credit this year?"

"You know, Donald, as we're sitting here talking, I'm thinking about how I taught high school Latin at one time. You'll be needing some of that when you go to the seminary to study for the priesthood. Do you think Ted would be interested in taking a class with you if we can find the time?"

I promised to talk to Ted and get back to Mr. Jackson. Ted was more interested in the extra credit than the Latin, but amenable. His sister, Beatrice, who was also in our class, liked the idea of completing high school in three years too. Jackson set us up for two classes a week to learn Latin, but not until our sophomore year. Beatrice and Ted thought their knowing Spanish would help them with the Latin—and it did. For freshman year, Mr. Jackson set us up with a tutorial on world history.

When Halloween came around, I did the dumbest thing in my life. I joined in a completely reckless tradition in Edgemont called gate night. On the night before Halloween, many teenage boys roamed around town and tore gates off of fences, tossed trash barrels, messed up woodpiles, and whatever other easy mischief they could find. Each year, the town marshal deputized about a dozen men, and they did their best to stop the mayhem. It became a dangerous game of cat and mouse. I had never participated before, as I agreed with Dad that it was wrong and stupid. But in 1948, with Dad gone and me feeling in an "I don't give a shit" mood, I joined in the mayhem. LeRoy Hudson and I went down an alley, dumped over a few trash cans, and pushed over an old outhouse. Just as we finished trashing the toilet, a car headed down the alley towards us. LeRoy took off running like a light. I was so embarrassed, I just stood there and waited for the car to pull up beside me. I didn't know what the punishment would be, but I would take it because I was guilty.

The driver shined his spotlight on me and yelled, "Hey, you're the Hanley boy, aren't you?" I nodded, and he continued, "Your dad would be ashamed of you tonight, wouldn't he?" I nodded again. "Well, we're not going to arrest you, but we'll follow you home—got that?" Again, I nodded and started walking home. They followed me until I went into our little house. The next day, the same man called to tell me that the outhouse we dumped over belonged to an older couple, and it was their only toilet, and we must fix it or pay to have it fixed. I told him I'd fix it. LeRoy helped me find enough lumber. I continued to feel ashamed, but LeRoy just laughed about it.

With Bob and Glen making the house payments and the utilities, and our three Social Security checks, we were able to get by and even take in a movie each week. The movie tickets for kids were still ten cents. Before Christmas that year, Ted, his brother

Jayce, and I hiked up to a pine-covered hill just east of town. We chopped down two good-sized Christmas trees and dragged them two miles back to our houses. It had been a long time since we had a decent-sized Christmas tree, and it filled the little house with that wonderful ponderosa pine smell. We had been invited to Christmas dinner in Hot Springs but decided that the four of us would have our first Christmas in five years together in our own home. Bob brought gifts from everyone the day before Christmas. Jim and Kay joined Kay's family in eastern South Dakota.

The only money I was able to make that school year was for painting signs around town. I even painted the town's new fire truck—Edgemont Fire Department—on the two front doors of the cab. I didn't have any idea how much to charge, but I ended up making five dollars an hour for my work. To keep busy, I joined the school glee club, acted in a play, and joined the freshmen basketball team. Again, I invited Janis Hudson to go to the prom with me, and again, she was gracious enough not to comment on my awkward dancing. So, the year went by peacefully except for the Halloween fiasco.

I continued being my very independent self that year, just as I had been when I lived with Jim. Mom seemed to be too uncomfortable, or too tired, to tell me anything except what I needed to get at the grocery store. I thought of myself as an adult in our house, not as a child.

That spring, Bonnie graduated from high school. There were only thirteen students in her class, and she was the third-ranking graduate—only a couple of points shy of being the salutatorian. She seemed to be happier than I had seen her in years. When school ended, she headed to Wichita to find work, and I went to Hot Springs to work with Bob and Glen.

Eighteen

LAST HURRAH IN SOUTH DAKOTA

———❧———

During nearly all of June 1949, Ann and Elsie argued about whose turn it was to feed me. Bob said I ate like my sixteen-year-old body had two hollow legs. I worked mostly at the service station. In late June, Bob asked me to help him build a new house for Glen and Elsie, and I began staying full time with Glen, Elsie, and their two small boys. I enjoyed doing the carpentry work more than helping at the station, and I also enjoyed driving Bob's gasoline truck whenever I could.

One day in July, I pulled the truck up to a filling station with a truckload of gasoline. An old man who owned a store nearby saw me get out of the truck and hurried over to confront me. He yelled, "You're too young to be driving that truck, aren't you?" He said it like I was committing a crime, so I retorted snottily, "Well, I'm driving it, ain't I?" I later thought I should have apologized for my bad manners, but I didn't. Soon after, on one of my truck driving days, I discovered an interesting thing; if I hit the top of the viaduct in Hot Springs that went from a hill into the valley below and was going at least thirty miles an hour, I could let up on the gas at the top, and the truck's exhaust would backfire like a canon and echo all up and down the valley that contained downtown Hot Springs. That tickled my little adolescent brain. I did this four times before Bob heard about it. He had heard the shots but didn't know his truck was the source of them until a policeman showed up at the station. He was *not* tickled.

Bob did not stay angry with me, as the following day he had to take a load of gasoline to a station in the Pine Ridge Indian Reservation and asked me to go along with him. As we bounced along on a gravel, wash-boardy road going about fifty miles an hour, Bob said, "Let me show you how we changed drivers in the army." He opened his door and shouted, "Scoot over and take the wheel." I thought he was completely out of his mind, but I quickly moved over and took the wheel. The truck had slowed down to about thirty miles an hour, and the slow speed made the truck even more bouncy. Bob said, "Bring her back up to sixty, and we'll bounce over some of the bumps." He was right, and I looked over, and he had fallen asleep. That became the summer's scariest experience and did the most to build my self-confidence.

It seemed that every time I began to feel good about something, I did something stupid. The week after driving the truck to the Indian reservation, I decided to drive the truck to Bob's apartment by going down the alley between two rows of apartments. The alley was only eight feet wide, and the tank on the truck was six inches narrower. Each home had a coal-and-wood box next to the drive, and I managed to wreck one on the passenger side. Bob heard the racket when I hit the first box and came running out of his apartment. He was waiting for me when I finally made it through the alley. "Well, little brother, what have you learned?" He didn't expect an answer and added, "So, first thing in the morning, you'll repair that wood box, right?" It wasn't a question; it was a command.

Between the truck, the service station, and working on the new house, I was working about eighty hours a week. Fortunately, I was getting paid, under the table, close to a dollar an hour for most of them. The most irritating thing about working on the house was hearing a girl across the street playing *Chopsticks* endlessly on her piano. My most disturbing and sinful thing all summer was seeing Elsie in her summer pajamas. I didn't have to search long to find sins to confess in the confessional.

Going back to Edgemont on the Saturday right before Labor Day, I heard that the *Denver Post* needed someone to distribute their paper to the newsstands and a few homes every day. I took the job; it would begin the day school started. On that same day, I was walking home from the post office and saw some men struggling to move a meat showcase into a store. I went over and helped them. When we sat the heavy thing down, I asked the owner if he had anything else I could help with. He looked around the storeroom and said, "Well, yes. Look at this mess. Why don't you see what you can do with it?" I didn't ask him what he would pay, just hoped he would pay something. I realized I was often doing what Bob called wishful thinking, but it seemed to be a good thing most of the time.

The storeroom was a mess; there were boxes of different goods piled willy-nilly all over the place. I remembered Dad telling me I should do a job as if it was my own place and do it as well as I would want it done. So, I thought, How would I want this storeroom to be? The owner was busy elsewhere, so I didn't want to wait or bother him. I began putting all the canned vegetables in one area, canned fruit in another, and other like items together. It took me a little over three hours to have it looking as good as I wanted. I swept up the exposed floor and went to the door leading to the main part of the store. The owner came to the door, and I told him I was finished and hoped it was okay. He walked around the room, shaking his head. The headshaking worried me a bit. He came back to stand in front of me. "My good man, this room has never looked so good in the five years I've been here. Thank you. You have a knack for organizing. Do you drive?"

"Yes, sir. I used to drive the lumberyard truck, and I drove a gasoline truck in Hot Springs."

He leaned back and looked down his nose at me skeptically. I quickly added, "I can get a letter from each manager to prove it, if you'd like." I didn't tell him that both managers were my brothers.

"That won't be necessary. You don't look like the kind of young man who would lie. How would you like to have a job after school, driving the old Ford out back and delivering groceries and then stocking shelves and such?"

Every boy I knew around town was paid seventy-five cents an hour, so I asked, "How many hours a week would you like me to work, and how much would I earn, sir?" I had learned that adult men liked to be called sir.

"How about a dollar an hour, and you work two hours each weekday afternoon and five hours on Saturday?"

"That would be great. Thank you, sir." I floated home and thought of Bob saying this summer that nobody could say us Hanleys were ever afraid of work. He was including me in the group of Hanley men when he said it. The only worrisome thing,

I learned later, was that my grocery job put a man with three kids out of a job. I felt a bit of guilt every day as I passed his house walking to school. Every Friday, I received a check for $15, which just about paid the grocery bill for Mom, Patty, and me.

The day after Labor Day, I learned that the Edgemont Bakery needed a part-time worker for the morning shift. I applied for that too and got it! I would work at the bakery from 7:00 to 8:45 each morning, so it looked like I was going to have a profitable and busy year.

For my sophomore year at high school, I signed up for mechanical drawing, English II, geometry, and physics. I lost my job at the bakery in early October because they needed someone who could work more hours each day, so I talked with Ted and Beatrice, and we asked Mr. Jackson if he would begin teaching us the Latin class, which he agreed to do Monday through Thursday before first period. At noon, I would run to the train station and then take the *Denver Post* off the train to the three drug stores and Sam's News Stand. Then I would grab a sandwich that Mom made for me and hurry back to school. There was one free hour for study hall, and I completed most of my homework in that hour. At 3:30 p.m., I rushed to the grocery store to deliver groceries and stock shelves. Other than finding it difficult to wake up in the mornings, I was enjoying being so busy.

Just like in my freshman year, I continued having headaches. That year I had one or two a week; as a sophomore, I began having three or four, but they were manageable. Usually, I could knock them with one or two aspirin. One time, when I was visiting Jim and Kay in their rented house in Hot Springs, I had a terrible one. I asked Kay, a registered nurse, if she had two aspirin I could take. She said, "Sometimes, in the hospital, if a patient is in deep pain, we will give him four aspirin. It sounds like you are in deep pain, so would you like to take four aspirin?" I said, "Sure," and she gave them to me. That knocked the headache in only two hours, and from that time on, I always kept a large bottle of aspirin in the medicine cabinet.

I had to admit that I was glad to be able to sleep in a little longer for three mornings a week. Also, one of the physics students, an attractive senior who lived across the street from us, began to wait for me each free morning so I could walk to school with her. I felt very flattered.

In October, Bonnie found a good job as a secretary for a large insurance company in Wichita. She wanted Mom, Patty, and me to join her there. She said she had found a small, reasonable apartment near Marie and Jim. I told Mom that I thought we were doing okay and should, at least, finish the school year in Edgemont. Mom, Glen, and Bob vetoed my idea, and we prepared to move to Wichita in November.

I found a classmate to take over the *Denver Post* job and informed the grocery store owner that I would be leaving. I asked Mr. Rohlf in Casper, the grocery owner, and the bakery owner to write letters of recommendation for me for when I applied for a job in Kansas. They all wrote very helpful letters about how conscientious, honest, and hardworking I was. Of course, that made me feel very good.

Glen loaded up all our clothes and other stuff, along with the four of us, and transported us to Wichita in November 1949.

It wasn't difficult leaving Edgemont, as the only people I would miss were Father Groel, Ted Torres, and the Hudson family. My life had been full of goodbyes and new beginnings, which reinforced my feelings of never belonging anywhere.

Nineteen

ANOTHER NEW BEGINNING

It took us one very long day to drive diagonally across Nebraska and northern Kansas. Jim, Marie, and eight-year-old Suzie greeted us warmly and had food ready. Bonnie was especially glad to see us. After one night in Marie and Jim's small apartment, Glen headed back to South Dakota, and the rest of us moved four doors down the street to our new home. It was a strange apartment that had been jig-sawed around plumbing pipes and furnace ducts in the basement of an old but well-kept house. I got the bed under two heating ducts. In winter weather, it was always colder than the apartment proper until the furnace came on, and then I got roasted. The good part was the rent—only forty-five dollars a month.

On the first Monday after Thanksgiving, Marie took me down to Wichita's only co-ed Catholic high school. She had made an appointment with the pastor of Cathedral Parish who lived and had his office between the school and the cathedral. The buildings were all made of tan sandstone, and my first thought was not that they were beautiful but solid and permanent—something I needed in my life.

The high school tuition was $200 a semester, and, of course, I could not afford it. I really did not want to go to a Catholic school, but it was better, I thought, than one of the two public schools that had over 2,000 students each. The Catholic school only had 650 students, and that was going to be shock enough for me, as Edgemont only had eighty-three in all four grades. Hoping we could get a free ride, Marie told the monsignor-pastor that I was planning to become a priest. I hated to be a beggar again, but it worked and made me feel better when the monsignor called it a scholarship.

We then went over to the high school and met with Sister Laura, the principal of CSJ—I later learned that stood for Congregation of St. Joseph. Sister Laura told me I wouldn't be able to have a study hall because of the tough course schedule I signed up for. I wondered if I could handle it. She looked very surprised and dubious when I told her about my schedule in South Dakota, until Marie confirmed it. I was impressed with how professional and self-assured Marie was with both the monsignor and Sister Laura; then I reminded myself that she was twenty-two years older than me.

Sister Laura said that I might have a problem with physics because it had always been limited to seniors only. I told her that had been true in Edgemont too, but I got an A for the first six weeks. I didn't tell her that the teacher was fresh out of college and had never taught physics before. She took me to talk to the physics teacher. Marie, who was very pregnant, waited in the office. Sister

Laura knocked on the door, and a short and very stern older nun opened it looking angry. Even the principal seemed slightly intimidated by her as she explained the situation and asked about adding me to her class.

Sister Louise looked up at me—I was about nine inches taller than she was—like she was looking at a mouse or maybe a first grader. She said, "I've never taught a student other than a senior, but I'm willing to give it a try. If you cannot keep up, young man, you'll just have to drop the class. Is that understood?"

That was the first time I consciously realized that if someone said I could not do something, it became a challenge for me, and I wanted to prove them wrong. I wondered if my determination to become a priest became even more entrenched in my thinking because some in my family thought I couldn't.

So, I began the class with about thirty seniors and proved I could handle the subject by becoming the only student in the class to receive an A from Sister Louise. The homework for physics took longer to complete than the homework for all my other classes combined.

The city bus took me to and from school. I couldn't arrive in time to attend Mass before school started, but I would spend a few minutes visiting the cathedral and praying the rosary before the marble statue of the Blessed Virgin Mary. The beautiful cathedral had many magnificent and real marble statues of the saints. Almost every morning when I entered the church, a young but stern-looking priest named Father Strecker was finishing his private Mass at a side altar and leaving. He always walked stiffly with his hands folded prayerfully in front of him as he made his way to the sacristy. My brother Bob would say he looked like he had a cob up his ass. Only a few years later, I learned he had been made a bishop in Missouri and, after that, the archbishop of Kansas City, Kansas.

We joined the Abney clan for both Thanksgiving and Christmas dinner at the home of one of Jim Abney's siblings. That was a tradition of the family, and we were graciously invited. We crowded into Marie and Jim's '48 Mercury and headed to suburban Wichita. The food was delicious, but all the adults, except Mom, were at least two sheets to the wind, if not fully drunk—three sheets—and too wasted to appreciate it. The young children seemed to enjoy the day, but we teens were more than a little bored. Later, Marie asked me to get my Kansas driver's license so I could drive everyone home at events like these, which I did.

The big family event of the year was the birth of Jim and Marie's first son, James Phillip, or Jimmy Phil.

Marie stayed home with him for a few weeks, and then Mom became the babysitter and was joined by Patty after school each afternoon.

I enjoyed the classes at Cathedral High School but kept pretty much to myself. Most of the students seemed to come from affluent families and dressed up for school. I didn't have any dressy clothes to wear, and I couldn't afford to change that. I was sure that the other classmates thought I was a country hick, but I had no way to check it out. Originally, I didn't mind Marie telling the pastor and Sister Laura that I planned to become a priest, but somehow the word got around, and as a result, I was asked to be a ticket-taker at some social events, like dances. I would rather have been a dancer.

I enjoyed the religion class because it was better than what I had in the first grade, but nearly all the other students were bored to death. What I disliked about the class was that I was supposed to unquestioningly learn everything rather than discuss it and find its meaning in our lives. At least Sister Melissa, the teacher, was kind about it. My biggest regret of the school year was allowing so many of my physics classmates, all seniors, to borrow my homework. I wanted to be accepted, as in other times, but I don't think I ever forgave myself. I was still unconscious of my belief that I didn't belong anywhere, and I held onto it tightly throughout that year.

In May, we moved to a nicer and more spacious apartment across the street. It was above ground, and my bed was not under heating ducts. The rent was seventy-five dollars a month, so it was very important for me to find a job as soon as possible. I guessed my headaches hated seeing me not working because they were plentiful the entire school year.

Twenty

BACK TO WORK

———— ⌘ ————

After Memorial Day, I borrowed Marie and Jim's car so I could look for a job. With my letters of recommendation in hand, I started by visiting lumberyards. I spoke to two managers before lunch, but they didn't need any new employees. When I went home for lunch, I stopped by our old house to pick up a box of books we had left there and ran into our old landlord. I told him about my search for a job, and he told me to stop by the Earl Huston Lumber Company on Broadway. He said, "Ask to speak to Mr. Huston himself and tell him Sam Harrison sent you. That's where I buy all my hardware, paint, and stuff."

Mr. Huston's lumberyard was not imposing. It was in a 1910 one-story house with a glassed-in front porch and a well-kept front yard with a pretty flower garden. Behind the house was a concrete block warehouse with a large, wide-open drive-through doorway. I walked into the store, and a pleasant-looking, blond young man was behind a counter. I said, "Hi, I'm looking for Mr. Earl Huston. Is he here?"

"Yes, he is." He motioned to someone behind me.

Evidently, Earl had heard his name. He was a distinguished-looking man who appeared to be in his forties and wearing a suit and tie. He held out his hand.

I took his hand. "Pleased to meet you, sir. I'm Don Hanley, and I just moved here from South Dakota, and I'm looking for a job." Holding out a copy of Mr. Rohlf's letter, I added, "I worked in a lumberyard there for four years, so I thought I would start looking for work at lumberyards. This is a letter from the owner I last worked for. Oh, and Mr. Harrison encouraged me to stop here and meet you."

Earl smiled and said, "Sam is a good man. Let me take a look at this letter. I believe this is the first time we've seen a letter like this. Give me a moment." He went to a nearby room with several desks facing out into the store. A stout, well-dressed, friendly woman read the letter and said something to Mr. Huston, then followed him out to meet me. As she shook my hand, Earl said, "Don, this is my wife, Audra, and co-owner of our company."

I took her hand gently and said, "Nice to meet you, ma'am."

She smiled and shook my hand firmly. "We can put you to work part-time right now. How would that be?"

Of course, I hoped for a full-time job for the summer, but, for now, anything would do. "That would be fine, ma'am. When would you like me to start, and what time each day?"

We agreed to start at three o'clock each afternoon and one dollar an hour.

I did not express my excitement. Instead, I tried to match their business-like manner. Earl excused himself to finish an estimate and said Audra would show me around and take down all the necessary information.

She introduced me to Cliff Huffman, the friendly, blond, and kind of pudgy young man who worked in the store and dispatched the truck drivers. Then we went through an inside door where I met Mrs. Winnie Mishler, a pleasant, gray-haired lady who was the lumberyard bookkeeper, lunch cook, and part-time caretaker to Audra's mother, who was bedridden in their home. Her desk and office were also the Huston's living room. Behind the office-living room was a closed-in back porch that had been turned into a kitchen. There was a door leading back into the yard that was never open to the public. Mrs. Mishler looked like a woman who could easily juggle all her expected duties. We then went out into the warehouse, where I met the yardman, Floyd Eveland. Floyd was a tall, muscular, friendly fellow with a southern/western twang who looked to be in his forties.

While we were looking over the building and its contents, a flatbed truck drove in. Audra introduced me to the truck driver. Audra told me they had another storage yard near the railroad, about two miles away. When we went through the door, she pointed to a stack of boxes and said, "There's the hardware that needs to be marked up and shelved. I'll get the invoice and marker for you. We take 50 percent of the cost and add it to the selling price. Got that?" I nodded, and she added, "Now, let me see if you do. Let's say that the box with two hinges cost us one dollar; how much would you mark on the box?"

"One dollar and fifty cents."

"Why not three dollars? After all, there are two hinges in the box?"

"Because we don't sell one hinge, we sell a pair of hinges."

"Very good. Now I know you've got it. How does that compare with how you did it in South Dakota?"

She told me she'd been a grade school teacher, and I could tell. I started with the boxes and then helped clean up at closing.

I walked to work and back home each day, and my part-time status lasted only two weeks, as Earl asked me if I would be willing to help Mack Mishler, Mrs. Mishler's husband, build a new storefront on the store. He told me a bit about what he planned, and that evening, I put what I had learned in the mechanical arts class to work. I drew up a floor plan like I'd seen in architectural drawings and even drew a picture of the storefront. I showed it to Mr. Huston the next morning, and he liked it and made some additions. He showed my drawings to Mrs. Huston, and she was equally enthusiastic.

On Monday morning, I met Mack, a shy and friendly man in his sixties. He considered himself a handyman or farmhand rather than a carpenter. The various other employees stopped in to help with the project when they had time. I ended the first day after ten hours of work and rewarded myself by getting a Dairy Queen ice cream cone on the way home.

The next morning, Mack, Floyd, and I got busy on the construction project. I saw that Mack was hesitant to start things, so I took the lead and hoped that I didn't sound bossy when I made suggestions. Floyd could read invoices but could barely read anything else, so he was okay with letting me take the lead too. Of course, I enjoyed doing it, and my experience "bossing" Jim helped me out here.

I liked it when the other employees talked about personal stuff—that made them more real, rather than just workers, and helped me feel at home with them.

It was interesting hearing Mack talk about the war, where his sons served like my brothers. He was against his boys being cannon fodder. "War is only wanted by egotistical, old, white men who are power-hungry. That's what I think," he said.

Both Marie and Jim worked at the humongous Boeing plant

with over 24,000 employees, and I wondered if they felt like their coworkers were people or just worker bees. Bonnie often said that her fellow secretaries were pretty nice people, but the male bosses treated them like slaves sometimes.

We got the store completed before the end of August, and it looked great—at least we all thought so, especially Earl and Audra. We installed store shelves and fixtures right before Labor Day. I was going to ask them if I could continue working part time after school started, but I didn't have to ask. They offered, and I readily accepted.

I felt like hugging him, but that would not have been proper. Working all summer had been a wonderful experience, and the only headaches I had were on Sundays when I didn't get to go to work. School was fine, but I enjoyed working more, especially figuring out how to do things and build things. I hated being tied down and told what to do in school, but I still wanted to learn everything. My dad's constant refrain, "Don't waste time," came in very handy for me when I was working. I still had not realized that my ability to visualize a project was a gift and one that not everyone possessed. It took me many more years to realize that school, recreation, and nearly everything else in life were more than just stuff I needed to do in between the times when I was working. In the three and a half years I had been with Dad, the closest we had ever come to a vacation was that four-day trip to Nebraska. And it was much later when I connected my habitual thinking to the fact that many men die soon after retiring from the work they spent their lives doing. It seems a shame that, for many, work is what provides meaning to life rather than intellectual, emotional, and spiritual growth.

Twenty-One

ROME WASN'T BUILT IN A DAY

I jumped over junior year and joined the senior class. I needed six more units to graduate. The principal suggested I take American government in the fall and international relations in the spring by correspondence through Kansas University to finish what I needed. So, I signed up for them for ninety dollars each. I thought I could easily handle these and my regular classes and still work twenty-four to thirty hours a week at the lumberyard.

It didn't turn out to be easy at all. The only class that did not have homework was PE. South Dakota hadn't required it, so I had to take classes five days a week to make up for it. My fear of teacher-nuns was gone, and I looked forward to some of my classes, but the homework was a growing problem, and I tried fitting it in everywhere I could—mornings, on the bus, during lunch breaks, and late at night.

I continued to stop at the cathedral so I could say a prayer to have strength enough to survive the day. My headaches had become increasingly more painful each day for three weeks straight. On Sunday morning, my head hurt so badly that I couldn't raise my head from the pillow. I took four aspirin every four hours all day. It didn't seem to help. Mom was a very caring nurse for me, but I could barely move and threw up everything I ate. Drinking milk seemed to help me keep the aspirin down. By Monday, I was not much better. Mom insisted I go to the free clinic for children, so I took the bus to the clinic. After a brief interview with an intake person, I took a series of tests: EEG, EKG, X-rays, and a couple of others. In the middle of the afternoon, I finally got to see the doctor himself.

"Well, my friend, all of your tests came back negative," he said.

I felt confused. Everything wasn't okay because I still had a headache. Maybe negative meant bad, rather than nothing.

He went on, "I know you have an awful headache, so tell me, my friend, about what you are doing—like your schedule each day."

I named off my routine of work, homework, and school.

At the end, he said, "Hell, man, Rome wasn't built in a day!"

I remembered a line I heard my brother Bob say, and I repeated it, "Yeah, I know, but I wasn't foreman on that job." As soon as I said it, I hoped I didn't sound like a smart-ass.

The doctor laughed so hard he nearly fell off his chair. He asked why I was in such a hurry to finish school.

"I plan to become a Catholic priest. My dad died two years ago, and ever since, my older brothers have helped us three youngest kids, so I believe it is my turn to help out. My sister, just older than me, is now our breadwinner, and she doesn't make very much. So, I need to help now and save up so I can go to the seminary. And I really like to work."

"Do you know how to relax? I mean, to have your muscles relax and all that?"

"Probably not real well, I guess."

"Well, you are in good physical health, so I urge you to learn to relax and do it as much of the time as you can—while walking, sitting in class, riding the bus, and everything. I have a hunch you're not going to allow yourself to cancel any classes or cut down on your hours at work, so promise me you'll try this, Okay?"

He stood up and extended his hand. I shook his hand and said, "Okay, thank you, doctor."

Somehow, I got through school Tuesday, Wednesday, and Thursday, but I stayed home from school on Friday and returned to work on Saturday. Luckily, the Hustons were very understanding. I was also able to do two sets of correspondence course assignments over the weekend so I wouldn't fall too far behind.

On Monday morning, I still had about a five on a ten scale headache. My algebra teacher, Sister Louise, asked to see me after class. She said it pleasantly enough, but I still worried that she would say that I needed to drop the class because I had already missed too many classes, or I was too far behind, or something like that. At the end of the period, I went up and stood beside her desk and nervously waited.

She finished writing and looked up at me. "Donald, I suppose you are worried about your studies, aren't you?"

Actually, I hadn't been. Mostly, I was worried about losing my job and only a little about my studies, but I said, "Yes, Sister." I didn't want to contradict her.

"Donald, you needn't worry. You are an excellent student!" She smiled.

It felt like a thousand pounds had been lifted off my shoulders, and within an hour, my headache ceased. Sister Louise was the toughest teacher in the school, and her vote of confidence did wonders for me. While I did not stop doing any of the things I had been doing, by relaxing more and worrying less, I had only a few medium headaches the rest of the year.

At Thanksgiving and Christmas, we went back to join the Abney clan, with their delicious food and rather inebriated company. The Hustons asked me to work full time to help with the end-of-the-year inventory during Christmas vacation. That allowed me to have a merry Christmas, and I bought nice gifts for everyone, including Marie, Jim, and Suzie.

I always wore my work clothes—khaki pants and a plaid shirt—to school, which made me look more like a construction worker than a schoolboy. It would have taken me over an hour to go home and then walk back to the lumberyard, so I didn't want to do that. Most of the boys in our high school dressed in what Bonnie called preppy, but I didn't care. I wasn't interested in fitting in anyway. It was usually no problem, but one morning in April, the student council president stopped me in the hall and told me I needed to go over to the cafeteria to get my picture taken.

When I asked why, he said, "You are the top-ranked senior guy in our class, and they want you to join the top girls for a yearbook picture."

I had never heard of such a thing, and I thought he must be mistaken. I was not dressed for having my picture taken, but I traipsed on over to the cafeteria. There were ten beautifully dressed, attractive girls and the photographer waiting for me. I immediately thought I was a complete misfit for the picture, and I was. It was beauties and a beast. The photographer didn't know what to do with me. He couldn't find a place for me and finally just put me at the end of the second row, but I still stuck out like a sore thumb. When the yearbook came out in May, my name was listed as the top-ranked boy at the end of the list of ten girls, but no picture. I knew why.

I put nearly all my energies into schoolwork and the lumberyard, and I guess I kind of ignored my family. Bonnie had her closest friend move in with us, and she helped with the rent. She was more a part of the family than I was. Bonnie seemed to enjoy her work at the insurance company and was glad to have a close friend live with her. Patty was in the seventh grade and still Mom's baby, and although she was three years older than her classmates, she seemed even younger. I didn't do anything with them except go to Mass every Sunday and the movies once in a while.

My eighteenth birthday was on March 28, 1951. Mom baked a special cake for me, and Bonnie gave me a pipe with tobacco and all the accouterments that a pipe-smoker needs. I had almost forgotten that I had mentioned how much I admired how men looked who smoked pipes and that I planned to smoke a pipe when I grew up. Bonnie reminded me of that, and I spent several minutes each evening struggling to light the damn thing and keep it lit. It burned my tongue and mouth, but I was going to master the damn thing by God. I finally got it down, but I never smoked it at school or the lumberyard because I was sure Earl and Audra Huston would not approve.

Marie and Bonnie encouraged me to take part in the graduating seniors' festivities—especially the senior banquet and prom. Of course, in their view, I must have a date. The only girl I got to know in any way was MaryAnn Hahn, a beautiful, red-haired girl who was one of the brainy ones too. She and I had three classes together and often walked together from one class to the next and talked about current events and class assignments. The only personal thing I knew about her was that she had a brother in the seminary who was studying to become a priest. She was very proud of him, and I think she walked and talked with me because I had told her I hoped to go to the seminary someday. It took me about five weeks to ask her if she would go to the dinner and prom with me. I was sure she would turn me down.

But she said, "I've been waiting for you to invite me. What took you so long?" When I told her I was sure she would say no, she laughed delightfully.

The banquet was at the Broadview Hotel—considered one of Wichita's finest convention hotels. MaryAnn was as much of a wallflower as I was. She had been with the senior class for four years but didn't seem to know any more of our classmates than I did, and I had been in the class only that year. We both basically connected only with each other. The same was true when we went to the gaily decorated ballroom next door to the dance floor. We danced only the slow dances with one another. I had just learned how to do the jitterbug when we left Edgemont, and MaryAnn had never learned it, so we limited ourselves to a modest waltz-like two-step. We both chuckled when we agreed that we'd give the evening a C.

Mary Ann said, "I think we are better students than partiers."

The following Friday evening, I got another huge surprise. It was honors night, when special awards were passed out for various achievements. I was especially surprised to see that both Earl and Audra Huston were in attendance. That was quite an honor for me, but I was afraid they would be disappointed in me, as I didn't expect to receive any awards. I sat there bored while the head coach read off the athletic awards for seniors who earned four-year letters in football, basketball, baseball, and track. He also gave out the few awards for the girls' achievements.

Sister Laura took back the podium and announced the music and drama awards for different achievements in those fields. Finally, the last, and most important in my view, the academic achievements—salutatorian and valedictorian. Both went to girls I barely knew, and both received standing ovations.

Sister Laura said, "And finally, we are giving out our first outstanding student award to a student who has completed high school in three years with an A/B average in all of his course work, Mr. Donald Hanley."

I nearly fainted and barely heard the ovation as I floated to the podium and took the beautiful blue leather-bound award. I managed the trip down and back up to my seat without stumbling, which was a miracle.

The class of 1951 marched down the center aisle and stood in a line near the door as the audience came by and congratulated us. Jim Abney, Marie, Mom, Bonnie, and Patty all gave me a congratulatory hug, and many others I didn't know shook my hand. I looked for Audra and Earl, but they had already left.

The next day, Earl said that he thought I had received the best honor of the evening and congratulated me. The scholastic achievement award was like a flower blooming in my heart, and it helped me think I might be smart enough to make it in college and become a priest. I decided I needed to work for five years, until Patty graduated from high school in 1956, before I could go to the seminary. So, the year had started with a headache but turned out well, indeed. Maybe Rome *was* built in a day, and there were flowers to be found in our world.

Twenty-Two

A CAR AND OUR VERY OWN HOUSE

Our formal graduation ceremony included a Mass at the cathedral that was uneventful. The only personal experience was this: I was asked to sit next to other top male graduates, so I found myself next to the out-going senior class president. Fifteen minutes before the Mass began, he asked me to look over his type-written talk he was to give at Mass. It was full of pious platitudes, as expected, but I said it was excellent, and the only thing I would add would be for him to give a simple thank you to the Sisters of St. Joseph for their excellent education. I believed that was true for me and told him so. I was honored to be asked to look it over. The following fall, I saw him sitting alone at a café counter near the lumberyard. I sat down beside him, and we started talking about our high school experience. I told him I felt like everyone in the class looked down on me because I was a country hick among all the city slickers. He shook his head, and I asked, "How come you're shaking your head?"

"Because we all thought you were stuck up because you were such a brain." For the first time, I realized just how different everyone thinks about things—other people, experiences, everything. My classmates saw me as the exact opposite of how I saw myself. It was my turn to shake my head.

After graduation, I began a new and more leisurely work week. After my school-work schedule, I was glad to get back to some leisure reading. I got interested in science fiction, and I especially liked Robert Heinlein. Cliff Huffman, whom I met that first day in the store, had been serving in the Air Force Reserve and was called up for full-time duty and left the lumberyard. For a year, I was the only person, other than Earl and Audra, to wait on customers, answer phones, write out delivery slips, and everything else Cliff had done as well as sweep up in the evenings. The Hustons raised my pay to a dollar and fifty cents an hour—double the minimum wage at the time—and that was great. With several overtime hours a week, I made more than Bonnie was making as a secretary.

One of the truck drivers had a '37 Ford in his backyard that he didn't use because the brakes needed a little work. I bought it from him for thirty-eight dollars. The engine ran like a champ, but the "little work" on the brakes was an understatement. It had mechanical brakes, and I worked on them every Sunday for several hours, but I could still only stop the damn thing after I stomped on the brake pedal for half a block. In the third week, I ventured to take Patty, Bonnie, and her friend to play miniature golf in the brake-impaired vehicle. On the way home, the car ahead of us stopped in the middle of the block, and, of course, I couldn't stop in time and jerked right, jumped a curb, ran across a lawn, and stopped by bumping into a tree. That was the end of my excursions in the Ford.

The following Sunday, I started shopping for a car among the cheapest used car dealers. I found a '39 Dodge I thought I could afford, but they wouldn't take the Ford as a trade-in or give me a loan. I felt very down when I went home and damned if I didn't start crying like a baby when I told Mom about my encounter with the sales guy at the dealership. She unintentionally added to my misery by calling the dealer and talking to the owner of the car lot. She told him how hard I worked and reliable I was and that he should be ashamed of himself for refusing to deal with me.

When she hung up, she demanded that I go back to see him because he promised to find a deal for me. She sounded like she had when she refused to move into the little bungalow in Edgemont. I liked how she stood up for me but was ashamed of myself for feeling like a baby. I didn't understand how Mom could have such energy when she seemed to be needed and then almost immediately fall back into a depressed state otherwise. Her helplessness seemed to be her usual way of being in the world, unless she was needed by one of her children. With that said, I don't know what Patty would have done without her help. That day with the car, I ate crow and went back down to the car lot and came home with a nice Dodge and a twenty-nine dollars a month car payment. Anyway, I now had a car that I could trust to take me places, including to work.

Around that same time, I heard Floyd Eveland tell Earl that his family would have to move out of the house he was renting to buy from the Hustons. It was just too small for his family, and they all wanted to move back to the old house they used to rent near the rail yards on Wichita's poor north side. I asked about the house the next chance I got, and Earl said they had taken it to pay for a contractor's debt. I asked him if it might be possible for me to buy it for Mom, my sisters, and me. Of course, we had to have payments low enough for me, with some help from Bonnie, to afford it. He did some figuring and came up with a figure around $100 a month. I was making about $100 a week, and we were paying $75 a month for rent, so I thought it was possible.

I told Mom and Bonnie about it, and we went to look it over. The house was on a relatively large corner lot in a well-kept, working-class neighborhood. It had only two bedrooms but a laundry room large enough to hold a twin bed for you-know-who. Bonnie's friend had been staying with us and paid twenty dollars a month that could help with the utilities. We went for it, and Earl and Audra arranged for us to take over the original mortgage of $6,700, and they would hold a second mortgage for $320. Thus, we'd have a house for $9,900 with payments of $101 a month. The original mortgage holders wanted Mom to sign the loan papers with me. Bonnie did not want to be on the papers. I thought it rather interesting and humorous that Mom, with no money and no income, would be the primary landowner, at least until I turned twenty-one in three years.

I felt quite important having a reliable car of my own and a house to live in, even if I had to share a room with a washer and dryer. For the next two years, I took Patty over to Marie and Jim's on my way to work, and she went to Our Lady of Guadalupe School with Susie. Bonnie shared a room with Joyce, who worked for the same insurance company. Sometimes they took the bus, and other times Joyce had the use of a car.

I had just signed the loan papers when I received a notice that I was drafted into the army. Even though I was not friends with any of the other guys in my graduating class, I found out that nearly all of them had been drafted into the military so they could fight in the Korean War. At that point, that war had been going on for only a few months. Anyway, I was shocked. I did not want to go into the military and absolutely did not want to take part in the Korean War. There were only a few days before I had to report. I challenged the draft notice and helped Mom write a letter stating that I was her and Patty's sole support. Marie encouraged her to include that three of her sons had served in the military in World War II. Earl wrote a letter confirming what Mom had said and emphasized that I was a valuable and conscientious employee. The Franciscan pastor of Our Lady of Guadalupe parish also wrote a letter for me. I sent them to the draft board and later met with the three board members. I was extremely nervous entering the briefing room and sitting in front of the three men. The following week, I received a letter saying that I was deferred from the draft and given a rating of 4A. That was the same rating given to married men with children. I gave a loud sigh of relief.

Unless I was working, I was still incredibly shy. Partly because I had a fairly bad case of acne. It wasn't as bad as Bonnie, but I couldn't cover it up with makeup like she did. Despite my complexion, I joined Our Lady of Guadalupe choir, led by Father Omar, a young, good-looking, and friendly Franciscan Friar, who was the only male other than myself. I think all eight of the young women had a crush on him. The girls accepted me, and they didn't seem to be bothered by my pock-marked face. So, Wednesday night choir practice became my only social activity for several months.

I joined Bonnie and Joyce a few times when they didn't have dates and went honkey-tonkin' with them—bar-hopping—on a Friday or Saturday night. I was far too self-conscious to enjoy the scene. The very first stop on the first night with the girls didn't help. I had my hands in my pockets when we entered a seedy nightclub with a so-called comedian at the mic. The jerk saw me and yelled, "Hey you, there in the back, get your hands out of your pockets. I do the entertaining around here." I looked around as if I didn't know whom he was talking about. Everyone else in the joint stared at me and laughed. I encouraged Bonnie and Joyce to leave as soon as possible. Another time, in another seedy place, an attractive young woman at a nearby table kept looking at me. Both Bonnie and Joyce encouraged me to ask her to dance. After about fifteen minutes, I did. When the woman stood up, she was as tall as me—six feet—and probably weighed more. She immediately held me tight, and we moved out onto the dance floor. I got an erection, and the bigger it got, the closer she hugged me. She seemed to enjoy my embarrassment, but I did not.

I wondered why I was constantly bothered by impure thoughts, while at the same time so uncomfortable around women. I think part of the problem was my complexion. Jim Abney's sister-in-law set me up on a date with her niece, who was visiting from out of town. When I took her home and walked her to the door, she looked up at me, tilted her head back, and pursed her lips for a kiss. I bent down and touched her lips with mine, about like I would with Bonnie or Patty. When she went through the door, I ran to my car like I was running from a fire. Then Mrs. Mishler wanted me to take her granddaughter to her high school prom, supposedly because her boyfriend had been drafted into the army and couldn't take her. Even Audra asked me to take her niece to dinner and a movie.

I asked Bonnie why these people kept wanting me to date their young female relatives. She said, "Because, little brother, they think you are a good catch. You're hardworking, sensitive, nice-looking—at least in their eyes—and oh, yeah, serious. By that,

I'm sure they mean boring." In my family, you never just gave a positive message to another person without adding a dig.

Except for that one quick conversation with Bob when I was thirteen, I never had a single talk with any adult about what it is like to be a man. Dad was a good model as a worker, a carpenter, and a storekeeper, but definitely not on how to get along with women. I felt lost in that part of my life.

Perhaps I might still be holding on to my first confession warning from old, grouchy Father Bartrow in Paola. My recollection was that, in his book, almost anything to do with sex was a mortal sin and might send me to hell. Or was this some kind of sign that I was destined to become a priest? I really had no idea how God worked. I didn't think He micromanaged the world. If He did, I hated Him for sending tornados and diseases, especially to children. Maybe the studies in the seminary would have some answers for me. I was not going to find out until I got Mom settled and Patty had graduated from high school.

Twenty-Three

LEARNING TO BE A SINGLE GUY

———∞———

It was a good time to be in the lumber business, especially in places like Wichita, a boom-town during the war and the years afterward. We could sell everything we could get. I didn't spend much time working in the warehouses or the yard, but we were very short-handed one day, and I was needed to help unload an eighteen-wheeler filled with hundred-pound boxes of nails. I went to the unemployment office and picked up two day workers. They were in even worse physical shape than I was, and they could only take a box and drop it on the floor or place it up to the third tier. It was my job to put the fourth and fifth boxes on the pile. About mid-way through the task, while I was putting a fifth box head high, I felt a terrible pain in my back—like I had been stabbed. Instead of stopping work on the unloading, I just gritted my teeth and continued to carry boxes until we were finished. My back was killing me, and I limped into the store. Earl suggested I go up the street and see the osteopath physician.

The doctor saw me right away and took an X-ray that showed I had a slipped disc, which was causing my pain. He taped up my back so I could not bend very much and told me not to pick up or carry anything heavier than five pounds. I could take two aspirin for the pain as needed. I didn't tell him I was used to taking four aspirin for my headaches. I took the two he gave me and two more when I got home. That kept me out of the warehouse and yard for a while.

Soon after that, I awoke one morning with a swollen right leg. It was so swollen that it was as big as my waist and hurt like hell. I went to a doctor near where we lived, and he noted that I had some kind of bite on my thigh. He guessed it was a black widow spider bite. He gave me a heavy shot of penicillin and tetracycline and told me to come back to the clinic for another shot every day until the swelling subsided. I was also to stay off my feet and have my Mom look closely around our house for spiders. That very day, Bonnie turned my mattress over and screamed. There was a nest of black widow spiders in the bedsprings! The doctor had said that if I had not been young and healthy, the one bite could have killed me. I felt so fortunate that I had only one bite. What if two or more spiders had attacked me? I took a long time getting to sleep in bed that night. The only good thing about my week off was that the Dodgers and Yankees were playing in the World Series, and I got to watch it on the new black-and-white TV that I had just bought. Soon afterward, Mom got addicted to the TV soap operas, which she kept up with for the next twenty years.

A few months later, I began hanging out with my fellow worker, Cliff Huffman and Don Cutler, who co-owned the

Standard station that serviced all the lumberyard's vehicles. We went bowling, played billiards, played miniature golf, and hung out. It was the first time since Edgemont and my brief times with Ted Torres and LeRoy Hudson that I had leisure time with friends. I wanted to hang out but really did not know how to enjoy leisure time. Cliff was the oldest of our trio and had gotten out of the Air Force after only one year. I was worried he might take over all of my duties at work, and I was glad that didn't happen.

I was even happier when, one day, Earl called me down to the front of the store where he was talking to a man from Oklahoma.

Earl said, "Barney, I'd like you to meet our assistant manager, Don Hanley. Don, this is Barney Frank, for whom I worked for ten years, another lifetime ago." Neither he nor Audra ever told me I was their assistant manager, but Earl's comment to his old boss picked up my spirits—there was another flower. I guess the Hustons considered both Cliff and me as assistant managers. At the check-out counter, we each were given a separate cash drawer that we should use, and we were the only ones, other than Earl and Audra, who had a cash drawer.

The Hustons had bought an old house across the alley from the lumberyard, and I spent many hours helping to remodel it for them. One day, they hired a man to put Formica countertops on the kitchen cabinets that I had helped build and put plastic tile on the backboards. I observed how he did it until I decided I could do that in my spare time and make some much-needed extra money. The next day, a young couple came in and picked out tile for their bathroom and then asked if we had anyone who could install it.

I replied, "Yes, I do that in my spare time." We set a time, and the husband said no one would be home, but he told me where the house key would be. That first evening, I had completed one wall and was halfway through the second wall when the man came home. He pulled a chair up to the doorway and watched me work.

After a little while, he said, "It looks easy. I guess it is when you know what you're doing."

In one of my rare moments of chutzpah, I said, "Yeah." I came back two more evenings and made ten dollars an hour—including the time to travel to and from. I had a new occupation: tile setter.

The following week I installed a Formica countertop on a new set of cabinets I had built in a home being remodeled by a lumberyard customer. He was a fellow who made a living by buying fixer-uppers, remodeling them, and reselling them. I became his new subcontractor.

In 1953, Don Cutler bought a new Oldsmobile Rocket 93—the top-of-the-line model GM made that year. He mentioned that he wanted to make a long trip in his new machine. I told him that Mom had mentioned that she would like to visit my brother Bill and his family in California.

He immediately responded, "Hey, why don't we take the Olds to California with your mom?"

I also learned that one of the lumberyard's best customer's son, Bob, who had just graduated from high school, also wanted to visit his uncle and family in California. If we could take the boy along with us, he agreed to pay for half the car expenses. Don and I knew the young fellow well, and we both believed he'd be a trouble-free companion, so we were on for a two-week trip in June.

We made it to Holbrook, Arizona, on two-lane roads in ten hours. Don, Bob, and I took turns driving, and all three of us drove between 90 and 100 miles an hour, and it didn't strain the big Olds eight-cylinder motor even a little. Mom and Patty sat in the back, and Mom often spied over the front seat, and when I was driving, she would murmur, "You're going a little fast, aren't you, son?"

I kept responding. "Don't worry, Mom, we're all fine." We were eighteen to twenty-five years old and thought we would live forever—and we were nuts. I enjoyed being away from work and racing too fast down the highway. On the second day, we stopped long enough to gaze at the Grand Canyon. It was truly beautiful and amazing. Mom told us that President Teddy Roosevelt said that it was so beautiful it brought tears to his eyes. I saw tears in her eyes as she said it.

Without thinking, I insensitively replied, "Yeah, it's beautiful, but it sure don't make me cry." Later, I apologized to Mom in private. At the time, I didn't know why I didn't want my two stoic male companions to hear me. I was a long way from finding flowers in nature's beauty and from knowing how to relax and just enjoy seeing wonderful and interesting landscapes. So far, I had only allowed myself to work and study. Enjoy life and leisure time and the company of others—huh? What's that?

We drove into the vast L.A. metropolis in the late afternoon and found South Pasadena surprisingly easily. All we had was Bill Hanley's address and phone number. I called, and luckily, we were only two blocks from the house. Bill and Helen had a small three-bedroom home, which was comfortable for them and their young son, Steve, and daughter, Judy. Bob called his uncle, as planned, to pick him up. Bill had set up a double bed for Don and me in their garage. Mom and Patty slept in one of the kid's rooms, and they seemed okay with that.

On the first day there, I came down with a horrible number ten headache. I did not have any aspirin with me, so Bill gave me a full bottle, and I took my first four and followed with four every four hours. Don and Bob had made reservations for the three of us to take a boat ride over to Catalina Island, and I had to back out. Young Steve, I think he was about ten, wanted to take my place and was delighted when the guys and Bill and Helen were open to it. So, I stayed at the house, felt sorry for myself, and nursed the headache. By the evening, I felt a lot better. When the guys got back, Bill grilled steaks and potatoes for everyone, and we ate out in their backyard. We shot the breeze until fairly late, and then we all headed for bed.

I had not shared a bed with anyone since those few weeks in Edgemont. The first night, I was comfortable with it, but the comfort ended abruptly the second morning when I felt Don's hand on my penis. Horrified, I immediately turned over on my stomach, remained ultra-quiet, and didn't move a muscle. After what seemed like hours, I heard him get up and go into the house. I was shocked and insulted that he had touched me. At that point, I knew next to nothing about homosexuality and felt horrified that Don would think I was such a sinful person and that I would welcome his touching me like that. Not knowing what else to do, I acted like nothing happened, and the following day we went east of Pasadena to Lake Arrowhead with Bob's relatives, where I tried water-skiing and got a severe rope burn that put a huge damper on the rest of my vacation.

Mom and Patty were planning to take the train back to Kansas in two weeks, so the three of us young men took the southern route through Arizona so that we could visit Carlsbad Caverns in New Mexico. Luckily, I was well enough to enjoy the beauty of the caverns. When we returned to Wichita, I thanked Don for taking his new car to California with us. Our encounters after that were only for service station business, and nothing was ever said about the touching. I kind of missed the friendship I thought we had.

With no longer spending leisure time with Don and Cliff, I devoted my energy to my favorite pastime: work. The word workaholic wasn't in my vocabulary at the time, but looking back, I definitely was one. I realized I had put my plan to become a priest too far back on the back burner. It took a priest to remind me that I needed to do something about finding a seminary if I was serious. I had been stuck in some kind of rut as far as my intellectual and spiritual growth was concerned, and I wished I had some kind of education about human sexuality, especially homosexuality. All I knew was that it was a sin. My ignorance caused me to lose a friendship with a very good young man.

Twenty-Four

THE CHALLENGE OF MAKING ENOUGH MONEY

—— ∞∞ ——

In the fall of 1953, Father Omar, our beloved choirmaster, and the assistant pastor of Our Lady of Guadalupe Parish, was transferred and replaced by Father Michael, an even more handsome young Franciscan priest. He took Father Omar's place as choir director, and two of the girls said he reminded them of Ricardo Montauban, an actor Bonnie adored. He learned from the young women in the choir that I was planning to become a priest, so one evening, after practice, he said, "Hey Don, they tell me you are thinking of going to the seminary, is that right?"

"Yes, Father," I replied somewhat sheepishly, as I was sure that I looked foolish because if that was true, why was I, at age twenty, still dilly dallying about? I'm sure I sounded lame when I said that I was waiting for my sister to graduate from high school.

"Well, I think you should get started making applications, don't you?"

"Yes, I suppose I should." Fortunately for me, he didn't bring up the subject again, but I started making plans to get Mom set financially. I increased my tile work and remodeling jobs and made extra money by driving the Catholic school bus every morning. The bus was old and creaky but had a decent motor with good brakes.

On my first run, I picked up my first passenger, a first-grade girl. She climbed onto the bus, looked at me, smiled, and said, "Boy, Mr. Bus Driver, you sure have a big nose!" Instead of laughing and taking it in stride, I frowned and nodded for her to sit down. I filled the bus with kids, first through eighth grade, from the east side of the parish. I dropped them off at school and picked up a busload from the west side. All year I had only one scary incident: Halfway through the east side route, I turned back toward the school and took a different street than usual, and it took us across about twenty sets of railroad tracks. Halfway across the tracks, one kid yelled, "Hey, bus driver, where are we going? This isn't the way to anywhere?"

I said to myself, "Oh shit!" I shook my head and yelled, "Oh, thanks, I made the wrong turn." Thank God there were no trains coming on any of the tracks, and I turned around. I never zoned out like that again, and none of the kids complained to the principal or anyone. Other than that, I had a successful year, but I did not choose to repeat it. Working until ten or eleven and going to bed at midnight or one o'clock and getting up at 6:00 a.m. was proving too much. Yeah, I know; Rome wasn't built in a day.

In that same fall of 1953, when I was twenty and Bonnie just turned twenty-two, she began dating Jim White, a nice-looking fellow slightly younger than her who was enlisted in the air force.

He was well read and claimed to be an atheist. I enjoyed arguing with him about religion. One of his favorite authors was Philip Wiley, author of *A Generation of Vipers*. I read it and thought that Jim, having been raised in a very conservative Baptist home with a tyrannical dad who made our dad seem tame, had a good reason to criticize Christianity. In October, he was transferred to the air force base in Biloxi, Mississippi. In December, Bonnie went to visit him, and two weeks later came home for Christmas, married and pregnant. Despite morning sickness, she joined Jim when he was transferred to North Carolina, where she gave birth to a baby girl they named Terri.

With Bonnie no longer able to help with expenses, I needed to make more money. I told Mom of my concerns, and she mentioned it to Jim Abney. Jim mentioned it to his brother, Phil, who worked at Boeing, and there just so happened to be an opening in his department. Jim was an inspector for the U.S. Air Force, and Phil was an inspector for the manufacturing company, so basically, they did the same thing for two different entities. I mostly guessed that they moved around the plant and looked to see if everything being manufactured was being done properly.

I didn't know anything about any of that but figured I would get trained—if they hired me. So, I set up an appointment with the supervisor. He was a pleasant man, about the same age as the Abney brothers. I was surprised to learn two days later that I had the job if I wanted it. It paid a little over three dollars an hour, which was a dollar an hour more than I was making at the lumberyard. If I took the job, I wouldn't have to do all the extra jobs and would still have the same income. The downside was that I would be working the graveyard shift from midnight to eight in the morning. Being an inspector seemed like a very boring job, and I would go back to being a nobody working with 24,000 other nobodies. The Hustons had been extremely kind and supportive of my family and me, and I would miss them and the entire gang. I didn't tell anyone that the idea of joining several thousand others in that immense plant scared the hell out of me.

Audra invited me to join her for the lunch Mrs. Mishler fixed for her every day. It was like she was a second mother to me. So, feeling too close to Audra, I told Earl about my offer from Boeing. He asked me how much they were offering me, and I told him three dollars and twenty-five cents an hour.

He said, "Let me talk with Audra." A little while later, he walked over to where I was stocking shelves and said, "Don, we really don't want to lose you, but we can't afford to match Boeing's hourly rate." I took a deep breath and did my best to hide my disappointment, and then he added, "What if we raised your pay to two dollars and fifty cents an hour? With that and your overtime, your pay will be better than Boeings, I think?"

I quickly calculated the figures in my head and reached out and took his hand. "Thank you. Yes, sir, that would be very helpful, and it would be much better here than working for Boeing." I almost crushed his hand gripping it so hard.

"And Don, please keep all this to yourself. We can't give everyone raises like that, okay?"

"Yes, sir, and mum's the word. Thank you again." I would be the youngest and highest paid of the lumberyard's twelve employees and would have to work to not let that go to my head. I was never sure I succeeded, especially after one of the young truck drivers got angry at me for chewing his ass out for screwing up a delivery. He responded, "One of these days, Hanley, we're going to knock you off your high horse."

My humble response was, "You'll never find a stick long enough!" I was ashamed of myself for that insensitive and prideful remark for a long time.

I called the Boeing supervisor and told him I would not be taking the job. He had made a special trip to downtown Wichita to talk with me, so he sounded cross when he said, "So you were just job shopping, is that it?"

I felt scolded and ashamed for having put him to the trouble. "Well, uh, no, sir, that wasn't my intention."

In late summer, Bonnie called and asked me to come to Nashville, Tennessee, to pick her up and bring her and the baby back to Wichita because Jim was being sent to Germany. So, I drove to Nashville and immediately turned around and drove back. I went through the Ozarks and part of Tennessee and thought it would be nice to make the trip someday when I didn't have to be in such a hurry. I had missed her presence in my life, and I was glad she came without her Jim. The baby was Mom's delight, especially because Bonnie did all the caregiving, and Mom needed only be Grandma. She said once that she had done enough mothering for one lifetime.

A few weeks later, I decided I could set Mom up financially if I built a house on the back of our lot for her to rent after I left for the seminary. That was another good reason to stay working for Earl and Audra—they could help me find building materials at a lower cost, and I was fairly sure Earl could give me good advice on my project. I drew up plans for a 600 square foot, two-bedroom house. I figured I could finish the house for around $3,000 or less if I did all the work, except the plumbing. Earl suggested I get an FHA home improvement loan because I was improving my property, and it would be a low-interest loan. I applied for the loan and took my plans to city hall and got all the paperwork approved.

In October 1954, I began digging the footings for the foundation in the moonlight after choir practice. I never gave it a thought that I should be proud of myself for buying a house at eighteen and building a house at twenty-one.

I found a plumber who would do the plumbing for $600 if I provided the bathroom and kitchen fixtures. Jim Abney then helped me run the foundation concrete pouring. Being that it didn't have to be smooth, only correctly laid out, it went well. Two weeks later, Jim helped me with the concrete floor, and that was a complete disaster. I didn't know enough to know that the concrete needed to be liquid so that we could spread it out properly. By the time we got it spread out, we could walk on it like a gravel road. Jim asked, "Now what are you going to do?"

"I don't know." Jim left, and I went into the house and cried. I felt like a complete and utter failure.

At the time, I didn't give it a thought that my perfectionistic tendency was a hindrance to my growth as a human being.

Twenty-Five

OVERCOMING A FAILURE—SORT OF

On Monday morning, I told Earl about my concrete failure and asked him if he would take a look and tell me what I might do about it. All day Sunday, I visualized getting a jackhammer and turning the whole damn thing into real gravel, among other similar ideas.

When we got to the site, Earl got out of the pickup, looked at the floor critically, and then said, "It looks like you and your brother-in-law did a pretty good job of getting it leveled off. If it were my problem, I'd go ahead and frame it up and complete everything except the baseboard around the walls. Then I would mix up a concrete topcoat, cover the rough floor, make it as smooth as possible, and put asphalt tile over it."

He put a hand on my shoulder and continued, "What do you think of that idea, Son?"

I damn near cried again, "I think that is a great idea. I never thought of that. That's what I'll do. Thank you, sir, thank you."

With a lighter heart, I drove us back to the yard. He would have been a great dad, I thought. After work, I called Jim Abney and told him about Earl's suggestion, and he sounded relieved that our work had not been in vain.

By Thanksgiving, I had the walls up and ready for the ceiling joists. Thanksgiving Day, I started putting the joists in place. I took time off to take Mom, Patty, Bonnie, and the baby out to the Abney family dinner, and then I returned to complete the joist project.

At Christmas, I sang with the choir for midnight Mass but went back to work on Christmas Day and started putting up the roof rafters by myself. That was another penny-pinching mistake. I should have hired someone to help. After fighting an especially strong wind all day, I managed to get all the rafters nailed into place. It was only then that I noticed I had let the ridge pole board sag in the center, so the entire roof sagged in the center. I had to do the entire roof structure over again or do some kind of cosmetic work so that it did not look awful from the ground. I chose the latter, and if anyone noticed the problem besides me, they never mentioned it.

It seemed that I always screwed up something, so I could not take any pleasure in being able to tell myself, "Job well done." When it was all done, I *was* proud of completing the house. The only help I needed was the plumbing, the concrete work, putting up the walls, and the drywall on the ceilings. What prevailed in my thinking was the vision of my gravel floor and sagging roof. *Way to go, screw up, on your high horse.*

I finished my house building only a few days after my twenty-second birthday. Marie took a picture of me with Mom and Patty in front of my cute little house. The total cost, plumbing and all, turned out to be $2,200, plus hundreds of hours of my labor and about forty volunteer hours from my brother-in-law, Jim Abney. One weekend, after Jim White got out of the air force, he visited us, and after watching me work on the kitchen cabinets for a few minutes, he asked, "Don, where do you get the motivation to work like you do?"

Never having given it much thought, I just said, "I don't know," and he shook his head. I wondered why he didn't volunteer to help me. After all, we had provided a home for his wife and baby for two years. I have to admit that I felt superior to him because of that.

There were several small remodeling and tile jobs lined up, so I kept up my eighty-hour workweek schedule. Audra kept the contracts coming. Once, I heard her say, "Oh, Don can get that done in a few hours." It was wonderful to hear her encouraging words, even when they were exaggerations.

One of my high school classmates, a pretty brunette named Mary Blume, joined the Guadalupe choir in May. I was embarrassed to say that I didn't remember her, even though she remembered me. She had gone to St. Mary's Women's College in Leavenworth, Kansas, and completed a B.A. and earned her Kansas state teacher's certificate.

After a few weeks, she said, "Don, I know you plan to become a priest, but I was wondering if maybe we might do some things together like go play miniature golf? I don't mean that we'd be dating, just be friends who do things. What do you think?"

Although she was attractive, she was not sexy like my sister-in-law Elsie or even Bonnie's friend, Joyce, so I thought I could do things with her and not be afraid of her, as I seemed to be with so many young women. Maybe spending time with her might help me overcome that fear.

So, I said, "That might be all right, but I have a really heavy schedule, and I don't have many days or evenings free."

"Well, my time is pretty free until I start teaching school." She snapped her fingers and brightened. "I know; I just joined the Legion of Mary at All Saints Parish. They meet on Sunday evenings. You don't work on Sundays, do you?"

I thought she would think much less of me if I told her I had worked every Sunday for the past year and about half of them before that. I gave myself the excuse that I was keeping holy the Sabbath because working on Sundays would help me become a priest sooner. Feeling guilty about impure thoughts and masturbation was a pretty big sinning load without adding violating the prohibition of work on Sunday to the mix.

I said, "Not too often. But what is the Legion of Mary, and what do they do?"

"You've never heard of it?" She sounded incredulous. I shook my head, and she went on. "They meet twice a month and talk about the people they have seen since the previous meeting, and how many fallen-away Catholics are coming back to the church and going to Mass and getting their children baptized and stuff like that. They also visit the sick in the hospitals and rest homes and take food to those who can't get around. I think you would like the people in the group. Want to give it a try, or are you chicken?"

I don't know where she got the savvy to challenge me by suggesting I might be a coward, but it worked, and I agreed to her picking me up the following Sunday.

She seemed very pleased with herself.

On Sunday, we went and met in the church basement. Like about a half-dozen parishes in Wichita, the church was the future parish hall—whenever the parish could afford to build a "real" church. Wichita, in 1955, was about twice as big as it had been before World War II. I immediately did not like the priest, Father Eugene Robl, who was supposed to be the group's chaplain. He was a tall, fat fellow who seemed irritated to have to unlock the room for us. After giving an opening prayer, he grunted a "good evening" and then went to sit in a corner chair. He didn't appear to have any interest in the group he was chaplain to. I'm sure Mary and I were the youngest people there, and I was uncomfortable being the only male. I withheld judgment on the seven older women present. They sounded like a bunch of holier-than-thous as they narrated their visits to people during the week. Mary reported that she had talked me into joining the group.

Mary took an assignment for the two of us to visit two families who had fallen away from the church. They both had school-age children, and it had been reported that the children had not been baptized. We decided to visit them on the following Saturday evening. This time I picked Mary up in my 1947 Chevy that I had bought two years earlier. There was no one at home at the first address, and we met with the other family in a WWII vets' housing complex converted into cheap apartments. The young couple was sitting in lawn chairs and drinking beer in the small front yard. Three young children were running around and seemed to be enjoying themselves.

As we had agreed earlier, Mary took the lead and introduced us to the couple. The husband got up and shook our hands, introduced himself and his wife, then went into the house and returned with another lawn chair and a kitchen chair. We sat down, and I asked Joe what kind of work he did. He told us he was a carpenter and presently working on houses in a new development near Joyland, a nearby amusement park.

"Hey, I know about that development. I work for Earl Huston Lumber Company, and we deliver all the building materials to your construction company." He and I got into a conversation about building and carpentry. I glanced over at Mary, and she was nervously kicking her leg up and down and looking impatiently at me and her watch.

Joe finally broke the discussion of construction and asked, "So, Don, what brings you two here?" He looked over at Mary.

Mary smiled, "We're volunteers at All Saints Parish, and we've been asked to visit folks who are baptized Catholics but do not have their children baptized." She sounded too business-like for me, but I kept this to myself.

The wife, Irene, jumped in and seemed defensive as she said, "They're baptized as Christians. Both Joe and I were baptized Catholics, but neither of us liked how we were treated as kids, so we've been going to a church where the people are friendly. We're okay with God, and so are the kids."

Joe added, "About the only good thing they have in common with the Catholics is that they don't allow any n****** in their church, and I sure as hell like that."

I immediately jumped up and was tempted to punch Joe in the face, but only yelled, "I sure as hell don't like that kind of thinking, for a Catholic or anyone else who calls themselves Christian. I wouldn't call them real Christians. No one should believe that Black people should be excluded from any place or organization. I cannot say that it has been nice to meet you all. Mary, let's leave. Now!"

I nearly ran to my car ahead of Mary. I thought of the only Black man that Earl ever hired at the lumberyard and how he was hounded out by the redneck truck drivers. He was hardworking, polite, and conscientious, but the others constantly complained and lied to Earl about him. I asked Earl to please keep him on, but Earl said he would have to fire all the others, and he couldn't do that. I also thought about what this asshole, Joe, said about the Catholic church, and I was ashamed to admit that my church was too damn lily-white, even if it didn't have an official policy of not allowing Black people.

It made me mad to hear Mary say to them, "Please forgive my companion's rudeness."

When we got in the car, I said, "I don't need nor want their forgiveness. We don't need their kind of people in our church. And I'm ashamed of how we Catholics neglect to include Black people." After dropping Mary off at her home, I left without saying a word. The Legion of Mary was not for me.

How I remained interested in becoming a priest, I'll never know. My model was still the fictitious Father Chisholm in *Keys of the Kingdom*, and I held onto the idea of being able to change things for the better.

Right after Mass on Sunday, the young couple who had inquired about renting my new house came over and gave me seventy-five dollars for the first month's rent. They had been married only two weeks and seemed happy to be my first renters, with a new house as their first home. I happily put the money in my pocket. It would be my spending money on my first solo vacation.

I didn't know how Mary felt about my quitting nor what she thought about me because I didn't contact her on Sunday. I just left on my trip to visit Glen, Bob, and their families.

Twenty-Six

A VACATION AND A REUNION WITH SOUTH DAKOTA

———— ✳✳✳ ————

It was the first solo road trip I had ever taken, and I hoped my old Chevy was up to it. Glen and Elsie had moved to Lincoln, Nebraska, after he and Bob sold the Sinclair station. Bob had kept the Sinclair bulk plant in Hot Springs. Glen had worked as a draftsman for the Bureau of Reclamation office in Hot Springs, and when their work was done there, he was transferred to Lincoln. Lincoln was only 200 miles from Wichita, so I made it by dinner time.

Elsie seemed upset with Glen. She was polite to me and okay with Donny and Jerry. Donny was ten years old, and Jerry was six. Both were pleasant, fun children to be around. I learned that both struggled with very poor eyesight; each only had about ten percent vision—legally blind. I slept in on Monday, and when I got up, Glen had left for work and dropped the boys off at a special school for the blind on his way.

Elsie fixed me a nice breakfast of bacon and eggs, then poured herself a cup of coffee and sat down at the kitchen table across from me. "Donald, I understand that you've bought a house *and* built a house there in Wichita. That's quite an accomplishment for someone so young. How old are you now?"

"I turned twenty-two at the end of March. And thank you for the compliment." She seemed to see me as another adult, so I said, "You looked a bit out-of-sorts with Glen last night. How come?"

"You actually want to know?" I nodded, and she went on. "Still thinking about becoming a priest?" I nodded again. "Well, maybe what I'm about to tell you might help you on that."

I did my best to show that I was listening because I really was interested.

"As you know, both Donny and Jerry are nearly blind. Glen and I have gone to several doctors and have taken all kinds of tests, and we've been told that it's genetics. Both of our genes, in combination, create children who have this kind of eyesight defect. If we have any more children, they will also be nearly blind. So, we decided we should not have any more children. That is fine with me, two is enough. We were practicing birth control, and your dear brother got a case of the scruples and went to confession and told some asshole priest about our practicing birth control. And you know what that bastard told my dear, stupid husband?"

I shook my head decisively. I didn't know anything about that kind of stuff.

"He said that we would go to hell if we continued to use birth control, and if we wanted to stay married and not have more children, then we must live as brother and sister and not have sex anymore. And your asshole brother believed the bastard. So, little brother, that's why I'm more than upset with him. I'm pissed! And your dear Catholic church is completely out of its mind—if it has one at all."

I was stunned. "Wow, that's awful. I don't know what to say. I find myself agreeing with you, Elsie. Thank you for telling me all this. I wonder if that priest really knows what he is talking about?"

"I told a friend about it, and she was a Catholic once upon a time. She said that she'd heard that was the official teaching. So, Donald, do you still want to get into that mess?"

"Right now, I don't know. I really don't know. Damn."

Our little discussion put a pall over my stay in Lincoln. I went with Elsie to pick up the boys that afternoon. Glen got home around six and barbecued delicious steaks, and I played with Donny and Jerry until they went to bed. Glen, Elsie, and I talked about family until the ten o'clock news and then went to bed. The next day, I went with Glen to drop off the boys, and then he took me out into the countryside to see a Bureau of Reclamation project he was working on. He was very proud of his work, and I thought it seemed far more rewarding than running a filling station. I kept wondering why he believed that the celibate priest could threaten him with hell for being loving with his wife. Then I thought about my own fear of being around women who might be interested in getting married.

Maybe being threatened with going to hell made everyone gullible. The thought that the priest in *Keys To The Kingdom* went all the way to China to give the people there the kind of religion that put Glen in such a moral and spiritual bind—and which seemed to be so prejudicial toward Black people—haunted me as I drove toward Hot Springs, South Dakota. If I did become a priest, I would do my damndest to change things like that. I knew it was going to be a hot day, so I left Lincoln early, and that was lucky because my car, with its broken speedometer that never told me how fast we were going, threw a rod about forty miles south of Hot Springs. I called Bob, and he and one of his friends came down to get me, and they chained my Chevy to Bob's truck. Bob knew the owner of the Chevy dealer, so he towed my car there.

While my car was being fixed, I stayed with Bob, Ann, and their two kids. Bob Jr. was eleven, and Vicky was six. They had moved into a grand old home that was a bit run-down. Ann complained about it but kept it immaculate and seemed to be constantly on Bob and the kids' case for messing something up. I still smoked the pipe, and Bob smoked cigarettes. Whenever either of us put something in an astray, Ann immediately dumped it out and cleaned the ashtray. It was difficult to relax in their house.

I borrowed Bob's car and drove to Edgemont to visit Father Groel. We sat down for a chat in the rectory's screened-in sun porch. He looked quite frail, and although it was hot outside, he kept his sweater on. I told him about buying a house for our mom and building the rental so she would have a little income when I left for the seminary. When I mentioned the seminary, he raised an eyebrow, but that was his only response to my story. He never had been much of a talker, and he seemed even less so that day. He was a wonderful preacher when he gave his Sunday sermon, but socially, he was terribly shy. When I was younger, I thought his quietness was a sign of his holiness, but that day, I realized it was just his personality. I wondered if he was happy that he had become a priest all those years ago. I didn't ask him though.

Part of the reason I wanted to become a priest was thanks to the two nuns at the hospital where I had worked and where Dad died. They were the most caring people I had found. I should have asked the priests I knew about the seminary and college, but I was very fearful that they would laugh at my lack of knowledge.

I was glad that Bob volunteered to pay for getting my car fixed because I didn't have enough money to pay for it. He said, "This will be my contribution to you for providing a home for our mom. You've done quite a bang-up job. You really have been serious all these years about becoming a priest, huh? Remember that summer when you worked for us, and I kept teasing you about getting a little nookie for you, and you'd turn pink as a blooming rose if anyone was around?"

I didn't want to talk about things like that, so I said, "Yeah, and the time when we went to Pine Ridge and you suddenly climbed out of the truck and yelled for me to take over the wheel? You could have killed us both."

He just laughed and said, "I didn't though, did I? And now you're even ahead of me in buying a house and all that. We're renting this one, and I hope to get started on building our own next year. I've already bought a lot up near the high school."

I left South Dakota on the following Saturday and was only mildly glad I had made the trip. It seemed to be that both Elsie and Ann were unhappy, and that added to the belief that I had developed the summer Mom and Dad divorced: that to love a woman is to hurt her. I wasn't a happy camper as I headed home.

Twenty-Seven

WORKING UP THE COURAGE TO CHANGE MY LIFE ENTIRELY

———— ∞∞∞ ————

I had eight dollars in my pocket when I returned to Wichita. On the trip, I'd only paid for a few meals and gasoline, which was nineteen cents a gallon, so it was a cheap trip. I decided I wanted to pay off the loan for the new house before I went to the seminary. If I got enough remodeling jobs, I could get that done. Before I had left on my trip, I had made a bid on remodeling a bathroom for a family. My bid was for $600 plus materials, and the plumbing would be done by someone else. The couple said I was the lowest bidder. The next lowest bid was from Sears for $1,600. I was more than a little afraid that I would be working for peanuts if it took me too long, but I said I'd do it for $600, so I would. I sketched out what I thought it should look like. The couple approved it, and I got started my first week back.

I still went to choir practice, and Mary was there. I was relieved that she seemed to be in good spirits and friendly toward me. She asked me if we could play miniature golf sometime soon. When I told her I needed to work Sunday after Mass but could do something Sunday evening, she frowned.

She frowned even deeper when she told me on Sunday that she was uncomfortable with me sinning against the Lord by working on Sunday.

I responded, "You know, Mary, I don't think that offends the Lord. He has more important things to worry about, and I'm doing this so I can serve Him and His church for the rest of my life. That should be enough."

She shrugged. "I still think you're a bit too loose with God's laws."

"I honestly don't think they are all God's laws, but let's not argue about it, okay?"

She shrugged again, "Okay." I beat her at miniature golf, sixty-seven to seventy-three. I missed practice on Wednesday and found Mary waiting with Mom when I got home from my remodeling job at midnight. She had visited Mom three times while I was away. She said that she enjoyed visiting with Mom, and she thought Mom liked it too. That was true. Mom liked people but would seldom take the first step. She said she really did like Mary. Over the following months, Mary would find out where I was working in the evenings and weekends and visit me there. She never got in the way and often helped me clean up. I guessed she alternated between visiting me and Mom.

I made ten dollars an hour on that bathroom job—enough to repay almost a third of my FHA loan. Mary visited me only once when I was working at that place, and when she left, the teenage daughter asked me if she was my wife. I could feel my face burn but didn't know how much it showed. I simply shook my head, and she said, "I get it. She's just your girlfriend."

My next job was building out the basement of one of Audra's friend's houses. The friend had seen what I had done for Audra's basement and wanted hers to look like that too.

When I finished the work, the woman came down the stairs to see her new basement and said, "Don, you really turned the sow's ear into a silk purse." I had never heard that expression before, and it took me a minute to figure out that it was a great compliment, and then I laughed.

In early January, I inquired about what I needed to do to join the Maryknoll religious order. In March an elder Maryknoll priest from St. Louis came to Wichita to meet with me. He came to our house one evening and met Mom, Patty, and me. Mom and Patty stayed in the kitchen, and the priest asked me about my grades and what I had been doing since high school. I told him about buying the house and took him into the backyard to show him the one I built. He didn't seem very interested, but thought it looked like quite an accomplishment. He then explained to me about letters of recommendation and all the other requirements for applying. At the end, he said that it was too late for me to get enrolled in the fall 1956 school year, but if I wanted to get started, I could do my first year at a Catholic college like St. Benedict's in Atchison, Kansas. He said it was a men's college, and young men often interested in the priesthood went there for their first year or two. He said that I probably could get a scholarship there.

Disappointed, I decided to check with that college. No one in the family had ever attended college, so I was sort of flying blind. I learned that there was a St. Benedict's alumni group in Wichita, so I applied for their scholarship and received one that would cover tuition, room, and board for a semester, and I could apply for the second semester in December. My out-of-pocket expenses would be books, transportation, and incidental spending.

Earl and Audra were disappointed to hear that I would be leaving in September, but they were understanding because they had known for years that I was planning for it. In July I told the lumberyard crew. A few days later, the foreman, Floyd Eveland, came up to me when I was alone and said, "Don, uh, I have a question. Really, I think we all have a question, and the guys asked me to ask you: Are you, uh, well, uh, are you one of those, uh, queers?" Floyd took a step back, as if expecting me to hit him or something.

I got really angry, and at the same time, I was hurt and embarrassed that they would think such a thing. Three other fellows were standing a few feet behind Floyd, waiting to hear how I would respond.

I could feel Floyd's embarrassment; he really didn't mean to hurt my feelings. So, I did my best to swallow my feelings.

"No, Floyd, I'm not a homosexual. What gives you that idea, anyway?"

"Well, we noticed you don't date girls, and you get mad at us when we tell dirty jokes and stuff. And priests don't get married and, well, we wondered."

I thought of Don Cutler touching my penis, and then of Elsie's comments about the priest that told Glen he couldn't make love to his wife. For the first time, I wondered about homosexuality. I was still years away from being tolerant about a lot of God's creation.

I finally replied to Floyd and our audience. "Thanks, Floyd, for asking me rather than just guessing, and I'm happy to tell you I'm not." I felt proud of my answer.

My last remodeling job that summer was to convert Mary's mother's garage into a recreation room. Her brother wanted me to do it while their mother was on vacation, and he was going to pay for it. It was quite an undertaking, as the floor had to be raised to match the floor of the house, and the outside walls were brick that had to be covered with drywall. I worked every evening and, over Mary's objections, on Sunday. I made enough money to pay off the FHA loan, and their mother was surprised and pleased with how wonderful it was.

Patty had graduated from Cathedral High School at the end of May, and I hoped she could find a job to help with her and Mom's living expenses. I was disappointed when she applied to become a Sister of St. Joseph—the same order that taught at Cathedral High. She was accepted and would begin in September. Over the summer, Bonnie, Jim, and their baby moved into a house in Wichita. Jim was out of the air force and found a job at a loan company, and Bonnie got her job back at the insurance company. I found a reasonable apartment for Mom near downtown Wichita. It was close to stores and church. I found a one-woman agency who handled rental properties and would take care of the renters.

As I figured it, Mom's income from the rents and the $100 that she could withdraw from our joint bank account each month would still leave her needing over $150 a month. I wrote this all out for Marie, Glen, Bill, Bob, Jim, and Bonnie, and asked them what they could contribute to Mom's living expenses. I talked to each of them, and Marie said that she and Jim would help Mom with whatever she needed each month, and they did not want to set a monthly amount. Glen and Jim promised her twenty-five dollars a month each, Bill and Bob fifty dollars each, and Bonnie said she didn't think they could contribute anything but could take

Mom places. So, if they all sent their promised amount, Mom would have $150 a month, for sure.

I never figured out why I felt that seeing that Mom was taken care of was exclusively my responsibility. I guess I held on to what I had told the doctor when I was in high school: that my older brothers had taken care of us when I was young. In reality, it was only Glen for only a few years and Bob for a shorter time. I don't know why I didn't think of talking with the two kindly priests I knew about college and college living. I was pretty sure that I was smart enough to become a priest, but not at all sure I was holy enough—or even what the hell holy was.

The last weekend before 1 left for St. Benedict's, I moved Mom into her apartment and helped Mary fix up her fifth-grade classroom at All Saints Parochial School. After I sold her my '47 Chevy, she took me to the train station in Wichita. I gave her a brief hug and a brotherly kiss, then climbed on the train with only minor fear and trepidation. I was heading into a completely new world.

Twenty-Eight

BECOMING A COLLEGE MAN

The Kansas City bound train stopped at Topeka, and I changed trains. The one I climbed into was the oddest looking thing I'd ever seen. It was a one-car train, more like a bus on rails. I later found out that I was on the very last voyage of the ancient train. It had an engineer-conductor and one other passenger. The other passenger was a pretty college-age girl. I settled in for the two-hour ride, reading a biography of St. Thomas Aquinas. At Atchison, a station wagon with St. Benedict's logo was waiting for me, and a second station wagon with Mount St. Scholastica College logo waited for my fellow passenger.

I was told to tell my ride that I was a Hilltopper, so they could tell me where to go. The driver, a young man who looked like he was about my age, said, "So, you're gonna be a priest, huh?"

"I hope." I responded with little enthusiasm.

Downtown Atchison looked a little run-down, but after we left the business district, the street leading up to the college was quite beautiful with large shade trees, well-manicured lawns, and shrubbery in front of old stately homes. The last building was a huge red-brick church in front of a four-story building like I'd never seen before.

The driver announced, "The church is St. Benedict Parish Church, and the big building is Freshman Hall. It was the original monastery."

As was often the shameful truth, I didn't know what a monastery was, even though I had seen the word in various books.

"Now I'll take you to the administration building at the top of the hill. That's why they call its residents Hilltoppers." He dumped me and my luggage off at the side of the three-story building. "You guys have the entire top floor here—you're the kings of the hill." He chuckled and climbed back into the station wagon.

I lit my pipe and walked over to the side of the bluff. I could see the Missouri River. It was a beautiful view. Then I headed up to the third floor. The building did not have an elevator. At the top of the stairs was a handsome young priest in a black robe with a hood, reminding me of the Franciscans at Guadalupe. He held out his hand. "Hi and welcome to St. Benedict's. And you are?" He looked down at his clipboard.

"Don Hanley," I shook his hand.

"I'm Father Marcellus." He turned to a very muscular fellow going into a room to my right. "Hey, Tim, would you mind helping Don bring up his luggage?"

Tim was a handsome guy and introduced himself as Tim Senecal.

On the way down the stairs, Tim said, "I'm a sophomore, and I'm studying to join the monastery. Are you joining the Benedictine Order too?"

"I'm hoping to join the Maryknoll Fathers, but I applied too late, and they recommended I do a year here."

"I think you'll like it. At least I hope so." We took my trunk down the wide hall to the locker room. Tim looked at a list on the door, and he pointed to a wide locker with hangers on one side and shelves on the other. He said that I could start unpacking, and he'd go down the hall and bring back my suitcases.

When I finished unpacking, a fellow student who introduced himself as Dick Steinbrenner showed me where to stow my luggage.

"I'm from Burlington, Iowa, and I'm a freshman. You a freshman, too?"

"Yes, and I'm from Wichita, Kansas."

We exchanged information about ourselves, and he began showing me around. His parents had brought him across Iowa the day before. I thought it would be nice to have parents who could drive 400 miles and take me to college, but I didn't share my thoughts with my guide, who looked far more like a college freshman than I was sure I did. Dick showed me the shower room in the basement and lavatories on the second floor, and I wondered if the planners on all this wanted to make sure the Hilltoppers would get enough exercise. Back on the third floor, he showed me our desk room and told me to pick out a desk that would be my daily home base. I chose a north-facing desk below a window and was relieved to learn that smoking was allowed in the room.

Next door was our community bedroom—for all twenty-some guys. I sure as hell didn't share my thought that so many bunk beds would put a crimp in my habit of masturbation—along with nearly everyone else if Kinsey's research was correct that 90-some percent of males did it. Everyone had been asked to put their name on a piece of paper and placed it on a bunk. I felt lucky that I was able to choose one of the two vacant lower bunks. The next morning, I didn't feel so lucky, as the guy who slept above me was an eager beaver who jumped out of his bunk two seconds after Father Marcellus rang the bell at 5:30 a.m. He landed with a loud thud, right by my head. I wanted to reach out and punch him. I was sorry to learn that the remaining open lower bunk had been taken before I could change my bed.

Our chapel was across the hall from the locker room. It was far warmer and more pleasant to the eye than any of the other rooms. Steinbrenner told me that Father Marcellus would tell us where we were to sit before prayers at 5:30 p.m. Last, but definitely not least, we had a dining room of our own down the hill in Freshman Hall.

In the desk room, I met around twenty more guys hoping to become priests. Tim had an identical twin named Tom. There were four fellows who looked as old as my twenty-three years, or older. One had one of the most pleasant voices I had ever heard, and I learned that he, fittingly, had been a radio announcer. His desk neighbor was also older, and both had already earned degrees and were at St. Benedict's to learn Latin and some philosophy required by the seminaries they had applied to. I liked them both immediately and felt a kind of kinship, even though they were more educated than me. Fifteen of the twenty-two were here for their second year, and seven were freshmen.

At 5:25 p.m., we all trooped into the chapel, and Father Marcellus introduced himself and informed us he was also working on his own graduate degree at the University of Kansas and wouldn't be with us at every moment to see if we were behaving ourselves. One of the older students said, "Thank God," and everyone chuckled. Marcellus told us of the schedule and then led us in a prayer called Vespers.

I walked down to the dining hall with the two older guys and learned that Marcellus's predecessor was an old pain-in-the-ass Benedictine priest who acted like he was God. They thought Marcellus would be a breath of fresh air for all of us. The food was served cafeteria style and was quite good—really better than I had been used to. Mom had left most of the cooking back home to Bonnie and Patty, and they were barely adequate cooks. Their specialty was cold lunch-meat sandwiches. After dinner, we hiked back up the hill. I counted the eighty-one steps between the dining hall and our quarters.

The next morning, all the freshmen assembled in a large hall and were given a battery of tests. Before the tests began, a priest who announced that he was the dean of students told us about the college rules and that he and the faculty were in *locus parenti*—in the place of our parents—and that we were expected to be obedient to the rules. My immediate thought was that I was back to being fourteen years old—when Dad died. Oh, well, I'd wait and see if the rules were tolerable. We then took the test—for three freaking hours!

For the first time in years, I felt like I was always following others around and that they knew far more than I did about everything. So, I asked around and then one morning I met with a faculty member to determine my schedule. My mentor was the college registrar, the chief honcho, who signed me up for what I soon learned was a very rigorous academic schedule. When I exited the building, I saw a cluster of my fellow Hilltoppers and joined them. One of the older ones asked me how many units I signed up for. I didn't know a unit from a hole in the ground but noticed a number after each course and assumed that designated units. I counted them and said, "Twenty-four."

He almost yelled, "Aw, come on, Hanley, that can't be. Twelve is full time, man! Let me look at that." I handed him my list. He counted them up, then exclaimed, "Well, I'll be damned. Who signed you up for this?"

"The registrar. Four units are for choir and schola, and I don't imagine there's much homework for those."

And so, I began my college career. I wasn't worried about the load; after all, I had been working eighty hours a week for years. I was more concerned about the regimentation. It was a comfortable and friendly beginning, but I felt like I had gone backwards in my personal life—like I went from being an assistant manager and remodeling contractor to a school boy—emphasis on boy. I felt a bit more like a visitor than an actual participant.

However, I began to like the regimen of the seminary students more than I thought I would. I realized that I had put college students on a far higher plane of intelligence than I found them— or, maybe, I realized I was smarter than I had previously thought. It was an interesting and comfortable world for me. Flowers abounded.

Twenty-Nine

MAYBE I COULD BE A COLLEGE STUDENT

———∽∾∽———

My classes had me running up and down the hill. After lunch, I always headed to our desk room. One day I felt like taking a nap, but we could not go back into the bunk room unless we were sick. So, I sat down at my desk, put my head down on my arms, and fell asleep.

In my afternoon English literature class, taught by a priest who had a Ph.D. from some prestigious school, there were two sophomore football scholarship students seated right in front of me. Their questions and observations were so lame, I thought to myself, If these guys can make it in college, I sure as hell can too. After only a few minutes, I was sure the professor would teach me to read a novel in an entirely new and more interesting way. This was going to be a class I would enjoy.

History was also interesting, taught by an ancient priest who had stories for every part of the Western World since the time of the Babylonians. Another of my favorites was music. The priest was small, epicene, and serious. He encouraged everyone who wanted to learn to sing better to stay and for those who were only looking for an easy credit to just leave now. He put each of us through musical scales and assigned us accordingly. I was assigned baritone. The choir class lasted two hours and was followed by schola—a six-member group that chanted short refrains during Mass. I was singled out right away because I was the only non-tenor in the group. He had me run through various scales and decided that I could reach the high notes, so I'd do, because no other tenors had applied. I felt like I was a second-rater, but, what the hell, I'd see where it went.

Dick Steinbrenner and I began to hang together, and he urged me to join an intermural Hilltopper flag football team with him. I did and enjoyed it. With all the classes, Hilltopper prayer routine, the stairs, and football, I kept busy.

I found myself lightly studying my fellow bunkmates. Overall, I thought them to be a good bunch of guys, except for my top-bunk thumper and one other fellow. Both seemed to be about my age or older and, I hoped, far more odd. Thumper kept his eager-beaver enthusiasm at full steam all day long—rushing from here to there as if his pants were on fire. Even in chapel, he rushed to his place in a pew and quickly put his head down to pray. When the bell rang, he hurriedly did the sign of the cross. I once tried to talk with him, and he kept looking around like if I didn't hurry up and get lost, he'd melt or something. The other one was slower and moved like a plaster statue. The moment he entered the chapel, he folded his hands in front of him like a little boy making his first communion. Thumper and Cob Up His Ass seemed to be loners trying to mimic some saint they had studied. I hoped they never made it into the priesthood, for I was sure they would terrorize poor seven-year-olds like Father Bartrow did me.

Most of the guys were great company, and if we all became ordained priests, I hoped to work with them if they kept their positive outlook on life. I wondered which saints I would like to mimic and decided that I'd like to be smart like St. Thomas Aquinas, humble and a nature-lover like St. Francis Assisi, and get things done like St. Ignatius of Loyola. It took me years to realize that my greatest challenge was to become my own unique, authentic self.

I had a couple of classes with a fellow from Wichita. He was a few years older than me and came to St. Benedict's to see if he really wanted to go to a seminary. He drove his own car to Atchison, and I hitched a ride with him back to Wichita for Thanksgiving.

I had him drop me off at Mom's apartment, and I slept on her couch. On Thanksgiving Day, Marie, Jim, and their three kids—Suzie, Jimmy Phil, and Valarie, picked Mom and me up, and we joined the Abney's usual holiday dinner party. On Friday, I borrowed their car and visited the lumberyard. Earl and Audra asked me to help them out with the end-of-the-year inventory during Christmas vacation. I noticed that Cliff Huffman was not around and asked where he was.

Earl told me Cliff turned out to be a thief. "As you may or may not know, I check out the two cash drawers each evening. A few weeks before you left in September, I noticed your drawer was short a few dollars several times each week. I kept track of the amount and waited to see if the shortfall continued after you left."

I felt angry that he would even suspect me of being a thief, but I didn't say anything.

Earl had confronted Cliff with the register and some other accounting errors they'd discovered. He admitted he had taken the cash and embezzled the money. Earl fired him and he agreed not to report it to the police if Cliff paid the money back, which he was now doing in installments.

Many years later, after Earl had died, Audra offered to give me the lumberyard if I would simply allow her to use a desk and a phone. She said it was worth over a million dollars, and she wanted to leave it in good hands. I was very flattered and grateful for her offer, but I just did not want to be in the lumber business. I thought I could serve people better as a priest.

After talking to Earl that day, I stopped to see Mary Blume and her mother. My old Chevy was parked on the street, covered with dust. I knocked on the door, and Mrs. Blume opened it and looked annoyed to see me.

"Good afternoon, Mrs. Blume. Is Mary home?"

She gave me a quizzical and unfriendly look and said, "She's still in the hospital, as you should know."

"I didn't know she was in the hospital. I'm so sorry to hear that." The way she was looking at me, I got the feeling that she thought it was my fault. I fumbled around for words, "I, uh, what happened? Is she seriously ill? I'd written to her, but she never wrote back."

"She had a nervous breakdown. You know that she was in love with you, don't you?" With that, she slammed the door on me.

What? In love with me? I was stunned. We were just good friends; she repeatedly told me so. What had she told her mother? I stumbled back to the car. The rest of the weekend, I kept thinking of that old haunt of mine, "To love a woman is to hurt her." Did I love her? Well, yes, and no. I didn't love her in a way that would lead me to ask her to marry me, or, God forbid, even go to bed with me. I couldn't recall ever having an impure thought about being sexual with her.

My mom was worried about Patty. She didn't think Patty was doing very well in the convent as a postulant. Mom never told me how she knew this or why she felt that way.

I was quite happy to climb back into my fellow student's car and head back to St. Benedict's. Two weeks later, I received a letter from Mary. She wanted to apologize for the way her mother treated me and to tell me she missed me and would like to see me when I came home for Christmas vacation. There was no mention of love or if she ever told her mother that she was in love, and I never asked. She did invite me to go to a New Year's Eve party with her. Someone had given her two tickets to a dinner and dance shindig at the Blue Moon ballroom in Wichita. She went on that I was the only man she knew well enough to ask. It sounded to me like she was carefully couching her words in a way that did not say anything about being in love with me. But I was glad to hear from her and looked forward to talking with her about what her hospitalization was all about and what her mom had said. I wrote back that I would be happy to join her for the New Year's event.

At St. Benedict's, classes continued as usual, and the choir and schola practices increased. Performances in the parish church took up a lot of time, but that was okay with me. Finding myself comfortable in the college setting was a pleasant surprise. I continued reading novels and biographies in the evenings and developed an inner world very different from my "real" world. The fuller my daily schedule became, the fewer and less severe my headaches were. I averaged about two aspirins a day during the semester, compared to about one per day while working at the lumberyard.

On December 21, I took some books home in a suitcase with the thought of studying for the semester exams the second week of January. I had no idea what a storm was coming up for me when I got back to Wichita.

Thirty

OH SON, YOU'LL FIND A WAY

———— ∞∞∞ ————

I hitched a ride to Wichita with my fellow Wichitan on December 21 and had him drop me off at Mom's. I was surprised to see Patty there with her, but not surprised to learn that she had been told by the Sisters of St. Joseph that she was not suited for the convent. Patty didn't seem to be bothered too much by the rejection and said, "I really didn't like it there anyway."

I had barely put my suitcase on the floor when Mom started crying and, through her tears, said, "Oh, Son, you are going to hate this." I sat down opposite her and held my breath as I waited to hear what "this" was. "Son, everything has just come apart. I'm so sorry." She looked so pitiful as she looked up at me.

"Mom, what is 'everything'?"

She took a deep breath and began, "Well, the renters—they have both left. The young couple moved out right after Thanksgiving and said they couldn't afford the rent. They moved in with his parents, I think. And the people in the front house didn't pay the November or December rent, and your rental lady asked them to move out." The way she said it, I knew there was more, so I waited. "And Bill is the only one who is still sending me any money each month. Bob and Jim sent a little in October and then stopped. Marie and Jim made your mortgage payment on December first."

I wished that she would have said "our mortgage" payment instead of "your mortgage" payment, but I was glad that Marie had helped with it.

Still teary eyed, she added, "And that is not all. I had to borrow $600 from one of the ladies here in the apartment building to help me pay the rent and buy groceries the last two months." She put a tissue to her eyes and looked at the floor.

"Why didn't you tell me about all this at Thanksgiving?"

"I knew it would be very upsetting to you, and I didn't want to worry you when you wouldn't have any time to fix things. I'm so sorry to dump all this on you now."

"I guess this means that I'll have to drop out of school, doesn't it?"

"Oh, no, Son, you'll find a way. You always do."

First, I knew I'd need a car and some money. I thought of my old Chevy gathering dust in front of Mary's house and called her to see if I could borrow her car while I was home. I was pleasantly surprised when she said yes because she could use her mother's car over the holidays and would be glad to come over and bring the car. All I would need to do was take her home after I took her to dinner. I only had six dollars to my name, so I was relieved when she said she would pay for dinner.

At dinner, I worked up the courage to say, "Mary, I'm sure glad you are willing to talk to me, and I was so relieved when I got your letter and your invite to go to the New Year's shindig. At

Thanksgiving, your mom implied I was the one who caused you to have a, uh, a, uh, nervous breakdown and . . ."

She put up her hand, motioning me to stop, and said, "Oh, no, Don, you did not cause it. It was the teaching thing. I guess I was kidding myself when I thought I could be a teacher. I just couldn't control the kids. They drove me insane . . . well, not insane, but I became so anxious I couldn't sleep or anything. Mom insisted I go to the hospital. Mom really wanted me to marry you and have kids." I must have registered the shock I felt because she added, "I love you but not in the kind of way that, uh, you know, that would lead to marriage. You understand, don't you?"

"Yes, I do. And, Mary, I love *you* as a friend and, well, I hope we can remain friends. I, uh, think our food is going to get cold. I can pay you back for dinner, and I can put gas in your car."

"Don't be silly. You're sure not going to make any money at St. Benedict's."

It was Friday, and I called Audra and told her I would report for work on Saturday. When I arrived, she said that they had a high school student for a few months, but he wasn't worth a damn about cleaning the floor, or anything really, so she fired him. "Will you please give the floor a good scrubbing and then put wax on it?"

I spent all afternoon cleaning things up. Then I went to see about what I would need to do to put the houses back up to snuff. The older house was in shambles—the door and window trim had been busted in several places in every room, the floors looked like horses had run over them, and the kitchen cabinets were a mess and would need to be re-painted. Outside, several asbestos shingles had been busted, and others had been knocked off completely. I found a piece of paper and wrote down all the things I would need to fix the place up in order to rent it. The young couple who had rented my little house, fortunately, left it in very good and clean shape. So, I went back to the lumberyard and used the key Earl had given me to pick up paint, door trim, a floor sander, and everything else I'd need to start working on Sunday. I told myself that going to Mass every day for three and a half months allowed me to work on the Sundays of vacation.

After searching my brain for hours, I realized that the only people I knew who might have enough money to help me out were Earl and Audra. They had already done a lot to help me, and I didn't want to ask them to lend me $1,000—the amount I thought I would need to catch up on our debts and have some to send to Mom each month. I had given Mom $600 when I left in September and told her to only take out $100 a month if she had to—which I guess she did because she had only seven dollars and forty-five cents in her account. I decided I needed to have $600 again, but this time I would keep it in my account and give her $100 a month.

I thought of another couple I knew pretty well, and although they didn't have a lot of money themselves, they were related to people who did. Bill and Rita Gorges were very devout Catholics and really supportive of my efforts to become a priest. They already had three children, and Bill had a profitable milk business. I had gone to their wedding at the request of the Hustons. Their wedding was in a Catholic church and Earl and Audra thought I could better represent the company than they could. They had bought all the materials for their own house from the lumberyard and had referred many of the large Gorges family to the lumber company as well. They lived on a farm several miles outside Wichita, and Mom and I often visited with them. On Sunday, after I had worked several hours on the rental house, I visited them and told them of my financial problems. They couldn't stand the idea that I might have to quit my quest to become a priest because I lacked money. They said they were sure they could help me with a loan. I promised I'd pay it back the following summer.

Over the weekend, Mom, Patty, and I decided that we should all move back into the little house as soon as possible, so we wouldn't have to pay January's rent on Mom's apartment. I thought that is what I should have done in the first place—move Mom into the new house and rent out the front house, but hindsight isn't worth a damn. As they say, "Don't cry over spilled milk." The young couple had left some furniture in the house, and Marie and Jim had furniture they wanted to get rid of, so we found enough to move into the small house.

I worked as many hours as possible for the Hustons and, at the same time, put in many hours fixing up the front house. Just like before college, I was working eighty or more hours a week and did not have a single headache. I even found time to attend Guadalupe's choir practice and to sing with them at the Christmas midnight Mass.

I received the loan check, and Mom repaid the money she had borrowed. We moved into the house two days after Christmas, and I slept in the very house I had built—for the first time. That really felt good, and I didn't have far to go to work on the older house.

Mary dressed up for our New Year's Eve "date," and I even wore my one suit and tie. I thought that it was the first time I'd ever seen Mary look so, well, sexy. We had a delicious dinner and danced several dances. At midnight we were on the dance floor. The band immediately started playing Auld Lang Syne, and every couple around us began kissing passionately. I awkwardly bent down and pressed my lips to Mary's and held them there longer than I had ever done in my life. I glanced at others who seemed to be trying to devour one another's faces, and I was turned on by them, but I didn't want to be so sinful, nor did I know how to kiss that way anyway. I felt certain that Mary was as ignorant as I was, and I didn't try to find out. Anyway, we just swayed together and sang what we knew of the song and left shortly afterwards.

I found what I hoped were good renters for our house. This time I used the lumberyard's account to check their credit, and it came out positive. They paid the first and last month's rent, and I put most of the cash in my own bank account and changed the utility bills to come to me rather than the rental company. I also put my final paycheck of $500 from Huston's into my account. The best news, right before I left, was that Patty got a job as some kind of helper at St. Joseph's Hospital in Wichita. She only had to walk two blocks to catch a bus that took her directly to the hospital.

So, I took Mary's car back to her, took a deep breath, and climbed into Jack's car. As Mom said, I found a way.

I was glad to get back to the carefree life at St. Benedict's. Not surprisingly, I began to have regular headaches again. I never talked to anyone about my pattern of only having headaches when I wasn't working my butt off. I often wondered if my frequent headaches meant that there was something wrong with me emotionally or mentally, but I did not ever tell anyone about that worrisome thought. My most relaxing habit was smoking my pipe every evening.

Thirty-One

ON THE HONOR ROLL AND A BIG DISAPPOINTMENT

—∞∞∞—

After I buckled myself into my friend's car, he asked, "Well, Don, did you get any studying done over the vacation?"

"Hah! I didn't ever take a book out of my suitcase." I went on to tell him about my vacation woes.

He looked at me like I was crazy or something. "Please tell me why you are the one responsible for your mom?"

"Well, my brothers took care of Mom and the four of us youngest kids when our dad was in the hospital for three years, so I think it's my turn."

"Okay, but it still sounds like a bit much now. But, hey, you're doing it. I hope if and when you become a priest that you keep all this in mind when you ask the working stiffs in your parish to give more to your building fund."

I let the discussion drop, put on my college boy's hat, and rejoined the good old Hilltoppers.

I had a week of classes and time to review my notes before taking the semester's final exams. I had applied for, and received, the Wichita St. Benedict's Alumni scholarship while I was in Wichita. The first week of the second semester, I learned that I had gotten four As, two Bs, and one C and was on the honor roll—just like high school. The second semester, I took Introduction to Psychology. I wanted to figure myself and others out, but the course was not helpful. I learned some things about rats and pigeons and thought they should have called the course "ratology." Yeah, I knew that I was conditioned, but I did not live in a cage and pull a lever for food.

During the first semester, I got in the habit of visiting the construction site of the new abbey church. The marvelous white stone walls were about halfway up when I first visited in the fall. Before the end of the spring semester, they were putting up colored aluminum ceiling tile. I thought that was a big mistake—it just didn't go with the beautiful stone walls and graceful cut of the building. But the whole thing was a delightful diversion to the routine of the school year.

I felt quite honored in February when Earl called to tell me that he and Audra were planning to take a trip to Kansas City to see the new Cinemascope movie. He said they wanted to try out their new Cadillac and wondered if I would like to go along. I was always open to anything to break up the routine of our Hilltopper life, so I accepted their invite. Father Marcellus approved the trip. Dick Steinbrenner wanted to join me. As we went to Kansas City in the back of the luxury car, I thought, Here I am, the former assistant manager of the lumberyard and owner and builder of houses, riding along with an eighteen-year-old like a kid with a mommy and daddy. Who and what the hell am I? I wondered. We saw the new 3-D film and had a delicious dinner at a very nice restaurant. The film was interesting technically but not very engaging, but it was nice to have a break—despite my narcissistic mental gymnastics.

In March, I spent a weekend in the monastery itself to experience how the Benedictine monks lived.

My first reaction was that it was a peaceful and quiet place—so much so, it was eerie. I enjoyed hearing the peaceful chanting of the Hours in Latin and was puzzled by the monks bending down and touching the kneeler and then putting their fingers to their lips. When I asked why they did this, I was told that it was an act of humility and a reminder to pay attention and to chant correctly. I marveled that the chants and St. Benedict's rule had been obeyed, unchanged, for around fifteen centuries! Although I was impressed with the serenity of the place and the dedication of the monks, I just could not see myself following such a strict regimen. I returned to the Hilltoppers with a new respect for the fellows planning to join the monks.

In April, the elderly Maryknoll recruiter came to visit me. He inquired about my grades and life at the college. After a bit of discussion, he asked me how old I was. I told him I had just turned twenty-four on March 28.

The old bastard put a hand to his mouth and exclaimed, "Oh my, that old?"

I rehashed our previous visit when I told him my age back in Wichita. I wanted to raise my voice at him but told myself to calm down.

"Donald, I just have to tell you that you are just too old to enter the Maryknoll seminary."

I wanted to jump out of my chair and knock the smirk off his face. I don't think I had ever been so angry in my entire life. "You lied to me. You sit there calmly, knowing that you lied to me a year ago!"

"Oh, my son, I'm sorry you feel that way. That's just the way it is." I didn't say another word. I just got up and left. I learned years later that the old bastard was only interested in young boys and that Maryknoll never had an age limit as he declared.

I was more depressed than I had ever been—even worse than when I was faced with the money problems over the Christmas break. I was glad that Father Marcellus was available when I dragged my sad butt back up the hill. I told him of my big disappointment, and he was very comforting.

He said, somewhat jokingly, that the Benedictines never took teenagers as possible candidates for their order, "Maybe, you've chosen the wrong group, Don." He chuckled, then added, "From what you've told me about your struggles financially, maybe this was a blessing in disguise."

I looked surprisingly at him, and said, "What do you mean, Father?"

"I believe that every religious order requires a candidate to enter their house of formation and begin their year as some kind of postulant or beginner's residency. And if they stay a year and are accepted into the order on a provisional basis, they are there for good. There is no going back home unless you leave the order or are asked to leave. You would not be able to work during the summer or Christmas breaks to help your mom. Now, if you studied for the diocesan priesthood, you would have summer and holiday vacations to go home. So, I encourage you to think about that. You are a good man, Don, and I think you will make a good priest."

That didn't entirely heal my wounded feelings, but I had never even thought of the points he made. He was right, I did need to have those times off. I finished my year at St. Benedict's, and I had to admit that I really enjoyed the experience. And for the fifth and last time, I climbed into my friend's car and headed back to Wichita. I whispered, "Goodbye, St. Benedict," and thought that I had said goodbye to too many places and heard welcome from too few. On the way, I told my friend that I was going to work to become a diocesan priest and told him why. He told me that he'd given up the idea of studying for the priesthood. When I asked him why, he said that there were too many pretty and delightful girls at Mt. Scholastica and the world, and the idea of a life of celibacy just seemed absurd. He planned to continue college at Wichita University and get an MBA. I realized that I was foolish to have sold my car and given away all my tools.

Thirty-Two

THE SEMINARY

———◦∞∞◦———

I had better news greeting me in late May than I did in December: Patty still had her job at St. Joseph's and graciously gave up her bedroom for me and moved in with Mom. Audra had lined up a lot of work at the lumberyard for overtime pay as well as extra outside remodeling jobs for me to make the money I needed. I went to the old car auction and found a 1940 DeSoto that ran well and had functioning brakes for thirty-five dollars. I borrowed back tools from Jim Abney and Jim White. I was in business for the summer and ready for my eighty-plus hours a week and fewer headaches. Near the end of my time there, I was averaging three to four aspirins a day at St. Benedict's.

On the first week, I made an appointment to meet Mark Carroll, the bishop of Wichita, and went to the diocesan chancery office the following week. I was pleasantly surprised to see the bishop in a collarless, white shirt sitting at his desk with his black coat and white collar draped over a nearby chair. The two windows behind the desk were open, and I could feel a pleasant breeze. The bishop stood and held out his hand. I had asked Father Blanpied, the pastor of the new parish that our house was in, how to greet the bishop. He said if he holds his hands with the palm facing the floor, he expects you to kiss his ring, if he holds it vertical to the floor like a normal person, he wants to shake your hand. I liked it that Bishop Carroll wanted to shake my hand. After pleasantries, we both sat down.

"I've looked over your transcripts from St. Mary's High School and St. Benedict's, and it appears that you are quite gifted, intellectually at least," he said. "And your two letters of recommendation are also impressive. So now, tell me why you have waited so long to begin your seminary training?" He looked at me, grinned, and added, "I'm guessing some girl ditched you, and so you decided to stop that dating nonsense and become a priest. Is that it?"

"No, uh, er—do I call you Your Excellency or Bishop or . . .?" I felt a bit embarrassed for not knowing.

"Just Bishop is fine, never mind all the fal-de-ral excellency stuff. Please go on."

So, I told him about caring for my mom and thinking of Maryknoll.

"Well, young man, that sounds quite noble of you. And where is your father in all this?"

"He died when I was fourteen, Bishop."

"I'm sorry to hear that. Yes, you are noble indeed." The way he said this made tears well up behind my eyes, and I had a great deal of difficulty holding them back. But I did manage to.

"Well, I'm glad that Maryknoll wasn't interested in such an old man because the Wichita diocese needs you. I like Kendrick

Seminary in St. Louis and St. Thomas in Denver. Which one would you prefer?"

I didn't know anything about either one, but I'd heard that St. Louis was often hot and muggy, and my brother Jim lived in Denver. I had visited him once after high school, so I chose Denver.

Bishop Carroll stood up, came around the desk, held out his hand, and said, "Well, Donald, welcome aboard."

I was elated by his hearty welcome, and I really liked the man and thought I had made the right decision. I was in good spirits when I went back to the lumberyard.

I learned that Mary had joined the Marines and was now a lieutenant in the U.S. Marine Corp. I did not want to bother her mother for her address, and for some strange reason, Mary's going to the Marines made me happy. Another Mary, Mary Grice, whom I met at a choir practice, and her mother had begun visiting Mom every Sunday evening. Mary was about eight years older than me, a newspaper reporter, and I enjoyed bantering about the Church and society. As a journalist, she knew far more about nearly everything than I did—except construction and lumberyards.

The summer whizzed by, and I made enough money to pay off the loan from Bill and Rita Gorges and to save enough to send Mom a $100 a month throughout the coming school year. Bill, in California, promised to continue sending Mom fifty dollars a month, and Bob and Jim said they would do their best, but I didn't count on them. With Patty's salary and a bit from the renters, Mom should be okay. The renters I had found in January had proven to be very reliable and kept the yard in good shape. They planned to continue to do so. I even had enough money for my train tickets and school expenses. I could relax a bit, as the Wichita Diocese was going to pay for my St. Thomas tuition, room, and board.

The last week of August, I sold the DeSoto for forty dollars and packed up my two suitcases and steamer trunk, which now contained two black cassocks and white collars. I climbed aboard the three-car Missouri–Pacific train to Colorado. Two of my fellow passengers were also Wichita seminarians headed to St. Thomas in Denver. They were third theologians, or, in other words, beginning their third year of graduate school in theology and would be ordained in 1959. They were Gene Gerber and Gene Grabner, and I liked them both, especially Gerber. How strange, I thought—Gene and Gene, Gerber and Grabner—not related, both from Wichita and studying to be priests.

My brother Jim met me at the train station and took me to his family's home in Denver. I spent two days and nights with him and Kay and their two young children, Mary Kay and James Dennis. Our family was sure full of Jims as Marie and Jim Abney had also named their son Jim. On the Friday morning before Labor Day, Jim took me out to St. Thomas. On the way I looked over at him and smiled as I thought of my old hope of getting bigger than him so I could beat the shit out of him.

He glanced over at me and said, "Whatcha smiling at, little brother?"

"I was just thinking about how I used to want to get big enough to beat the shit out of you, and now you're still an inch taller than me and about forty pounds heavier, that's all."

"Now, why in the world would you want to do that?"

"To pay you back for all the times you were mean as hell to me."

"Like what and when?"

"Like lots of times. Like all the years you kept calling me stupid, and when I was sixteen and you put my head in an arm-lock and took your other hand and burned circles on my head."

"Oh, those little Dutch rubs. I probably did that to pay you back for being so superior when we were running the lumberyard. Yeah, that was it. It didn't hurt did it?"

"It hurt like hell, damn it."

"Well, now that you're going to be a priest, I guess I should apologize."

We got to the seminary and saw the old, three-story, red-brick building where I would check in. It was creatively named the ORB—Old Red Brick—building. Jim and I unloaded my luggage.

I said, "Thanks, Big Brother. As they would say back at the lumberyard, 'If I was as big and ugly as you are, I'd go bear hunting with a stick.' And now I forgive you for the Dutch rubs." Before he could reply, I turned toward the small crowd of guys at the bottom of a set of stairs.

When I arrived at St. Benedict's, I felt like I was just beginning a new adventure. But here, looking over at a bunch of guys, most younger than me and dressed in cassocks and collars, I felt like the Martian guy in Robert Heinlein's *Stranger in a Strange Land*.

Two of the older fellows came over and introduced themselves and helped me carry my luggage into the building. I was assigned to a corner room on the second floor, and there I met my two roommates, Steve Beatty and Art Grant. Steve looked more like a high school student than a college sophomore, and I learned about vocational order. Every student was ranked according to their age and when they entered the seminary.

I was happy to learn that smoking was allowed outside and in our rooms, but I wasn't the only pipe-smoker, joined by Art and Steve. When we all lit up, our room looked like downtown Los Angeles at noon. Fortunately, the room was large enough to allow each of us to have an open window above our desk. We rearranged the room so that our metal lockers provided some privacy, and it was better than the common rooms we had at St. Benedict's.

I put on my formal cassock and collar to go to lunch in the refectory. The large room was filled with rectangular tables for eight and each of us were assigned to a table according to, of course, vocational order. Our food was delivered by apron-clad students who, I was told, were second-year philosophers or college seniors. Every student would take turns waiting tables and doing dishes for a week, about once a semester for each. I wasn't looking forward to either one.

In the late afternoon, we again donned our cassocks and assembled in the chapel to hear the rector, Father John Danagher, welcome us and to explain the seminary rules. Danagher seemed like a kind and gentle man and, from what I could gather, he was a welcome change from his stern, pain-in-the-ass predecessor. The rules were quite simple: no student cars on campus, and cassocks were to be worn to all classes, the chapel, and in the refectory. Students were expected to be present and on time for all scheduled events, there was night silence between evening prayers and ten, and visiting other students' rooms was forbidden, as personal friendships were discouraged. This last one remained a puzzlement—especially after I learned that Jesus commanded that we love one another. I wasn't interested in friendships, nor really how to have them anyway, so that wasn't a problem. Lurking down in my frail social brain, was a genie that told me I was really full of shit and an imposter. So, as usual, I wanted to get busy and become distracted from such nonsense.

On Saturday we were all put to work setting up booths, tables, and such for the annual St. Thomas Fiesta—a fundraising event like a parish fair. Being one to like physical work, I welcomed the day's work. On Sunday, hundreds of good Catholic folks filled the quadrangle between buildings and gave lots of money for the great cause of educating future priests. I manned the ring-toss booth with another fellow.

On Monday, we were awarded a two-hour bus ride to a Catholic Boy Scout camp in Estes Park. We had a few hours of free time, and many of the upper classmen found cots in the camp building. I joined a bunch of guys who planned to hike up Mt. Meeker, behind the camp. We had hiked the steep trail for about an hour when we heard a loud scream behind us. We found one of the Colorado students who had been making fun of us flatlanders from Kansas and Nebraska, lying off to the downside of the trail and holding one of his legs. One of the more experienced hikers examined his leg and thought it was broken. Another fellow ran back down the trail to get help. I suggested that we make a makeshift stretcher with our jackets and sweaters, which we did, and six of us began carrying him back down the trail. We managed to carry him about a mile before we met three park rangers with a regular stretcher. I don't know what the others did, but I slept on the bus all the way back to Denver.

On Tuesday, we took down all the paraphernalia from the fundraiser, and I was informed that we would begin our regular seminary regimen on Wednesday. So, my first five days weren't very educational in any formal sense, but they were interesting.

The beginning of my seminary career was not what I had expected, but I enjoyed the informal interaction with this bunch of white fellows from six or seven states. At the time, none of us questioned the fact that there were no Black men and only two or three Hispanic men.

I didn't like the almost constant reminder that we were expected to act like obedient little boys. I thought that, over all, the classes at St. Benedict's were quite good but still believed the practice of having the students sitting in rows in front of an instructor was a poor way to have a real educational experience. I hoped it would be better at this smaller institution. I soon learned that it was worse. I continued to be puzzled by how we were taught to love one another but never to visit one another because personal relationships were forbidden.

Thirty-Three

EDUCATION OR INDOCTRINATION?

———— ∞∞ ————

The regular regimen began with a loud bell, better suited to a fire department, ringing at 5:25 a.m. and repeated at 5:30 a.m. to make sure we were awake. Then a third at 5:43 a.m. and another at 5:50 a.m., at which time we were required to be in our cassocks and in our designated place in the chapel. After ten minutes of recited prayers led by our beloved and chubby vice-rector, Father Johnny Vidal, another bell rang demanding that we begin our meditation. I didn't know beans about meditating and was disappointed to discover that I would never learn how to meditate while at the seminary.

A student, kneeling at a kneeler in the sanctuary, read our points of meditation. I guessed that I was supposed to think about the points for twenty minutes and thus somehow become more holy or enlightened or something. One of the points on that first morning was, "The eye is not satisfied with seeing nor ear filled with hearing. Try, moreover, to turn your heart from the love of things visible and bring yourself to things invisible." Huh? This was from T*he Imitation of Christ* by some medieval guy names Thomas à Kempis. I looked all around me and saw all the returning students' chins resting on their chests like a hailstorm had run through the chapel. I was sure this was not the invisible seeing the writer was talking about.

Another bell at 6:20 a.m. woke everybody up, and we had more morning prayers and then another bell to help us be ready for Mass. A few minutes after Mass, another bell summoned us to breakfast, and we lazily marched to the refectory for so-so food and the opportunity to be halfway human until an 8:50 a.m. bell summoned us to our first class. I learned that on most weekdays, we had to keep silence during meals while we were read to by one of the older students. On those four days, we weren't allowed to be human until after breakfast. By the end of the second week, the damn bells were driving me batty, and I was tempted to give up the whole damn idea of attending the seminary. After stewing over that idea for a few days, I finally decided that I was going to be a priest, come hell or high water, and by God, I would do it even if I had to crawl through horse shit every morning.

In science class, the teacher said, "As you know, the sun and the moon are the only self-illuminating bodies in our solar system."

I raised my hand, and when the teacher called on me, I said, "Father, I'm sure you know that what you just said is not true. The moon reflects light from the sun. It is not a self-illuminating body."

"Are you contradicting me, young man?" He very imperiously responded.

"I don't mean to be antagonistic, Father, but I'm sure what I said is true."

"Well, we'll see about that. What is your name?"

At the end of the class, we all stood as His Majesty stood and stepped down from the platform. Immediately Jack McCoy, a fellow student from the Kansas City diocese, rushed over and nearly yelled, "Hanley, you never contradict a professor here in the seminary." He seemed to be genuinely alarmed as the rest of the class went by us on the way outside or to the restroom.

"Well, Jack, I do if they are as completely wrong as this guy was."

"Well, I hope you don't get expelled."

I shook my head and went outside and lit up my pipe and thought Jack had to be exaggerating. I asked a couple of other guys, and they thought he was probably right. It seemed just too unreal, so I dismissed it. The next class was English. Our teacher seemed to think that he had discovered literary gold when he found the word persiflage and learned that it was a polite word for bullshit. His class was followed by a truly gifted Spanish teacher who could speak and read the language fluently. The Latin II instructor was as shy and inept as the one at St. Benedict's. Another shy priest taught moral guidance using a text by a Father Hardon—the name of the author received more than a few chuckles. The course didn't go much beyond learning about the seven capital sins: pride, greed, lust, sloth, wrath, and gluttony—with a heavy emphasis on lust. Another class, History of the Church, was taught by a short-sighted priest. He seemed to think that everything that happened was the Divine will of God—even "Baptism or the sword" practiced after the Roman emperors became Christian and imposed the religion on the entire population of Europe. Everyone was to be Christian, and if a person objected, he or she was executed. Yep, I thought, that would create good followers of the Prince of Peace.

A layman from the University of Denver rounded out our schedule with speech class. I was disappointed to learn that I would only have the opportunity to give one or possibly two speeches a semester. This was a class I was sure I would desperately need as a priest. My fellow new sophomore, Don Hartley, told me about his experience with Toastmasters and how they had extemporaneous short speeches every week and how much it helped him. I asked around and found out that we could start a Toastmasters group during evening recreation period, so we did and had ten volunteers the first week.

At the next science class, I nervously awaited the teacher. We stood as he entered the room and ascended the platform. He began, "Where is the student who said that the moon reflected the sun's light?" I nervously raised my hand, and he glanced at his notes and continued, "Ah, Mr. Hanley. I apologize. You are correct, thank you."

I looked over at McCoy and grinned, and he grinned back. If I were a bit younger, I would have stuck out my tongue at him. That helped me relax. A short time later, we learned the teacher had some kind of nervous breakdown in Chicago and was sent to Denver for a bit of R & R. I felt a bit ashamed, and from then on I kept my mouth shut.

The only other break from the routine was forced on me by my damn penis. It became infected and sore for some unknown reason. I went to our residence hall classmate and infirmarian John Costanzo, and he made an appointment for me with the seminary physician. I took a bus to his office and was told in a harsh way that I needed to be circumcised and that I would need to go to the hospital for the surgery. I wondered if the doctor just had a lousy bedside manner or perhaps thought that a seminarian should never have an infected penis. Again, I took the bus to St. Joseph's hospital near downtown Denver. The first morning my room was invaded by another seminarian. When we were told that we would be getting a sponge bath by the pretty nursing student, he pulled up his hospital gown, looked down at his naked self, put his gown back down, and giggled like a little girl. I was glad that the bath came before the surgery and that the pretty nursing student didn't ask me to turn over after she did my back and legs. The circumcision definitely put a damper on my impure thoughts for about a month.

I took a cab back to the seminary and arrived just as the class was having a break and most of the guys were assembled at the bottom of the outdoor stairs. They all greeted me warmly, and our oldest classmate said, "Hey, Hanley, do you know what a frilly dilly is?"

I frowned and shook my head. "No, tell me, what is a frilly dilly?"

"It's a circumcision with pinking shears!" Everyone, including me, laughed. I thought that was one for the ages. It hurt like hell, but the humor helped. Since the operation put a few weeks stop to my sinful habit of masturbation, I found a bit of solace when I started going to an elderly priest, who was retired and living at the seminary, for confession. He was very hard of hearing, and I think I could have told him that I shot the rector and stabbed the pope, and he would have said, "Now say three Hail Marys and three Our Fathers." Deep down, I was convinced it was a venial sin and good sleeping pill anyway.

My roommate Art Grant and I took walks together, and he liked to talk even more than I did. Our discussions were often quite lively. One morning in particular stands out. I said, "You know, Art, I've often wondered about the significance of the Mass.

We all sit and pray with the priest and witness a reenactment of the last supper of Jesus and witness his symbolic presence in the Eucharist. I went to daily Mass with my dad, and we only went to communion on Sundays, after we had gone to confession on Saturday and—"

Art stopped walking abruptly and interrupted me, "Did I hear you right? Did you say symbolic presence?" He sounded alarmed and completely incredulous. I simply nodded. He went on, "You are a heretic!"

"What the hell are you talking about?" I yelled back.

"Jesus is present in the Eucharist, dummy. He is not symbolically present, for God's sake. In the Middle Ages you'd have been burned at the stake for a remark like that!"

"I know he is spiritually present, but isn't that also symbolic?"

"No! He is physically present. Haven't you ever heard of transubstantiation?" I thought I had heard of the word, but I just shook my head. Art said, "Well, look it up." He turned and walked on.

I was still satisfied with my idea of Jesus's spiritual presence and walked on with him. I recalled the previous May when the St. Benedict's choir sang for a newly ordained priest's first Mass and one of the students said, "Father Whatshisname just performed his first miracle." One of the other choir members asked what he meant and was told that he had just turned bread and wine into the body and blood of Christ. I needed to give that more thought, I guessed. Art didn't write me off completely, and we kept taking walks after nearly every meal.

I joined Jim and Kay for Thanksgiving, and we were also joined by Kay's younger brother and sister from South Dakota. On Friday, Jim took the brother and me out to see the retreat house. He was the construction company's supervisor for the Diocese of Denver's project. I thought he was justified to be proud of his work. At twenty-nine, he was probably supervising many men older than himself. Jim and his family came out to the seminary on nearly every visiting Sunday and stayed for an hour or so. I appreciated the gesture but thought that Jim did it more so that he could see himself as a good Catholic and impress his kids than for me, then I scolded myself for being petty and unforgiving.

In December I enjoyed being in the seminary choir and singing Christmas songs during the nine evening novena. On December 20, I joined Gerber and Grabner, and we took the last ever Missouri–Pacific passenger train back to Wichita. Once again, I took Patty's bedroom and went to work for the Hustons and sang in the Guadalupe Choir at Christmas.

After the three-week vacation, a cousin took me to Salina to catch the Santa Fe train to Denver. I took the semester-ending tests and managed to get As and Bs in all the courses except Latin and Spanish. We were saddened to learn that our excellent Spanish teacher was transferred elsewhere and would be replaced by the Dutchman who was also our music teacher. He would be taking Spanish classes at Denver University while attempting to teach us at the same time. It didn't work. I wondered if the Vincentian Order of Priests assigned their best teachers to DePaul and St. John's in New York and sent their lesser lights to places like St. Thomas. I heard a saying that helped me relax and let go of some of the anger I felt: "How do you make a young man into a priest? For eight years you dress him like a girl and treat him like a boy." I guess that our lesser light profs were good enough for that process.

I thought that the only fellow student I had really gotten to know was Art. I felt ashamed to admit to myself that I envied two classmates: Jack McCoy, who was a very gifted athlete and musician, blessed with good looks and a likeable personality; and John Costanzo, who was intellectually gifted and had such a magnetic personality and smile that invited a friendly response from everyone. All in all, it was a great group of guys to be around, but the educational experience was definitely less invigorating than St. Benedict's. I hoped that the third year, known as First Philosophy, would be an improvement.

At age twenty-four, I was living two lives: one as a boy away at college and the other as a responsible young man when I was on vacation. I felt more authentically myself when I was on vacation than when I was at the seminary.

At the end of that first year, I felt that I didn't learn much academically but could be more patient than Mom thought I could be. When I got back to Wichita for the summer vacation, I bought another old car at the junker auction, moved Patty back into Mom's room, assembled my tools, and started life again at the lumberyard. Audra had set up a bunch of jobs for me to supervise at the lumberyard and extra outside jobs. I was home and headache free. I heard that Blaine, Audra's nephew, and a yard hand, had told the new employees, "Get all your loafing done before Hanley gets back here, cuz he's going to work your asses off." I hate to admit it, but that made me proud of myself. I happily worked my ass off for three months of eighty hour weeks and made the necessary money for the coming year. My summer income was still necessary as Patty had been laid off at the hospital and was limited only to occasional babysitting jobs.

I became better acquainted with Bob Blanpied and his assistant pastor so I could become more familiar with the life of a diocesan priest. I liked Bob, but not his assistant, who when I ate dinner at their rectory always seemed too worldly as far as I was concerned—always talking about vacations, cars, golf, and how backwards Kansas was compared to his home town of St. Louis. He once said, "Stick with me, Hanley, and I'll have you farting through silk." I wanted to sock him one.

My brother Bill invited me to visit him and the family before school started and sent a train ticket to get there. So, I sold the old car I had been driving all summer and caught the Southwest Santa Fe Chief headed to South Pasadena. Just before I got on the train, I got the bright idea of lowering my anxiety about meeting people. I would sit by as many people as possible and see how many would start a conversation with me within three minutes. If they would not talk, I would try to start one. I kept track of how many I would start, and it was twenty-six, the same as the number of hours on the train. Only one nice, gray-haired woman started talking with me first. One young man wearing a navy uniform would not talk at all. One interesting one was with a pretty young woman in the dining car at breakfast time. She was sitting at a table for two, and I asked if I could join her. She was heading to California to join a Catholic convent, so we had a lot we could talk about. The exercise for reducing my anxiety did work, and I learned that most people were reactive rather than proactive when it came to conversations.

The most memorable thing about my visit with Bill and his family was my experience taking Bill and Helen's three youngest daughters to Disneyland. Barbara was the oldest at age twelve and led the way. Janice and Nancy were five and six. The three helped me enjoy the Magic Kingdom more than if I had been with a bunch of cynical young adults. I felt quite relaxed as I took the train back to Denver.

Thirty-Four

BECOMING A PHILOSOPHER–SORT OF

———⁂———

Back in Denver, the beginning of the school year was a repeat of the first year, but the climb up Mt. Meeker was, thankfully, less eventful. I was sorry to learn that Art Grant and Don Hartley did not return to the seminary. I would especially miss Art, but our class was enhanced by the arrival of Joe Lavoie, Bob Merz, and two others who were older than even Gene Murphy. Joe and I began taking regular walks together. Joe and the two others were military veterans. One had been on a battleship in Pearl Harbor when the Japanese attacked in 1941. They all had some great stories to tell. The only one of this trio of vets that was younger than me was Joe. My only disappointment was that none of them said anything in our classes. I think they just tried to put their noses to the grindstone and treated the seminary as a lengthier and softer boot camp. One had completed a bachelor's degree in business, but I guessed his bishop wanted him to learn some Catholic philosophy.

I had asked Mom what she thought of when she heard the word philosophy. She answered, "I guess it would be that everyone has a philosophy of life, or about life. Like, I think you, Son, have a philosophy that includes always working hard and taking care of your mother." I especially liked that last part. I was surprised at the thoughtfulness of her answer and the compliment. I looked it up and found that it was the search for meaning, values, beliefs and concepts of a society or group.

Looking over our schedule of classes for the fall semester, it looked like we would be getting our fill of philosophy, including its history. Each morning, we were regaled with the meditations of Thomas à Kempis. One of the earliest would be helpful, I was sure: "Try to bear patiently with the defects and infirmities of others, whatever they may be, because you also have many a fault which others must endure." I would need to remember this one, as all the professors were solemn, closed, often very impatient, and put-down artists. I hardly understood anything the philosophy professor said, and when I asked around, no one else seemed to understand it either. Whenever I tried to formulate a question, the answer I always seemed to get was, "Read the text, and when you can ask a reasonable question, try again." Thanks for nothing, I thought.

I don't know if it was accurate or not, but I gathered that there was a real gulf between science and religion and that we needed to know the scientific stand on things but were always expected to defer to the official Catholic interpretation if there was a conflict. For example, the Church taught that the universe was created by God the Father and that many thinkers in recent years believed that all of creation *did* go through some kind of evolutionary process but that humans were created separately from every other life form, and therefore, those who said that we evolved from apes were heretics. It was nice to know that the Church did finally admit that Copernicus and Galileo were correct and that they had been exonerated—centuries after they were condemned, imprisoned, and had died, unfortunately. Understanding the universe should not have been as difficult, I thought, as it was presented in the books and by our esteemed, pain-in-the-ass professor. Of course, I didn't dare say this last thought out loud. And ol' Thomas à Kempis was right about this.

I kept up my novel reading each evening but had stopped reading science fiction and moved to Morris West, John Steinbeck, and other more socially conscious writers. During our evening spiritual reading time, I was relieved to discover that no one checked-up on what I was reading. My first year's reading included Simone de Beauvoir's *Second Sex*. I learned, for the first time, the real plight of women in our society and how sexist the Church was. This book woke me up a little, but none of this was ever discussed in any of the classes. I learned far more about morality in this book than the entire year of so-called moral guidance. I also read a former Passionist priest's book entitled *I Was A Monk* and I was glad I hadn't chosen that route to the priesthood. I tried to read two of Thomas Merton's books and slogged through them but really didn't understand what he was trying to say. After the *Seven Story Mountain*, he seemed to soar into some kind of spiritual realm that I couldn't relate to. It seemed to me that Gregory Peck's Father Chisholm was doing great work for the people in China. I wondered if he understood and meditated on the ideas of Thomas à Kempis and Thomas Merton and if that had kept him going, and maybe I was just too dumb to follow?

I was working in the library's book bindery. The student manager, two classes ahead of me, asked me to take over as manager, which I gladly did. Now, that is my element, I said to myself. I continued with the seminary magazine, Toastmasters, choir, and intermural sports. At Thanksgiving, I invited Bob from Milwaukee and Joe from New Hampshire to join me for Thanksgiving at Marie and Jim Abney's. Jim Abney had asked for and received a transfer to the Lockheed-Martin plant in Denver, so they had moved to Littleton, Colorado. Jim, Kay, and family also joined us. Susan Abney, their daughter, visited the seminary one visiting Sunday and declared that it was a total waste to see all these handsome young fellows becoming celibate priests.

The classes droned on, and it seemed that if Thomas Aquinas didn't say it in the thirteenth century, then it wasn't true. I didn't learn anything about atomic physics or its nature, but I did learn about transubstantiation. As Aristotle saw it, and Aquinas adopted it, everything had a substance that is an essence of what it was. For example, a spoon has the essence of a spoon, and it has different "accidents" such as its color, its size, what it is made of, and so forth. So, the communion bread was just a flat piece of bread about an inch and a half round. It had the essence of bread, but after the priest repeated the words of Jesus, "This is my body," the bread kept the accidents of bread but became the essence, or substance, of Jesus. And a minute later when the priest said the words over wine, it became the blood of Jesus, but remained looking like wine. Ah, so that was what Art was talking about. And what that fellow meant when he said that the newly ordained priest had performed his first miracle. I still liked my idea of the spiritual presence of Jesus in the bread and wine better, but I didn't say that to anyone.

The other main course of study we were introduced to in the third year were courses in education, taught by Father Gaydos. I learned that we would have enough courses in philosophy that we could say that we majored in philosophy, and enough courses in history and education that we could say that we minored in those two subjects. Years later I learned the value of those two things—majors and minors. There was very little discussion of the material presented, as if everything was already known about education and how to teach anything and everything. One of our earliest courses was education methodology, and in the introduction of the required textbook there was a cartoonish picture of a student's head with the top opened like a jar lid and someone pouring facts into his head. I was sure it was a joke until I read it, and it said something to the effect that it would be great if teachers could do this—simply pour facts and information into students' heads. And the damned course proceeded to tell us the best methods of getting those so important facts into our heads. This textbook was a common one in teacher's colleges and education departments throughout the country. Of course, that is indoctrination and *not* education. Father Gaydos was critical of the text but did not give a better explanation. I didn't know how education should be at that time, but I continued being critical on the inside while outwardly conforming because I wanted to become a priest, and this was part of the boot camp.

At Christmas time, I again took the train to Salina. This time, Earl met me at the station. I felt very honored, indeed. Patty moved in with Mom again, temporarily, and I occupied her bedroom. The Hustons had purchased the house and lot on the south side of the lumberyard and had built another warehouse next to the first one. I had helped layout the building and was happy to notice that my plans were followed. Audra talked of vague plans to expand the store part of the operation, but there was nothing definite. She asked me to think about it and, later in the school year, asked me to draw up some plans and send them to her if I had time. I made time and enjoyed doing it, even if nothing came of it. This was at least something concrete to think about rather than all the abstract philosophy and education stuff we were being fed.

I have often wondered how I would have turned out if I had gone to a religious order seminary where I would never have gone home and had a responsible job during the summer and Christmas vacations. In some ways, I believe that these jobs gave me a second kind of education—an education that exposed me to the thinking and experiences of ordinary people and their life experiences.

I was so disappointed in the absolutistic philosophical thinking that was being presented by the textbooks and by Father Connelly. He sounded like he really believed that every bit of creative thinking had ended with the death of Thomas Aquinas in the 1200s. I couldn't believe that a course in metaphysics in the twentieth century would not include the thinking of Einstein and other modern theorists. I studied the concepts in order to pass the courses, but I was not inspired. There was nothing said about the beauty and radical amazement (a title used by a twenty-first century lay theologian, Judy Cannatu, writing about our wonderful cosmology) of the universe. Only a few years later, I found journal articles and books that were printed around my time in the seminary college. Those books were far more educational and inspirational than anything we had in our courses, and they were never referred to. We were being fed a barn-full of bullshit. Our new Pope, John XXIII, saying that he wanted to open the windows of the Church, gave me hope for the future.

Thirty-Four

EARNING A BACHELOR OF ARTS—SORT OF

———— ᙏᙦᙏ ————

When I got back to Wichita in May of 1959, I was disappointed to learn that I was too late to attend the ordination of Gene Gerber, Gene Grabner, and two other ordinands from other seminaries. However, I was glad to learn that Mary Blume's mother wanted to sell her 1951 Mercury. I needed a car for the summer, and she sold it to me for $100. Mom was doing okay, and Patty was earning her own spending money with babysitting gigs.

In June, I did two extra tile jobs that Audra had lined up for me. She and Earl both liked my plans for expanding the lumberyard offices and store by 5,000 square feet, but they could not agree whether or not they should build it. All through June they battled back and forth over the idea. Finally, on July 3, Earl called me into his office.

He said, "Don, I told Audra that we could go ahead with the remodeling project that you laid out for us, on one condition." He looked up at me as if sizing me up for a prizefight or something similar and continued, "We'll go ahead, if you can get it built and finished before you go away to school in September—using our present employees and only one more hired hand. Of course, the brickwork, electrical, and other specialized work will be contracted out. Now, I'm sure that this is quite a challenge, so what do you think? Can you do it?"

I stood there and thought about everything we would need to do to get this done in about eight weeks.

"Will I be able to work as many hours a week as needed to get this done, along with Floyd Eveland?" I asked.

He agreed to that plus the hours of an additional hand and said he'd secure a building permit and backhoe right away.

I passed Audra's desk, and she smiled encouragingly and said, "I told Earl you'd take the challenge—of course, we'll still need you to wait on customers and do all the other things you usually do." I stood in mock attention and saluted her. She chuckled and waved me on.

I discovered that the bricklayer who had done the work on the storefront in 1949 was still in business and would be able to start on our project the following week. Floyd got the foundation and footings trench dug by the end of the day on July 5. Earl and Audra's nephew Blaine managed to pour the concrete that week. The bricklayers began laying blocks the following week, and I got the glass company to schedule the window and door framing in two weeks. I would get home late and outline, in my head, a detailed plan of what everyone would do the following day. I should have added those hours of planning to my payroll time sheet, but I didn't.

My arrogance caught up with me when we were constructing the roof and putting up the ceiling joists. In one place, we needed a large beam weighing over 200 pounds to be raised twelve feet and connected to two walls. While I was waiting on a customer, I noticed three guys standing around trying to figure out how to get the beam up where it belonged. When I was finished with the customer, I impatiently went up to the three guys and told one of them to grab one end of the beam, and I grabbed the other end and said, "Now, let's put this damn thing where it belongs." I started up the ladder on my end, and he went up the other. I felt my back go out about half way up, but my arrogance would not let me stop, and we got the damn beam up in place. I yelled, "There, now get to work putting those joists in place, we need to get the roof in by the end of the week." I was sure I had slipped another disk as I had done with the shipment of nails years earlier. I should have gone to a doctor, but I didn't. I did my best to hide my pain and tried to walk straight as I headed back into the store.

I continued working without stopping, but my back hurt like hell the rest of the summer and beyond. I was headache free since May, but the back pain made me start taking four aspirin every four hours.

Jim White, Bonnie's husband, lost his job when his company closed the Wichita office, and I needed an extra hand to nail roofing boards on the new addition. Jim was a thin office worker and had done very little hard labor. He struggled through one day and then quit. He said he just wasn't cut out for this kind of work. I was surprised, as I never thought of any kind of work as something I wasn't cut out for, maybe unqualified for, like running a backhoe or fixing some electronic thing, but not just working hard. Anyway, I found someone else, and Jim found an office job.

The biggest challenge was getting the addition's roof completed and attached to the wall of the old house, while keeping the store open and ready for business. I planned this one out very carefully and assembled a crew of eight to move all the store fixtures away from the store wall and into the new store, then shore up the house roof and the new roof with, basically, two temporary walls. Then we needed to take down the old house wall, windows, doors, and all and replace them with a steel I-beam fifty-two feet long with five steel posts sitting on the old house foundation. We started this project when the yard closed at 5:30 p.m. and had it completed by 2:30 a.m. the next morning.

Building the addition was even more challenging than building the house six years earlier and was the first time in my life that I had completed such a complex project without having some higher-up telling me how to do it. Of course, Earl was a lot of help advising me on certain things, but I was responsible for the construction. I was very pleased with myself, bad back and all.

We did get almost completely finished—stock on the newly painted shelves, floor tile, air-conditioning on, and doing business by the Thursday before Labor Day. Blaine was putting ceiling tile on the ceiling of the addition on my last day of work at the lumberyard. I had worked between eighty and one hundred hours a week during July and August. When Audra gave me my last week's paycheck she also told me that she and Earl wanted to cancel the second mortgage on the house I had bought from them in 1951.

She then added, "And Don, this is not a gift, you have definitely earned it." I almost cried but didn't. So, my summer earnings for 1959 was a little over $6,000.

With all that work, and with the help of the renters in the front house, I managed to arrange for renters for the house that I had built. Soon after, Marie and her Jim moved to Colorado,

Bonnie and her Jim moved to the Kansas City, Missouri area. So, Mom and Patty decided to move to the Denver area. They got everything ready to load into the car for our trip to Denver. That included Oggie, aka Little Lord Oglethorpe, the little terrier-spaniel mutt someone had given to Mom when she first moved into the little house.

Near Kit Carson, Colorado, the Mercury blew a tire. There was only one Texaco filling station in the small town, and the two old codgers there told me that they would sell me the tire but wouldn't have time to put it on for me. I was afraid that the nearly bald spare would not make it to Denver, so I bought the tire, borrowed their tools, and put the tire on the wheel and on the car while they sat there and watched me. I was sure they weren't too old to help. When I got ready to go, Oggie got loose, and I had to drive all over town trying to find him and get him into the car. I was getting so upset, I said, "Maybe we should just leave him here and go!"

Mom, who rarely made demands about anything, responded that I'd have to leave her too. So, I kept chasing Oggie until I think he got wore out. I treated Mom like she was a sick old woman. I don't know when I realized she was only in her early sixties. But I think I was proud to be noble (as Bishop Carroll said) enough to take care of her. It took me many more years to learn the difference between taking care of someone and being a caring person.

Mom, Patty, and Oggie were going to live with Marie and Jim and their kids until Patty found a job, and they could move into their own apartment. I asked Jim Abney to take me out to the seminary and keep the car at their house until the holidays.

Again, we started the year with the bazaar and trip to the mountains and began classes on the Wednesday after Labor

Day. What made this year different from previous years was that it snowed three inches that Labor Day night, and I got my own room on the west side of the philosophy building. It had a view of Mt. Evans—a great picture to wake up to.

I was proud of my classmates, as six of us headed up various activities that served the students, such as the bookstore, snack shop, student store, and so forth. Classes droned on with the same know-it-all professors and non-dialogical classes. I was very disappointed that the History of Philosophy course essentially ended because the text and Father Connelly thought that all good and necessary philosophy ended with Aquinas, so all the rest were given short shrift. Mr. *Cogito ergo sum* Descartes was the exception. Kant, Hegel, Marx, and the existentialists were set up by the philosophy professor and dismissed as "straw men."

One good development for me was the addition of Father Cahill for a philosophy course and our first course in theology. I especially liked him because he was open for discussion of the topics presented. Before each class, I would look over the textbook pages that he would lecture—translate: read to us—and then I would come up with as good a counter argument as I could. Trying to prove Catholic dogmas by citing scripture, church tradition, and reason seemed to me to be a shallow way to defend any idea. Only Christians could say that the Bible was true because we believed it was true because God said so. And the same could be said of Church tradition—just because people believed something for many centuries didn't mean it was true either. Anyway, it was fun debating with Cahill. Years later, he said to me, "We had some good classes, didn't we?" I agreed. When I did not prepare an argument, one of my fellow students would ask me why I didn't challenge Father Cahill. I always responded, "Why didn't you?" No one ever joined me.

We got our first really good course of the four years from Father Vawter, who was a true Bible scholar. He spoke and/or read nine languages, had gone on archeological digs in Palestine, and written a book entitled, *A Path Through Genesis.* In his Introduction to Scripture class, I was relieved to learn that the Bible is not one book but a collection of books, and that the biblical story of God creating in seven days was only one of two creation stories in the Bible, and both should be considered myths that contained truths, but were not history nor archeology nor any kind of science. Now, that made sense, even if some traditionalists thought that Bible scholars were heretics.

My classmates Bob and Joe again joined me at Marie and Jim's for Thanksgiving. On Friday, after turkey day, the three of us drove down to the Air Force Academy near Colorado Springs.

We were given a guided tour and arrived a few minutes before lunch and saw the cadets line up in the parade grounds and, in uniform, stiffly march to their dining hall. We commented to each other that at least we didn't have to stand at attention and then march to meals. The most imposing building on the campus was the chapel. It was a huge A-frame building with beautiful stained glass windows on the top main room as the inter-denominational chapel. Under that was the Catholic portion—also beautiful—and the floor was shared with a synagogue and a mosque.

At Christmas, being I had a car available to me, I planned to drive back to Wichita. I told Jack McCoy and two others from Kansas that I would be glad to give them a lift if they wanted to ride with me. So, four of us piled into my Mercury, and we made it nearly to Limon, Colorado, about a hundred miles from Denver, when the car threw a rod. I heard a clunk and pulled over to the side of the road. Luckily for us, the Santa Fe train stopped at Limon, and a highway patrol officer stopped shortly after we broke down. The patrolman pushed the Mercury to a junkyard in Limon, and we planned to catch the train. Unfortunately, I was the only one who had enough cash to buy a train ticket. We checked around and found the Catholic owner of a restaurant who was willing to cash a check for enough to cover the train tickets.

Audra and Earl invited me to stay with them over the holiday time. I enjoyed working in the new addition that I had a hand in building, but I still wanted to become a priest. Father Blanpied asked me to be the straw subdeacon for the Christmas midnight Mass. A Solemn High Mass usually requires three priests, or it could get by with one priest, a deacon, and a subdeacon—the latter two were usually ordained a year before being ordained to the priesthood. As a straw subdeacon, I put on all the vestments of a priest except a stole. I had to admit that I felt like some kind of special person in the world—and a bit of an imposter.

Back in the seminary, we limped through the rest of our senior year that did not feel like the year we would truly earn a bachelor's degree. I wondered what discipline you could consider complete that ended the field's thinking in the thirteenth or fourteenth century? Our diplomas, without envelopes, were slipped under our doors, and I stepped on mine before I even noticed it being there. So much for ceremony.

Three of our classmates were going to the North American College in Rome for their theology graduate work. One was going to Louvain, Belgium. A small part of me was envious of them for receiving the honor of going to Europe for graduate work, but the bigger part of me was glad that I was not chosen for two reasons: first, that I would be able to work during the vacations and, second, in Rome, the subjects would be taught in Latin, and I was a terrible student of Latin.

Thirty-Five

BEGINNING TO BE A NINTEENTH CENTURY THEOLOGIAN

—— ∞∞ ——

For living quarters during the summer of 1960, Gene Gerber had given me the address for a room with an older couple, Mary and Tom Armstrong, who rented only to Catholic seminarians. I had my ride drop me off at the lumberyard, then I noticed a car that I had seen one of Audra's friends drive was now for sale. It was a beautiful forest-green 1952 Chrysler New Yorker with Fluidrive. I remember my brothers calling Fluidrive, Slushamatic. It was affordable for me, and I bought it. That first evening I drove it out to my new digs and met the very pleasant couple, the Armstrongs. My apartment consisted of a large bedroom, living room, kitchen, and bathroom combination, and the rent was thirty dollars a month. The couple had four grown children and a bunch of grandchildren, most of whom I got to meet over the summer. The only negative living with the Armstrongs was that they attended Mass every morning and that made me feel guilty when I didn't.

Audra had lined up several tile jobs for me, and I soon realized that I should have told her that my back hurt constantly ever since the previous summer. I never told anyone about reinjuring my back by lifting that beam. But she had promised the people I would lay the floor tile, and every evening for three months, I limped back to the apartment and melted into bed. I did manage to make enough to pay the rent, buy the car, save up enough to give Mom a monthly check, and pay for my own expenses.

I made one trip to Smithville, Missouri, where Bonnie and Jim and their two girls had moved. I spent the Fourth of July with one of the Armstrong's son's family on a water-skiing outing and got severely sunburned. That's where I learned that if I poured vinegar over the burn, it would not blister, and it would considerably reduce the pain. I smelled like a pickle, but it worked.

I was glad that I had the comfortable Chrysler to drive back to Denver, because my back hurt so badly. I didn't have headaches during the summer months, but I continued taking four aspirin every four hours for the pain in my back. I drove directly to the seminary and nearly crawled to the infirmary. The student infirmarian immediately called the seminary physician, and I drove to his office. Thankfully he was younger and friendlier than the one who gave me the frilly dilly. He told me to go to the hospital immediately.

At the hospital I was hooked up to a wide corset-belt with two ropes tied to pulleys with weights that hung over the end of the bed. The intention, I was told, was that the traction would pull the vertebrae apart and ease the back pain. The doctor said that someday I would probably need surgery.

I ended up spending thirteen days in traction—time enough to read two books I had grabbed off my desk at the seminary— Teilhard de Chardin's *The Phenomenon of Man* and Erich Fromm's *The Art of Loving*. I liked both of them, and when I got tired of wrestling with the difficult prose of Chardin, I would switch to Fromm. Chardin, to emphasize that he was definitely veering away from Thomas Aquinas's philosophy, coined his own words. He was a Jesuit priest and a paleontologist and seemed to be far more devoted to Darwin's theories of evolution than to the Church's devotion to absolute, static truths. I especially liked his ideas of the evolution of consciousness and that Jesus revealed a whole new level of human consciousness. As I understood him, all creation had some level of consciousness— even rocks and plants—and he called the level of vegetation and animal consciousness the biosphere. Above the biosphere was the level of noosphere that allowed us humans to think, reflect, create, and invent at a level of consciousness above the biosphere. It even allowed us to grow above that level and be in touch with the highest level of human consciousness or the level of amorization that led us humans to lovingly connect with God the Father in an entirely new, or at least different, way. He baptized it by calling it the Christianization of creation. And if we followed Jesus's teachings about loving others as we loved ourselves we were being "mystical" Christians. I thought that Chardin also implied that Buddha, Lao Tzu, and others taught the same. I wasn't surprised to learn that he was not allowed to publish his writings. He had given them to Thomas Huxley who published them posthumously and I was happy to learn that some of the theologians at the Vatican II Council were promoting his thinking.

I had never liked the theory that Jesus, the Son of God, died for our sins and was happy to learn that theory had been concocted in the eleventh century by a medieval monk named Anselm. It was a theory, damnit, not a fact. Chardin talked a lot about the power of love and that it is a force that humans need to grab on to and change the world—with and for Jesus. Jesus died because he was a menace to the religious Jews and Roman political leaders in Palestine. And Fromm put some practical psychology into it, and that made a lot of sense to me—especially when, in scripture class, we studied the Gospels and Epistles that constantly promoted God's love. My favorite passage in the entire Bible: *"God is love and he who lives in love, lives in God, and God in him."* Now I had to learn how to love, especially love myself. How in the hell do I do that? A big part of me still felt like a worthless pile of shit.

My main human contact in the hospital was Jeanine, a beautiful student nurse, who came in to give me a back massage every afternoon. She also came by to visit several times a day whenever she found a break in her routine. I regaled her with my new found theories of love and Jesus and God. I never mentioned this to anyone, but I thought Chardin really was implying that Jesus was not our savior, but a prophet that was introducing us to a new force and level of being human. I didn't even dare mention this to Jeanine, who was a devout Catholic, and I feared she would stop coming to visit me if she thought I was a heretic. I hated when she had one of her days off. Was I feeling love for her in a way that Jesus taught? Did I love either of the two Marys back in Wichita in that way? What in the hell was love anyway? Wanting to pull Jeanine into bed with me surely wasn't it but that was part of my confessions.

I kind of felt sorry for myself when, after thirteen days, I realized that my sister Marie had brought Mom and Patty only once to visit me, and my brother Jim only came once too. For the first time, I realized that I had put on a kind of rugged individualism that told everyone in my family and the world, "I don't need anybody."

I left Mercy Hospital with a back brace that kept me straight and helped me feel less pain. I wore it every hour of every day except when I was in the shower or in bed. I especially missed Jeanine when I left the hospital. I don't know what I would have done if I had to pay for the humongous hospital bill. As a good boy who was studying to be a priest, it was a gift to me. I guessed I was important to some people who ran the church.

Back at the seminary, I parked my car on the street outside the school grounds and used the elevator reserved for the faculty. Both of these acts were against the rules, but I never asked for permission and no one ever said anything. In May I had chosen a small third-floor room rather than one of the basement rooms with the rest of the first theologians, because I didn't want to sleep in the basement again. I didn't give a thought to the fact that I was distancing myself from the rest of my classmates because I never visited with them in their rooms anyway. I was still taking four aspirins four times a day for headaches and back pain.

I had missed the first two weeks of the first theology semester, but the only class that really mattered was Father Vawter's scripture class. One of my classmates let me use his class notes. Scripture seemed to be the only class that suggested a non-medieval philosophy and theology and could fit in with Chardin. Even in the Old Testament there were hints of the power of God that was love, rather than condemnation and eternal punishment. The church history droned on about popes and the Church's expansion through the work of missionaries. I was surprised to learn that mandatory priestly celibacy hadn't been imposed until the eleventh century. The textbook and instructor said that it was to enhance priest's devotion to Jesus and His teachings. Later, I learned that the real reason was to stop bishops and priests from leaving church property to their children. I wonder if that revelation would have encouraged some of the seminarians to leave the seminary? The missionary priests seemed to be more interested in preaching to the pagan natives of other lands about the Church's teachings than in providing basic human needs like Father Chisholm did in *Keys of the Kingdom*. I knew there were exceptions, but they were not highlighted by the history books. It was much like my South Dakota history book in the sixth grade that idolized General Custer who literally savaged the Native Americans.

Both textbooks in dogmatic and moral theology were written in Latin, and we were required to purchase them. I could ponderously make out what the dogma book was saying, but not the moral theology. It really wasn't important for two reasons: the lectures for both courses consisted of the professor sitting on the platform and translating the pages for us. And second, there were mimeographed "ponys" or English digested notes for each course. The first semester's course in dogmatic theology was bearable because it was taught by Father Cahill, and I could debate with him, but the moral theology class was a complete waste of time.

One day I mentioned to a classmate how discouraged I was, and he said, "Before you start thinking of leaving the Sem', let me give you a little book to read." I followed him down to his room, and he handed me Viktor Frankl's *Man's Search for Meaning*. I read it in three days, and I said to myself, "If he could make it through three horrible years in Auschwitz, I can make it through this f—king place for three more years."

A third-year theology student had gone to Catholic University to complete his bachelor's in philosophy and when he returned to St. Thomas, he started a set of evening discussion groups on various subjects. I volunteered to start a group on pastoral counseling and got eight students to join me. We met every Monday evening during rec time and discussed a book on the subject. I thought it was pathetic that this was as close as we would get to having an established class on pastoral counseling. So, I had two rec periods taken up each week with this and Toastmasters. And I continued with my other volunteer jobs, so the year went by with my back pain, my evenings, and the classes. I looked forward to the vacations, especially since I had comfortable transportation back to Wichita.

Thirty-Six

UNCONSCIOUSLY BECOMING A LIBERAL

———⊶∞⊷———

Back in Wichita, for the summer of 1961, I was joined by another seminarian at the Armstrong's home. They had two bedrooms on the second floor, and we shared the kitchen and dining area. He had also completed his first year of theology in a seminary back east and was studying for the Wichita diocese. He was five years younger than me; he had entered the seminary right out of high school. Someone found him a summer job at a construction site, and he constantly complained about how much he hated it. I did not find him very companionable, and that was fine with me, as I kept busy at the lumberyard and the remodeling projects Audra had lined up for me. I'm a little ashamed that I didn't make a greater effort to get to know my bunk mate, but I just didn't particularly like him. He reminded me of Father Blanpied's assistant at St. Margaret Mary's, who seemed to be more interested in the role of priests rather than service or even what was going on in the Vatican Council.

During the summer I got to know Gene Gerber a bit better. One evening he invited me to go to the movies with him. As we were watching *Camelot,* a scene came on depicting the leading lady in a very sexy way. I squirmed in my seat, and Gerber whispered, "Don't race your motor, Don, if you're not going anywhere." I chuckled and wondered if the actress caused him to race his motor.

Wichita had been given a new bishop, Leo Byrne, who was called a coadjutor bishop. From what I learned in the diocesan monthly newspaper, that meant he was sort of an assistant bishop who would become the ordinary, or head honcho, bishop when Bishop Carroll stepped down or died. Carroll stepped down a year or so later. I had yet to meet Bishop Byrne but liked him because he appointed Gene as vice-chancellor the following year. Gene later became bishop of Dodge City, then Wichita. My back didn't act up too much during the summer, and I did several remodeling and tile jobs that helped me with finances. I took Gary Kennedy, a new seminarian for the diocese at St. Thomas, back to Denver with me.

The classes began with basically the same lineup of Father Vawter continuing to inspire and enlighten us, and the rest of them making us wish we'd stayed in bed. After a few weeks, our dogmatic theology professor told us that he was going to divide us into small groups for our Friday class. The class combined second-year theology students with third-year students. I was delighted with the arrangement and jumped into the discussions with gusto. He visited each group for a few minutes, and after three weeks he noticed that two or three students in each group seemed to do all the talking, so he asked us to write down the names of each student in our group and put a number after their name indicating how we rated the talkativeness of each one. Those getting a ten or a nine, the most talkative ones, were assigned to one group and on down the line. I was in the ten group and the only second-year theologian to go into that group.

I soon discovered that the six or so third-year fellows were more conversant in the new theology than I was, and I was glad I was with them. After only two weeks, we all decided we'd learn a hell of a lot more if we just met in the group every class.

We met with the professor to see if that was possible and he said, "If you fellows do this and agree to write papers on the subjects I assign and take the final exam with the other students, then I'll allow it. One other thing, I expect you all to get an A in the class. If you get a B or less, your grade will be reduced to the next lowest grade. So, a B will become a C, you got that?"

We all accepted the challenge. At the end of the semester, I think we all got As. I'm sure I learned a lot more than I would have if I attended the formal class.

One time our group was given an experimental educational film-strip from St. John's University's Religious Education Department. We were asked to view it and give them an evaluation of it. The first slides depicted Jesus's passion and death on the cross with a voice-over stating that Jesus died on the cross in order to gain divine grace for all humanity. Then it showed a humongous, glowing, golden tank in the sky emblazoned with large, white, sparkling letters "Divine Grace." The tank had seven golden pipes descending from the tank to the earth with spigots depicting the seven sacraments.

When I first looked at it, I kind of thought it was quite clever and depicted how I was taught to look at the sacraments. But, at the same time, it didn't seem to be right at all. I didn't say anything but several of my fellow discussants bellowed their disdain at the lousy piece of work.

One fellow said, "That is terrible in many ways. Grace is not a quantifiable *thing*, it is a spiritual gift, a force, a power, and the sacraments are not pipes with spigots spurting out a liquid elixir."

Another fellow from Nebraska, added, "And the idea that Jesus died on the cross to *earn* back grace from God the Father is only a theory put forth by a bunch of medieval theologians."

These were exciting ideas that I had not heard so clearly before. I realized if that film-strip were true, it would put the role of priests as some kind of spiritual filling station operators managing the sacramental pumps and making sure that the people were properly prepared to receive the grace from God. Oh, Lord, what a bunch of horrible ideas! Those ideas couldn't fit on the same planet with Teilhard de Chardin's ideas on the evolution of consciousness and human transcendence into his idea of the divine milieu.

I don't know if the other second and third-year students had seen this film-strip or not. It was not mentioned at our refectory table. I tried to start a conversation about some of the ideas, but one of my classmates interrupted me, "Hey, Hanley, can't you ever talk just plain talk? Do you always have to talk shop?" He sounded scolding and some of the others nodded in agreement. So, I gave up and looked forward to another meeting with my discussion group.

Another serious encounter that year was in moral theology class with a pleasant older priest who translated the Latin text first written in the nineteenth century. It read like an expanded elementary catechism text on justice and Catholic morality. This class, like dogmatic theology, combined us second-year students with the third-years. One of the third-year fellows liked to talk shop, and we decided that the class was missing some very important aspects of the study of justice—especially social justice—including fair and living wages and the extremes of capitalism. Several classes, for instance, spent time examining such heavy issues as how much bread is acceptable to steal from a wealthy person versus a poor person and how much constitutes a venial sin and how much is a mortal sin. We considered this a complete waste of time.

Every day our kind and boring professor came into the classroom, stepped up on the platform, sat down at the table-desk, opened the Latin textbook, and began to translate the words where he had left off the previous class. No one challenged him on anything, and most of us just slept through the class. My fellow conspirator and I decided that we needed to challenge him, and that social justice was just the right issue to bring up. We began to take turns asking questions about the church's position on things like the minimum wage, labor unions, and poverty. His answers were off-putting. He'd say, "That is not in the text," or, "We'll go into that later," but it never led to any kind of dialogue. After about the third day, he came into the room looking very grim. He mounted the platform and before sitting down, he sternly said, "Mister Fischer." My friend nodded and prof turned to me, "And Mister Hanley." I nodded and he went on, "If either one of you interrupts my lectures one more time, I will see that you are expelled from this seminary. Do I make myself clear?"

We nodded. I still wanted to be ordained a priest and hated giving in to this guy who I thought was just a timid, obedient, old man. I was ashamed that I felt I had to nod to the old goat. I felt miserable, and my friend and I commiserated with each other after the class. I thought he had more support among his classmates than I did in mine. Everyone in our discussion group was on our side, and that helped a little.

At Christmas vacation, I agreed to take the daughter of the lumberyard's bookkeeper, Mrs. Mishler, with me back to Wichita along with Gary Kennedy. She was a very pretty young woman about a year older than me. She had a beautiful voice, and we spent the entire trip singing Christmas songs as well as dozens of others. After we dropped her off, Gary said that she was flirting with me. I felt flattered, but a bit uncomfortable; after all, I was the straw subdeacon at our parish's midnight Mass.

At Easter time, I got a surprise letter from a Monsignor Smith in Wichita. He was the director of Catholic Social Services, aka Catholic Charities of Wichita, and pastor of a small parish a few miles northwest of Wichita. He asked me if I would be willing to come to his parish and direct the new Holy Week liturgy and train the altar boys. He would arrange plane tickets to and from Denver. I immediately wrote back that I would like to do it and gave him the dates for the Easter vacation. I was sure that I didn't know any more than he did about the new Holy Week liturgy, but I could read up on it. I was looking forward to my first commercial plane ride. My brother Jim once took me on a small plane ride when we were working in Edgemont, and that was all.

Monsignor Smith himself, surprisingly, picked me up at the airport and took me to the St. Mark's rectory. It was the first time I would spend a night in a parish rectory, and he showed me the guest bedroom. It smelled a bit dusty but clean. Smith was a large man, about two inches taller and a hundred pounds heavier than me. He seemed a bit aloof and impersonal. He never told me his first name and seemed to prefer monsignor. I had never met a monsignor before, and I had asked around the seminary before I left Denver and learned that it was simply an honorary title given to some priests for special roles like diocesan chancellor and such, or simply because the bishop liked him. I thought it harked back to the ages of kings and queens. It was years later that I found out that the entire church hierarchy was modeled after the Roman Empire and the medieval feudal system that had given birth to kings and queens. Monsignor introduced me to the housekeeper and cook and then gave me a tour of the large sandstone church that looked like it could hold four or five hundred people.

St. Mark's school was an interesting parochial-public entity that I learned was quite common around German-Catholic parishes in Kansas. It was public in that the state and county taxes paid the schools expenses, and Catholic nuns ran the school and were the teachers. Everyone in the parish were Catholics, and so both the parish and school district saved money, as the nuns worked for smaller salaries and the parish did not have to pay for the buildings and supplies.

This decades old practice was outlawed a few years later. The monsignor took me over to the school, and I met the ten seventh and eighth grade boys who would be the altar boys for the Holy Week services. I dressed up with a cassock and surplus and acted as master of ceremonies and over-grown altar boy each day. Everything went well, and the monsignor was pleased. He took me back to the airport on Easter Sunday.

Two weeks later, Monsignor Smith sent me a letter asking if I would be willing to help the agency place Cuban refugee boys in Catholic foster homes in and around Wichita during the summer. I would be paid the current social worker salary. I was pretty sure that he had me come to St. Mark's for the Holy Week services to size me up for the summer position. Anyway, I thought that would be a good experience and wrote back that I would take the position, if I could also work about twenty hours a week at the lumberyard. So, in late May, Gary and I headed for Wichita in my Chrysler.

"Fools rush in where angels fear to tread," was an expression I heard from somewhere. And it definitely fit me many times over during my early years. I don't know where I got the chutzpa to believe that I could do anything related to work. If someone else could do something then so could I. So, I took on the role of professional social worker with no training whatsoever. As new priests, I realized that we were all put into roles in parishes that we were not trained for—school teachers, pastoral counselors, administrators, youth organizers, and on and on. We were only actually trained to be sacrament dispensers and spreaders of pious platitudes and moralisms.

Thirty-Seven

MY ATTEMPT AT BEING A SOCIAL WORKER

— ❦ —

As usual, the Armstrongs welcomed me warmly and informed me that the other seminarian who had stayed with them the previous summer was not planning to return. That was fine with me.

On the Tuesday morning after Memorial Day, I drove over to the offices of Catholic Social Services, just west of downtown Wichita. It was housed in a one-story, buff-brick, office building. Parking was in the rear of the building and the one door had a small sign, Employees Only. I assumed I was now an employee, so I entered and found a long hallway. On my left was a large office and I heard voices. I looked into the room through the open door.

Monsignor Smith yelled, "Good morning, Don, come in, come in!" He introduced me, first to the assistant director, Lou Antonelli; then to Marie Dasher, a licensed clinical social worker who had been with the agency for several years; and another new employee, Susan Olds, who had just received her master's in social work from Kansas State. Both women were already working on placing Cuban girls in foster homes.

Before Smith could say another word, Antonelli said, "Well, Monsignor and ladies, I want you to know that I do not want any part of this fiasco." I looked at him with amazement and then to the priest. Antonelli went on, "Putting a completely unprepared and uneducated young fellow in charge of placing refugee children in foster homes is criminal. Marie, here, can work with him if she wishes." He got up and stalked out of the room.

I'm sure I looked totally bewildered because I was.

Monsignor said, "Never mind him, Don, he's just mad at me and looks for opportunities to show me how much more he knows about social work than I do. Lou did not want us to take on the responsibility of placing the Cuban children in the first place, and that's part of it too. Anyway, Marie will help you as much as you will need. Do you know anything about the refugees coming from Cuba?"

"No, Monsignor. Only that many Cuban families and children have come to the U.S. since Castro took over the government there."

So, he explained that, because most of the thousands of refugees were Catholic, the Federal Immigration Service had given Catholic charities all over the country contracts to take care of the refugees. The Diocese of Wichita had agreed to take approximately 200 children and a few dozen adults. He handed me a folder with several pages in it.

"Here is a list of families who have extended an interest in taking foster children. Marie will go over the list with you. First I ask that both ladies tell you about their work so far, and then you can go over to Marianna House, next door, and meet the boys."

I followed Marie and Susan down the hall. Marie showed me the office that would be mine. It was sandwiched between theirs. She looked to be in her mid-forties and was dressed very professionally in a dark suit and white blouse. She seemed warm, friendly, and pleasant. Susan looked to be in her mid-twenties and was dressed in a navy blue skirt and light blue blouse modestly buttoned up to her neck. She had naturally blonde hair and was quite pretty with a friendly smile. Susan was very pleasing to look at and I hoped I did not have to spend too much time with her so I would not be led into temptation. Some wise guy once said, "I don't need to be led into temptation, I easily find it myself."

They both seemed comfortable being with me, so I said, "I'm guessing that you two do not share Mr. Antonelli's view that I should not be here and should not be working on the project?"

Susan shook her head and Marie said, "Please don't take his words personally, he is just a bit grumpy at times. Monsignor told us that he has met you and that you are a bit older than other students studying for the priesthood. He believes you have the kind of self-confidence and relational skills needed to work with us. So, let's give you an orientation. First, this dictaphone."

She pointed to the gadget on a typing table and showed me how to use it. "Each afternoon you'll need to dictate into this thing what you have done during the day—so take notes when you interview people, then we'll have a record of what you are doing. You'll then give the dictation to the secretaries, and they will file a copy and give you a copy. Here's a copy of a couple of my dictations, so you'll have some idea."

The orientation was quite complete, and Marie did most of the talking. Susan's comments about her first week were very helpful. Both let me know that they were available whenever I had questions.

I got a list of about eighty boys, ages seven to seventeen, and was told the five boys under age seven had already been placed by Marie and Susan. They said that I should begin with the boys under thirteen because they were more in need of a home environment and the teenage boys would be more difficult to place. I picked up the list and headed over to Marianna House. It had been a student nurses' house for the Wichita Hospital two blocks away. The nurses training program had been closed, and the diocese took it over.

The main entrance faced the social services building, and I entered there, crossing the dining room, through the hallway and into the kitchen, where I met with Molly Kelly, a motherly, round, and delightful woman in her late fifties or early sixties. Molly was the boys' cook for breakfast and stayed thorough lunch. I would later meet the Lopez family, the shy Cuban couple who were the part-time "house parents." Molly offered me a cup of coffee, and I accepted. I was mostly worried about my lack of fluency in Spanish. My two years of Spanish allowed me to read simple Spanish sentences, but I had almost no speaking ability. Molly said that she didn't speak Spanish at all and still got along well with the boys because there were enough of them who spoke English, and they helped her with the ones who did not. She gave me a walking tour of the home. The long hall bisected the building from the front to the back, and it was over a hundred feet long. On the right side, past the dining hall, were five rooms that held four to seven boys under thirteen. Surprisingly, Molly knew all their names and pronounced them in passable Spanish.

I asked Molly to slow down so I could do my best to have a fairly good but brief study of each one. All of them gave me a smile—mostly genuine, I thought. The smiles got bigger as they began to realize why I was taking their names and checking them off a list. Only one, Jesse, seemed hostile, and I made a mental note that he might be difficult to place. By the time I had met all of the boys, it was close to lunch time, and Molly excused herself. I decided to join them for lunch. I wandered around the house and then sat down in the middle of the dining hall and watched the sixty-plus boys wander in to eat. Four older boys served platters of sandwiches, sliced tomatoes, and chips, along with bottles of Pepsi. They seemed to tolerate my presence well enough. The boys made the house more than full in every way.

After lunch, I went to the lumberyard and checked in. I had told Earl and Audra that the most I could do was work around twenty hours a week. I thought that the best time of day to call and visit the prospective foster-home families was in the afternoon and evenings. Audra said that they would take any hours I could give them. After coming in each morning that first week, I realized that I really would need all day, every day, to make even a dent in the foster-home project by the end of August. Also, I felt the social work was far more challenging than the work at the lumberyard, so I quit the lumberyard. The Hustons, in their usual gracious way, respected my wishes.

In that first week during the afternoons and evenings, I scheduled home visits with twenty couples. Following my coworkers' advice, I had chosen those who were married, had young children, and owned their own homes. All of my appointments were in and around Wichita. Although the refugee program paid the families for fostering a child, I was encouraged to choose, first, those couples who did not need the money to take the child. I gave the list of those whom I had called to the secretaries, so they could check their credit ratings. I noticed they used the same credit services used by the lumberyard. Also, I gave preference to those who could have both husband and wife present for the first meeting.

Having made some deliveries for the lumberyard and directing truck drivers over the years, I knew Wichita quite well. On the first day, I dressed casually in a pair of black pants and a short-sleeved, blue, plaid shirt and called on my first couple only a mile from the office. Nothing I had learned at the seminary was helpful, but my years of experience waiting on and talking with lumberyard customers turned out to be very helpful.

I sat down in the living room to talk with the pleasant couple facing me. The house was a one-story, ranch-style home that had been built in the 1930s. I was nervous, but I did my best to explain the proposed arrangement well. They were in their late thirties and had one boy and one girl, ten and twelve, respectively, and were open to a boy of almost any age as long as he was in school. The latter requirement was because the mother worked in the school library during school hours. They showed me around the house. With a recent addition of a recreation room and a bedroom, they had four bedrooms, so their new guest would have his own room, which was a state requirement. I was sure they would be good foster parents, and I told them so. The husband looked pleased when I told them how much they would be paid for their trouble and extra expenses.

That afternoon and evening I met with two more couples. One was similar to the first, but the husband of the other was more than a bit grumpy and couldn't figure out why his wife would want to upset the family by bringing a foreigner into their house. After a brief visit I wrote them off. When I returned to the office and was dictating my day's work, I got a call from the wife of Mr. Grumpy. She apologized for his behavior but insisted he was a good and sweet man. I told her that I would keep them on the list but that it was important that everyone in the family be in favor of the foster care project.

I had found a reasonable burger joint for lunch and looked around for an equally reasonable diner for dinner. During the summer I had learned of all the fair to good diners in Wichita that served a reasonably priced meal. A few times I joined the Hustons for dinner, as they ate out every evening—usually at better restaurants than I could afford, but they insisted on paying. I appreciated that very much.

I placed five boys in homes the first two weeks, and everyone—hosts and guests—looked to be happy campers. One boy at Marianna House—Jorge, age sixteen—was having real difficulty getting along with the other fellows. He was portly and soft looking, like he didn't spend enough time out in the sun. Monsignor asked me to see if I could find a foster home before he was beaten-up at the house. I looked at his file, and he was the only child of a wealthy couple in Havana and had gone to a private, exclusive boys' prep school. When I shook his hand, I didn't feel even the hint of a callous, and I was sure he had never done a day's work in his life. He was polite and spoke a school boy's broken, but rather good English. I had told Bill and Rita Gorges about my summer job with Catholic Charities and placing Cuban children. They told me that Bill's sister and husband, Tom and Kathy Grendon, who lived near them, might be interested in an older boy who could help them around the farm, so I asked Jorge if he would be interested in living and working at a farm.

He said, "Sure, anyplace away from these guys."

I didn't think that was a very good reason to move to a farm where he would be expected to work hard. I did my best to tell him about the work on a farm and how hard it would often be. Then I went out to visit the farm and the family and to learn about their expectations. I told them about the city boy who needed to get away from the boys' home.

They said, "As long as he's willing to work, we'll do our best to help him fit in."

I liked them and their three young children, and I was dubious that Jorge would work out for them, but they did seem willing to give it a try. If he didn't work out, we'd just find some other place. I took Jorge out to see the farm and meet the family. He packed everything he owned and brought it with him. He liked them and they liked him, so I crossed my fingers and left him there. I dictated my doubts, and they were put on file.

Six days later, I got a frantic phone call from Kathy that Jorge had been run over by a tractor and hurt very badly. She asked what they should do. Without hesitation nor checking it out with anyone else, I told her that if Jorge was able to ride in the car, they should bring him into St. Francis Hospital in Wichita. If he couldn't stand a car ride, to call 911 for an ambulance. She checked and told me that Tom thought a car ride would be the best because they could get to the hospital more quickly. I told her to tell Tom I'd meet them at the emergency room.

They lived twenty miles west of the city, and the hospital was in the middle of town, but Tom made it in thirty minutes. I went to the hospital ahead of them and alerted the emergency staff, and they had a gurney and a physician ready. When they arrived, Jorge was conscious but obviously in a lot of pain. Tom told me that he and the boy had been out in a field and were stopping for the day. They had both the tractor and a pickup with them, and Jorge said that he could drive the tractor back to the house.

Tom said, "I was so damn stupid, I believed him when he said he could handle it, and I left first in the pickup. He was supposed to follow me, and I told him to take it slow. I got back before him. I should have gone behind him to make sure he was doing okay, but damnit, I didn't. Anyway, he fell off the tractor, and the big rear wheel ran over him. The only good thing was that it was over a recently plowed field, so he was sort of pushed down but, well, I hope he is not hurt too bad."

I told him I'd stay at the hospital and give them a call as soon as I learned how bad Jorge was hurt. I sent him on home. I called over to the social service's office and talked to the monsignor.

He said, "Don, how in hell did you know what to do?"

"What do you mean, Monsignor? I just did what needed to be done, that's all. Oh, and, of course, I told the hospital that the Catholic Social Service would handle all the expenses. There's no problem there, is there?"

"Damn, Don, you did well. Now I'm sure that I made the right decision choosing you to work with us. Thank you for everything." He sounded quite sincere, and his compliments felt very good. At the same time, I thought that anyone in my position would have done the same as I did.

I thanked him and told him that I would be here long after the office closed, so I'd see him in the morning and tell him all about it. I learned that Jorge had been taken into surgery and that he would be having a splenectomy and that it was very serious. An attendant came out and asked me who would sign to give the hospital and doctor permission to perform the surgery. I told her about his refugee status and that as the social worker, I was the responsible person. I felt a bit like an imposter for using the designation of social worker, but I didn't want to say that I was a seminarian doing a summer job. Anyway, the young woman took my word for it, and I signed the paper. I didn't want to tell anyone that I didn't have the foggiest idea what a spleen was. Monsignor's complimenting me for taking charge of things gave me carte blanche to sign the paper, I thought.

The next challenge was to find a new place to put Jorge when he got out of the hospital. I had talked to a delightful, recently-retired couple, Steve and Karen Bauer. They lived across the street from the Armstrongs, and they had shown an interest in the foster-home program. They had two college-age boys and thought it would be nice to have a young foster girl. I told them about Jorge and his accident and the need for a home after he was released from the hospital. I told them I would still work hard to see that they got a girl before the end of the summer but wondered if they would be so kind and take care of him for a little while—just a month or so. After cajoling them a couple times, they agreed. Then, after a week in the hospital, I took Jorge to their home. They welcomed him warmly.

I took a weekend off and went up to Smithville, Missouri, where Bonnie, Jim, and their two girls had moved. Teresa, the oldest, was then about ten years old and Shelly was around seven. I arrived before lunch, and the girls were busy doing housework with Bonnie supervising. Jim was out in the yard, mowing the grass. They both looked like they had already had two or more beers. Both seemed unnecessarily harsh toward the girls, whom I found to be very friendly and delightful. I had to work not to intercede for them when they were being scolded over something I thought was trivial. I mostly enjoyed the early hours of Sunday morning when I could quietly play board games with the girls before Bonnie and Jim got up. When they did get up around mid-morning, they went to the fridge and got beers and then scolded the girls for not getting some work done. I couldn't say that it was an enjoyable visit.

Back at social services, Marie told me about a seven-year-old Cuban girl, Sara, who was acting out at her foster home. Marie said that Sara was embarrassing her foster parents every time they had company of any kind—friends or family. Sara would come into the room and put her hand under her dress and begin masturbating. They had three girls of their own—eleven, nine, and five, all quite pretty blond girls.

I said, "I wonder if being right in the middle of a group of very white girls, she unconsciously felt she needed to do something to get attention?" I don't know what made me think of this possibility.

Marie snapped her fingers and said, "My Lord, I never thought of that. I talked to Monsignor, and he said she was just a sinful little girl."

I chuckled and she said, "Why are you laughing?"

"That's typical of a priest; they're all at war with sex and touching."

We both chuckled, and she added, "I hope you'll be different."

"I have the perfect placement for her." I told Marie about the Bauers. "They are a delightful, retired couple who want a girl foster child but were willing to temporarily take in Jorge, the boy who was hurt out on the farm. They have two college-age boys, but they really want a girl. I bet she would really love to be with them and vice-versa. Want me to ask them?"

Marie looked doubtful but said, "Sure, ask them, but be sure to tell them about Sara's problem."

That evening I went across the street and talked with the Bauers. I told them about Sara and her "problem." Neither of them was prudish in any way and asked only if she was pretty well behaved in other ways. Marie had said she was, and I told the Bauer's that Marie would bring Sara by to meet them. She did, and Jorge and one of the college boys were also very welcoming.

In late August, before I left for Denver, I visited with the Bauers and asked them about Sara's problem. At first, they looked puzzled, and I reminded them about her masturbating. They laughed and said they had forgotten all about it. She was doing fine and was looking forward to the third grade. Jorge had also done well at their house and had asked for, and received, a transfer to Miami. He had left in early August.

As I waited for Gary to arrive from Chanute, Kansas, I reflected on my summer's work as a social worker and felt quite good about myself. I had placed thirty-one boys in foster homes and, except for Jorge, all of them were working out okay so far. Monsignor Smith was very pleased with my accomplishments, and even Lou Antonelli, who hadn't even said hello all summer, smiled and shook my hand when I left. I thought that this was really doing Christ-like work even if the seminary had done nothing to train me for it. Working with a bunch of non-Catholics at the lumberyard had been good training.

I was aware of the lack of training for real pastoral work even then. The seminary seemed like an aggravating boot camp to see if we could be conforming, obedient servants of the Church. Looking back, I think that the evolution of human consciousness, championed by Teilhard de Chardin, would have come further along than it currently has if we had learned how to creatively do some social work like I had done that summer.

Thirty-Eight

LEARNING PATIENCE—OR TRYING TO

—∞—

Back at good ol' St. Thomas, I tried to tell some of my friends about my summer experiences, and the responses sounded a lot like my mom's, "That's nice." I did receive several encouraging responses to my thoughts about us needing more training to help us in our future pastoral work. One fellow from Denver, a couple of years behind us, joined my pastoral counseling discussion group and talked about his work with migrant workers. He was the only seminarian that had a summer job as challenging as mine, and I thought that was sad.

I tried to get enough interest in a seminar in dogmatic theology like I had with last year's third theologians, now deacons, but none of my classmates seemed to be interested. So, we patiently plodded on through the classes. Father Vawter, the scripture professor, was once again interesting and challenging. I especially liked the study of the Gospels, and I began to formulate what I thought was a better theology of salvation than the one I had learned growing up Catholic. Jesus was teaching and introducing the then radical idea that our purpose in life, as human beings, was to create a world-wide community of love, peace, and justice, not just a bunch of people and members of a church who all worshiped the same and kept the same divine laws and practices. I felt more than a little stupid when I learned that my thoughts were centuries old and that they were the core beliefs of nearly all of the saints. Right then, in 1962, there were quite a bunch of theologians counseling the bishops at the Vatican Council in this "new" theology. That was very exciting and promising.

Again, I tried to get a discussion going on the topic around our meal-time tables but was told that no one wanted to talk shop. The idea of bringing love into the world was revolutionary to me because most of my own religious education seemed to be how to be good and follow the commandments and church's teachings without question. Surely those good and conforming Catholics and Lutherans in Germany who obeyed and followed Hitler weren't creating a loving world. The spirit, and the Spirit, didn't seem to be reflected in the reality of the church in the world and in life as I knew it. I hoped the Second Vatican Council would effect a positive change—for everyone's sake. None of the faculty ever even mentioned the council, and we got most of our information from articles by Xavier Rynn—the anonymous name for a priest attending the council. His articles appeared in the National Catholic Reporter—a new tabloid printed in Kansas City. From the seminary's point of view, the council wasn't happening, and I couldn't understand that at all.

I had given up my job as manager of the library book bindery and put my part-time energy into being a cabinet maker. I built cabinets for the sound systems in the refectory and the gym stage. I also built shelving and counters for the student bookstore and general store. My friend and classmate, Bob Merz, asked me to build a display case for precious, old books for the library. That was a nice challenge, as I was to pattern it after the oak furniture in the library. The head maintenance man at the seminary broke a rule and allowed me to use his workroom under the tower—the first time a student was ever allowed to do that. The case turned out to match well with the library furniture. Out of curiosity, I visited the library twenty-five years later and was pleased to see it was still in use.

At Christmas, I returned to Wichita, stayed at Father Blanpied's rectory, played subdeacon at Christmas midnight Mass, and worked at the lumberyard to make some extra money. At Easter vacation, I invited Bob to go with me to visit my brother Bob and his family in Hot Springs and Father Groel in Edgemont. My brother had built a very nice three-bedroom home a few blocks from the house we had built for Glen and Elsie. I met their third child, a boy named Bruce, who was a preschooler. Bob Jr. was in high school and Vickie in junior high. Father Groel was retired and, of course, much older and in assisted living in the Sisters' Hospital in Hot Springs. The trip was a pleasant, nostalgic break for me.

In the spring I auditioned to play in the dramatic play, Agatha Christie's *Ten Little Indians*. I was chosen as one of the stranded men on a deserted island with a murderer. During the final week of rehearsal, I learned that the man I was playing was the murderer. He had killed each of eight other guests by different means—poisoning, stabbing, smothering, and so on, until the last one, who was to be hanged. At the performance, I put the rope around the victim's neck and threw the rope over a ceiling beam and began to pull, shouting, "I need my hanging," and then I was shot by the previous man whom I only thought was dead. I was surprised that I really felt a deep down emotional urge to hang the guy. I got a standing ovation at the curtain call. It was a small flower on my life's journey. Several classmates said it was type-casting.

During the year the seminary was invaded by a troop of professors from other colleges to study the curriculum, faculty, and students to see if the seminary college and graduate school were qualified to be accredited by the North Central Accreditation Association. Having little or no experience with higher education, I had no idea how important the process was. I learned it was especially important for us if we wanted to go for a graduate degree from another college or university. And it was very important to students who left St. Thomas and wanted to continue their education elsewhere. Thankfully, we learned before the end of the semester that St. Thomas passed muster and was now accredited. Even then, I suspected that the examiners were not really looking for good education.

I think accreditation may have been related to the fact that in May, several fourth-year and-third-year theologians were invited to take three comprehensive tests in theology to see if we qualified to receive a bachelor's in theology from the accredited Catholic University in Washington D.C. I was among the four or five in my class who had sufficiently good grades to be chosen. It cost $300. I received the additional degree to go along with St. Thomas's bachelor's and master's in religious studies. Another significant event that spring was getting ordained a deacon—the last step to getting ordained a priest. It also carried the obligation of praying the Breviary, or priest's prayer book, every day. It was a series of biblical psalms and passages that took about an hour each day to read. Fortunately for me, it had been recently published in English, rather than Latin. I thought the elevation to the deaconate was more of a burden than an honor—but I never told anyone about that thought.

Right before summer vacation, Bob, Joe, and I discussed attending the World's Fair and the Catholic Ecumenical Council in Seattle at the end of summer vacation. I volunteered my Chrysler for the trip. The Ecumenical Council conference was a big deal organized by liberal priests and lay people all over the U.S. to promote the changes in the liturgy, theology, and the church's interaction with other religious organizations. It sounded exciting, and I looked forward to it. On the Saturday before Memorial Day, I headed back to Wichita and to working with social services—this time with placing the older boys in foster homes, or so I hoped. I knew it was going to be a challenge, but I looked forward to it.

Thirty-Nine

BEING A HOUSE MOTHER

———∞∞∞———

In May 1963, I met with Father Bob Kocour, the new director of Catholic Social Services. He was new to this role and looked to be around forty years old. He was thin but not skinny and handsome, I thought, with a pleasant smile. His smile seemed more natural than the one Smith had. I liked him right away. I guessed he saw the question on my face.

"Monsignor Smith has moved to California, I think," he said. That was the only and last word I heard him utter about Smith. Later I heard that he was involved in some kind of scandal.

Kocour continued, "So, I'm the new director around here. Lou Antonelli, whom I'm sure you know, told me about the fine work you did last summer placing the Cuban boys in foster homes. He said that, to his surprise, you successfully placed thirty-one boys in foster homes and only one boy had to be moved over the entire year. And Marie Dasher told me that you helped her place one girl, and it was a wonderfully successful placement."

He took a deep breath, scrutinized me, and went on. "So, I guess you are expecting to work with the foster-home program again this summer?"

I nodded and replied, "I think placing the older boys will be a big challenge. Oh, and I'm glad to hear that Mr. Antonelli had some good words for me. He wasn't very keen on me working here last summer."

"Yes, he told me about his reservations, but I guess, as my mother used to say, 'The proof is in the pudding.'" He chuckled. "So instead of working to place the boys in homes, how would you like to be their house mother?"

"What happened to Mr. and Mrs. Fernandez?" They were the Cuban refugee couple who took over as the house parents and had arrived the day I left for Denver in August. "Where are they?"

Kocour looked at his watch and said, "Right now they're on a plane to Miami. The last time I saw them was last Saturday night." Again, he looked at me questioningly, "They were holed up in the kitchen at Marianna House, and the boys were outside the kitchen door brandishing knives. Mr. Fernandez called the police from the kitchen phone and the cops called me. So, I went over and arranged for them to go to a hotel and then get on a plane. I've stayed there the last three nights. I'm hoping you will take over for the summer. What do you say?"

"When would you like for me to start?"

Again, he looked at his watch and said, "It's now 10:15 p.m. How about 9:00 a.m.?" He chuckled.

I wasn't afraid of the boys or the role of being the house mother. I would do what I needed to learn like I had been doing all of my life, so I easily said, "Okay, I'll do it. But please, tell me what happened?"

"I had heard that the boys called them Mr. and Mrs. Castro, but I didn't realize how dictatorial they were until they left, and I talked with Molly and Grace, the cooks. Remember them?" I nodded and he continued, "So, you want me to go over with you now?"

I thought for a moment and then said, "No, I'll just go over there and mosey around and then let them know I'm the new mother." I chuckled, and he joined me.

I walked across the vacant lot that separated Marianna House from social services. I walked through to the kitchen where Molly was cleaning up after breakfast. I knocked on the door jamb, and she smiled her friendly Irish smile and waved me in. I gave her a hug and leaning on the counter told her I was going to be the new house mother.

She clapped her hands together and said, "Oh good!"

"First, I need one of the boys to be my assistant: one who speaks clear English and has some leadership abilities. You're a good judge of people, Molly, so who would you recommend?"

She put a finger on her chin and looked down. She seemed to be in deep thought for a full minute and then said, "I think you would do well to get Lazaro San Martin. He's only fifteen, I think, but he's a big guy, and friendly, and the others listen to him. The only negative thing I can think of is that I think he is kind of lazy." I asked where I could find him and she said, "I'll bet you'll find him in bed." She pointed down the hall to our left. "He's in the second room on the right. Give it a try."

I thanked her and headed down the hall. I knocked on the door and then opened it. I didn't expect it to be locked, and it wasn't. The room was uncomfortably warm, and a big fellow was asleep on the lower bunk. I yelled, "Hey, Lazaro, wake up, I need to talk to you." He didn't stir, and I went over and patted him on the shoulder and yelled again.

He grunted and mumbled, "Go away." I repeated that I needed to talk to him, and he opened his eyes a little and mumbled, "Who are you and whaddaya want?"

"I'm Don Hanley, we met last summer. I want to talk to you." I raised my voice and nearly shouted, "So get your ass out of bed, get dressed, and come down to the dining room. And if you're not up in five minutes, I'm going to come back with a bucket of ice water. Got that?" He growled a little, and I went back down the hall.

I found a bunch of guys in the recreation room at the other end of the building, and I introduced myself. I recognized almost all of their faces but not their names. I asked each of them their names and repeated it back to them until I got fairly comfortable saying each name in Spanish. The room had three ping-pong tables and various board games and books on a row of shelves on one wall. The floor needed a good cleaning, and there was a bunch of candy wrappers and other stuff on the floor. I was going to ask them who cleaned up the room when I saw a sleepy Lazaro in the doorway. I went over to him and held out my hand. "Good morning, sleepy head."

He gave me a limp hand and mumbled, "Mornin'."

"Let's talk, okay?" I pointed to the dining room to our right, and we headed down the hall. I sat down at a table, and he sat down across from me. "Lazaro, Father Kocour asked me to be the house mother for the summer. Now I'm going to need some help and I asked Mrs. Kelly who would be a good person to help me, and she said you would be her first choice." That seemed to wake him up a bit, and he smiled a little for the first time. I continued, "So tell me what were the big problems with Mr. and Mrs. Fernandez, and what needs to change?"

He looked at the ceiling and around the room and finally back at me and said, "Kinda everything. They were dictators and wanted us to be slaves. We complained to the monsignor, but he didn't listen. I'm glad Father Kocour is listening and that they are gone." He kept eye contact, and I asked him to give me some specifics. He said, "Well, first, is food. They wanted us to be Americans and eat like Americans and have hamburgers and hot dogs and all that shit."

I asked him what kind of food the Cuban boys liked, and he gave me a list of foods. I wrote them down. Black beans and rice seemed to be the most important; he said they could be served at every meal, even breakfast. After several minutes, I asked him to give me the names of two more boys who could form a three-person advisory council for me. He gave me the names, and I asked him to invite them to a meeting that afternoon.

I went to the mother's room that was now mine and used the phone to find black beans and rice in bulk. After several calls I found a market on the east side of town and headed out to get them. I stopped at the Armstrong's home and told them that I would not be staying with them during the summer and about my new position. They wished me luck, and I picked up my two suitcases. When I got back to Marianna House, I carried in a fifty pound bag of black beans. The boys were all in the dining hall eating lunch. When they saw what I was carrying, they stood and clapped. I had them! From that moment on, I was their friend and savior. My council met and helped me to understand the boys and what they would like to see happen at the house.

Having been ordained a deacon, I was obliged to pray the breviary every day. It took most of an hour, so I rose before six every morning and read my breviary as I walked to St. Joseph's parish church for the 6:30 a.m. Mass. I had a long day every day—usually spent hauling the boys around to baseball games and physician appointments in the house's station wagon. I usually did a bed-check each night at eleven. Often there was one boy missing, and I was told he was probably on a date of some kind. He was seventeen, so I didn't worry about him. His last name was Romero, and the other boys called him Romeo. One morning as I was entering the church, two elderly women informed me that they saw one of my boys fooling around with a girl on someone's front lawn. They saw them as they were coming to church and thought I should do something about it. I asked them what he looked like, and they described Romero and asked what I was going to do. I replied that I was just surprised that Romero was up so early. They looked at me like I was totally disgusting and incompetent.

Each day was full and, for the most part, went fairly smoothly. There were two unusual incidents. One involved a young Cuban fellow named Gonzales who often visited Mariana House. He was in his early twenties, so could not stay there, so I had often had to just run him off when he stayed too long. I thought he was a harmless adolescent himself. One day he was all upset and worried, and tried to tell me, in his broken English, that the police were after him. He didn't make a lot of sense, and I asked Lazaro to help me out. I learned that he had been stopped by a policeman and given a ticket for a broken tail-light on his old car. He was ordered to get it fixed. He did and put the receipt in the mail box instead of the box for such papers in front of the police station. So, they didn't receive it, and he was summoned to the traffic court. All the Cubans were scared to death of the police, and he asked me to go to court with him. Being that he was not fluent in English, and I wasn't fluent in Spanish, I asked Lazaro to go with us in case I needed a translator. I put on my black suit and clerical collar, and we headed for the courtroom.

When Gonzales's name was called, we got up from our chairs and headed toward the judge's bench. I led the way, and while we marched, everyone in the courtroom started laughing and giggling. I was sure we were an amusing sight—a priest leading a nervous Hispanic young man and a portly teenager did look unusual, but I couldn't figure out what they were laughing at. When we got to the judge, I explained to him what had happened, and he turned to the kid and asked if that was true. Lazaro translated what the judge had said, and Gonzales shook his head vigorously and said, "Yes, yes, si, si, si." There was more tittering as I assured the judge that the tail-light had been fixed. When we got outside, I asked Lazaro what the laughter was all about, and he told me that all the way up the aisle, Gonzales was constantly doing the sign of the cross over his chest. He guessed that the two of them following a priest up to the judge really looked funny.

The other incident wasn't so funny. Mariana House had a community shower room with six shower heads. One day, as I was walking down the hall, I heard loud laughter, shouting, and screaming coming from the room and stopped to see what was going on. One boy, a fourteen-year-old named Diego, was cowering naked in the corner of the room, and five guys were snapping him with their wet towels while Diego screamed. I could already see welts rising on his pale skin. Diego was very skinny and often was a real pest to the others. He seemed to have a Hit Me sign on his back, but he should not have been treated so cruelly as he was being treated. Being the youngest of five boys in my own family, I knew how to snap a towel. I grabbed a wet towel and began snapping the snappers, hitting each one viciously, and it was their turn to scream. It didn't take long for them to raise their hands in surrender. I was, of course, protected by their belief that they could not, ever, raise their own hands against a priest.

After they, and I, calmed down and Diego escaped, I gave them time to get dressed and assembled them and Diego in the dining room. I asked them to tell me what they were thinking and feeling while they were attacking Diego and then asked them to individually apologize to him. If the apology seemed insincere to me, I asked them to repeat it until I felt it was more sincere. I also asked Diego to verbally forgive each of them. Of course, I became Diego's savior for life.

I was present at Marianna House twenty-four seven all through June and July, and the days were full and long. I was very relieved when Father Kocour told me that another seminarian, Ron Gilmore, would be joining me August first. Ron was about twenty-two years old and between his first and second year of theology. He was a very intelligent and pleasant young man. He was also very cooperative and flexible, even willing to share a room with two of the boys for three weeks. My room had only one single bed and also had to serve as the office for the house, so there was no room for a second bed. My first priority was to take a couple of days off to visit Bonnie and Jim in Smithville. Again, I got the most enjoyment from playing with the kids, rather than being with Bonnie and Jim because they were usually three sheets to the wind by early afternoon each day.

Father Kocour decided that he would take on the task of being house mother after both Ron and I went back to school. He would also continue as director of social services. He somehow learned that I had some carpentry skills and asked me to build an office next to the mother's bedroom. I enjoyed the challenge of doing some "real work" for a change. With the help of two boys who volunteered, for a little pay, I began the project. We built the room out of one end of the adjacent recreation room and completed it in a week. The boys were astounded to see me pounding nails, hanging doors, finishing drywall and painting. They never did seem to learn the difference between a deacon and a priest. I had gotten used to being greeted each morning with, "Good morning, Father, how are you today?" I enjoyed the way they said, "How are you today?" It sounded like "how you fold today?"

The day before I was scheduled to leave, Ron asked to use my car for an afternoon. He had always used the Marianna's station wagon, so I was surprised by the request but figured he must have a good reason. I was bowled over when, a few hours later, Ron returned with the car, and I saw two brand new seat covers on both seats of the Chrysler. The boys had donated enough money to defray the costs. They all stood around the car when he drove up and clapped when Ron gave me the keys. I had to work to hold back tears. I guess the black beans and rice did it!

Looking back, I had gained a new enthusiasm for working with people and a realization that I had a knack for social work and community organizing. Father Kocour was amazed at how fearlessly I had handled my job as house mother. It appeared that I had a gift for getting things done that were more than just building things and selling building materials—I could help create good things for people as well.

My first ride in my newly upholstered Chrysler was to the Wichita airport to pick up Bob Merz, who was flying into Wichita from Milwaukee to go on our trip to Seattle. Our first stop would be Denver to pick up Joe LaVoie and Paul Sandorf for the trip. I was glad that we were going on the trip in my car because I was uncomfortable being dependent on someone else's good will and timing. I liked being in control—as you may have noticed. We stayed at the University of Seattle, a Jesuit university, because we got a price break for our two rooms. We divided our time between the Liturgical Conference and the Seattle World's Fair. None of us had been involved in the conference before and were fascinated by the enthusiasm for all the changes being generated by the Vatican II Council. We didn't have very much time to spend at the World's Fair other than walk through some of the exhibits. We were told many times that we were fortunate to have five full days of sunshine during our stay in Seattle.

We took a long route back to Denver, going south through Oregon and California. We stopped in San Francisco to visit Paul Sandorf's sister. She lived with two other young women, and I embarrassed my fellow seminarians following a visit to the women's bathroom which had panties, bras, and hosiery hanging from the towel racks and shower curtain rod. When I came out of the bathroom I said, "I really like the way you girls decorated your bathroom." All three of my mates said they were so embarrassed by my comment. I don't know if it was related to their scolding, but I had a blockbuster migraine after sleeping on the floor of the women's apartment. We headed south on the beautiful Highway 1 along the Big Sur California coast, and I missed most of the passing scenery because I was laying down on the back seat. We stayed overnight with Bill, Helen, and their kids in Los Angeles and then headed east via the Grand Canyon. Between the canyon and Farmington, New Mexico, the transmission on the Chrysler began to make an ominous grinding sound. We made it to my brother Bob's driveway in

Farmington, and the car quit entirely. Bob agreed to get it fixed and loaned me his car so we could get back to Denver in time for the first day of the fall semester at good old St. Thomas. The car problem did not detract from the grand vacation we all had and the full summer I had.

Forty

AT LAST: THE FINAL YEAR OF THE SEMINARY

—⊛⊛⊛—

The June death of Pope John XXIII cast a certain pall over the beginning of the fall 1963 semester. Little was said by the faculty at St. Thomas, but we seminarians were very hopeful that the windows of the church would stay open, as John XXIII wished, and the Vatican Council would continue with some fresh air and spirit.

The course load for the last year of theological studies was light and uninspiring because we no longer could look forward to Father Vawter's scripture classes. We had a canon law class taught by Father Danagher, the seminary rector, and he droned on five days each week all through the first semester. There were several classes on the Church's laws on marriage and human sexuality. I liked my classmate's comment that Danagher talked about sex like it was cold turkey in the refrigerator—yep, *very* personal, and inspiring. I thought one law we learned about completely obliterated all consideration of the others. It was this: A wife commits a mortal sin if she fails to render the debt by refusing to have coitus with her husband. I said to no one in particular, "You mean to tell me that we're to tell couples, planning to marry, that the wife-to-be will be risking going to hell if she doesn't feel like having sex with her drunken bastard of a husband? Give me a break!" No one argued with me about that. We all just laughed.

As far as the Church was concerned, the only positive sex act was coitus between a male husband and female wife. And they must NOT use any kind of artificial birth control. Under the pain of mortal sin all sexual intercourse must be open to conception. There was no mention of masturbation, homosexuality, birth control, abortion, or gay marriage, except to say that they were all grievous sins and could send a person to hell. This is the kind of teaching that the idiot priest gave to Glen that ruined their marriage. Because of the stupid "law," Glen had gotten a divorce the previous year.

When I visited Mom at her apartment in Denver after that enlightening class on sex, she looked very sad and depressed when she said, "I don't know where I went wrong." I asked her why she said that, and she replied, "You know Glen got a divorce, don't you?" I nodded and she added, "I must have done something wrong." I did my best to assure her that she was in no way responsible for Glen's divorce and besides, Glen was forty years old! I had read articles about sex and the Kinsey reports and was sure I needed to find more research outside the seminary if I was going to be helpful to anyone.

I felt I really did need to grow closer to God, or the Cosmic Christ, as Teilhard de Chardin suggested, so I made an appointment to talk with Father Cahill. Cahill was the kindest and, to me, the most spiritual priest at the seminary. I asked him if he would be my spiritual director for this, my final year at St. Thomas. I was surprised and disappointed when he said, "Well, thank you Don, but I really don't know anything about being a spiritual director."

I sat there in his small office feeling quite stunned. After, what I'm sure was a full minute, I said, "Well, Father, I don't either. Could I just come in and talk with you, say every other week or so?"

"Oh sure, we could do that." So I did come in to talk with him once in a while during the year but never did learn how I could really *know* how to be in the presence of God or the Spirit.

Besides Pope John's death, there was another extremely sad and more violent death that fall. A few days before Thanksgiving, President Jack Kennedy was assassinated in Dallas. We were all in the refectory listening to a student reading to us when Father Danagher rang his little bell and announced the terrible news. Students were not allowed to have radios or TV sets in their room, and the only TV available for students was in the recreation hall. Knowing it would be crowded, I went with my classmate to the student store's radio. We turned it on just in time to learn that the president died.

As they had done for years, Joe LaVoie and Bob Merz joined me at Marie and Jim's home for Thanksgiving and for a very somber meal. Like nearly everyone else in the country, we were all glued to the television all during the vacation.

A few days later, I wrote my first Christmas card lamenting Pope John's and President Kennedy's deaths and said something about how I hoped to continue their work of promoting peace and love in the world. I heard that one of my fellow seminarians was critical of my linking my coming ordination to the death of such luminaries, and I wondered if I was really guilty of doing that. That certainly had not been my intention; I honestly did not think of myself as intelligent, courageous, or spiritual enough to be mentioned in the same breath as these two men. At age thirty, I wondered if I would ever be.

I returned to Wichita, and, for the first time, I stayed in the rectory. Bob Blanpied had been appointed pastor of the Cathedral Parish and given the title of monsignor or papal chamberlain. I asked him what that meant, and he said, "I'm appointed the honor of emptying the Pope's chamber pots." That was typical of his sense of humor and disdain for titles. I continued working for Earl and Audra at the lumberyard and taking the annual inventory. Bishop Mark Carroll, bishop of Wichita emeritus, was retired, but he still lived at the cathedral rectory. I joined him for breakfast each morning, and he called me "the lumberjack," which I didn't find funny, though I'm sure the bishop was in no way making fun of me.

In January we began a one-unit class on the liturgy, which turned out to be a set of lessons on how to properly conduct the sacraments and enforce canon law—the natural and church laws. The course was taught by Father Johnny Vidal, the vice-rector. I didn't take it too seriously because I was sure we'd be performing all the ceremonies in English and unlike Father Vidal, I didn't think performing the sacraments were the most important duties of any priest. I'm quite sure that I'm the only one who received a C in the class.

In March I tried out for a part in the musical *South Pacific* and got the part of Emile de Beque, the French plantation owner on the South Pacific island. After I got the role, I learned that it was the leading role in the play and that I would have to sing multiple solos. I had sung in choirs and glee clubs, but I had sung solos only when I walked or drove around by myself. I had never had a singing lesson in my life. The sailors in the cast sang a raucous song, *There is Nothing Like a Dame*, to the delight of the guys in the chorus. After a week or so, the rector learned of it, and he was not delighted. They had to drop it. There were three leading ladies in the cast: Nurse Nellie, Bloody Mary, and her daughter. Bloody Mary was wonderfully played by a small Hispanic fellow from Cheyenne, Wyoming, and he had a beautiful tenor voice. Nurse Nellie never appeared, but messages were given to her by her brother. Mary's daughter never showed up either, and Lieutenant Cable sang to her non-presence. The actor who played Bloody Mary had taken singing lessons and patiently coached me several times. Unfortunately, my attempt to sing the songs with a terrible French accent failed miserably. I did receive mild applause after the performance but not the ovation I had received playing the murderer the year before. My classmate, Jack McCoy, played Lieutenant Cable. He had a great baritone, and he was very believable.

Father Vidal rushed up to the stage after it all ended and exclaimed—mostly directed at Jack and me, "Oh, oh, I don't know about these deacons singing all these love songs, oh my, oh my." Both of us laughed as soon as he turned around. Interestingly, Jack and I were two of the first four of our class to leave the priesthood.

That spring, Bishop Byrne, the administrator of the Wichita diocese, called me at the seminary and asked me to pick him up at the Denver airport and take him to Regis College, then the following day to St. Thomas and back to the airport. Of course, I was glad to do it, but I was a bit embarrassed by the gray primer on the hood of my Chrysler. When my brother Bob drove it back to Denver from New Mexico, the hood blew open and remained with primer, but the bishop didn't seem to mind. I was glad that he was not finicky, and I wondered how he knew I had a car at the seminary. I never asked him.

Every seminarian who is to be ordained is expected to purchase a new silver chalice to celebrate Mass. I knew that one would cost around $600—money that I did not have. I told my brother Jim about it, and he and Marie asked four of our siblings to help. They all agreed to pay for it if I would design and order it. As was the style at that time, I chose what I thought was a beautiful sleek design and ordered it and gave the invoice to Jim. I didn't ask nor ever learn who paid what. I only knew that Patty, who did her best just to pay for her own expenses and whatever both she and Mom needed to live on in their small apartment in Denver, could not help pay for the chalice.

We were all expected to send out announcements to friends and relatives and, with it, a "holy card" with the place, time, and date of our ordination and a meaningful saying. I believe most of my classmates choose something from scripture or some saint. I came up with my own motto. Thanks to my years of studying theology, especially the New Testament, I firmly believed what I wrote: "No matter what great things a man may do in life, unless he becomes a loving person, his life is a failure." I really didn't know much about love, but I did know that I didn't want to be known as someone who just built a school here or a rectory there, as I saw in the obituaries of many priests.

I was proud of that slogan then and still use it now. I looked forward to being ordained on May 23, 1964. I also knew I had a lot of work, effort, and praying to do if I were to become a truly loving person. I was sure I knew what love was, but looking back, at that point I really didn't.

Every one of us deacons had to give a sermon to the assembled student body In the last few weeks of our final year, I gave a sermon that I thought was honest, but I immediately wished I had not given it. I scolded my fellow students for not encouraging me and one another to be better scholars and co-educators. Not a single one said a word—good or bad—to me afterwards, but a new, younger priest faculty member visited my room the next day and asked me if I had told the students, in my sermon, that I would not recommend that my bishop send any new seminarians to St. Thomas. He was not scolding me; he was curious whether or not I had said it. I told him that I did say that, and he sadly looked at the floor and frowned. He asked me to explain why I had said that, and I told him that I really wanted to scold the faculty, not my fellow students, but I was afraid I might be prevented from getting ordained. I began to realize I was thinking and walking a kind of tightrope between conformity and honesty. I didn't realize that it would be something I would continue to do for years.

Forty-One

A KING FOR A DAY

———⊶⊷———

Everyone who was scheduled to be part of the solemn ceremony of my ordination to the priesthood assembled in the cathedral rectory. It turned out that I was the only one to be ordained at the Wichita Cathedral in 1964. The one who went to Rome for his theology courses decided not to go through to the priesthood, and the one who had roomed with me at the Armstrong's was being ordained in his home diocese somewhere else. So, it was my day, and I was to be king for a day!

A crowd of several dozen priests, wearing cassocks and surplices, were standing in the long, wide hall and began the procession. The most honored participants brought up the rear, and that included the presiding bishop, Bishop Leo Byrne, right behind me. Right in front of me was Bishop Mark Carroll, and in front of him were all the priests. We walked solemnly out through the rectory front door, down the sidewalk, and into the cathedral. An organ and choir were performing a Latin anthem I don't think I'd ever heard. I suppose I should have had some ultra-holy thought or prayer on my mind as I proceeded down the aisle of the cathedral, but when I saw my entire family standing in the front row, I just thought about how happy I was that they were present (only the second time I was aware of all eight of us being together at the same time) and the times each of them tried to help me, and I'm ashamed to say that I also thought, "I made it despite you sons of bitches."

What impressed me most was that Earl and Audra and all of the lumberyard employees whom I knew well over the years were all present behind my family. They had to close down the lumberyard in order to come to my ordination. It must have cost them many thousands of dollars! That was the first time that I realized that, in a way, I was the Huston's adopted son. I had sent announcements to every aunt, uncle, and cousin that I had an address for, and a bunch of them showed up. None were as meaningful as having the crew from the lumberyard there. None of the crew were Catholic, and I wondered what they thought of all the Latin songs and prayers. None of the lay spectators understood Latin either, but they were used to hearing it.

I had to lie down in the middle of the huge sanctuary as the bishop said a bunch of Latin prayers that I didn't understand either, but they sounded regal and solemn, so I guessed that they were what was needed to elevate me out of the ranks of the common man. I suppose I was to feel some kind of spiritual bolt of lightning or something, but I didn't. I was only glad to get up from the hard terrazzo floor and kneel on the solitary kneeler in the middle of the sanctuary in front of the bishop.

After the bishop said the magic words, he laid his hands on my head followed by dozens of priests, all of whom were conveying the power and grace of the Holy Spirit onto me. I realized, I think, that this was all done to impress upon me, and everyone else present, that something special was happening because I was becoming someone special—an ordained priest!

After the ceremony, all present were invited to come up to the communion rail and receive my blessing. It was my turn to convey the spirit onto everyone as a newly ordained priest. I was more than a little embarrassed to be doing this, especially when I was putting my hands on the heads of people I thought were especially holy, like the Armstrongs. I was glad that the lumberyard crew had left before this ceremony was performed.

After that ordeal, relatives and some clergy assembled in the Cathedral High School cafeteria for breakfast. The bishops and my immediate family were at the head table. Mom was sitting next to Bishop Carroll, and I was next to Mom.

The bishop said to Mom in his usual folksy way, "Maggie, I think you've raised a very fine son."

Mom responded. "Thank you, Bishop, but I think he really raised himself."

That was a wow for me. I didn't realize she felt that way, and I realized for the first time that it was quite true.

She followed it up with a bit of a downer, as she whispered to me, "You know, Son, I really never believed you'd become a priest until today."

It was a downer because I felt disappointed that she did not seem to realize that all my work and effort with the houses and overtime work was to help her so I could go to the seminary. It was, I suppose, a good lesson in humility for me.

The next day, Sunday, I celebrated my first Mass, a Solemn High Mass at St. Margaret Mary's—my home parish. I needed four priests besides myself, so I choose Bob Blanpied to give the sermon—because he knew me best, Bob Kocour to be my deacon, Gene Gerber to be my subdeacon, and the new pastor of my home parish as my archpriest, Father Joseph Hagan. The archpriest was sort of the master of ceremonies who followed me around the altar to make sure I didn't screw up. Everything went off smoothly, and I felt a bit more celebrational than I did with the ordination ceremony. Mass was followed by a lunch in my honor at the parish hall. Usually, the father of the new priest gives a laudatory speech, and being that Dad had died seventeen years earlier, I choose my brother Bill to give the speech. Glen, the oldest brother, did not want to give it because he was officially excommunicated because he was divorced and remarried. I should have chosen Marie, but I was not sufficiently emancipated to ask a woman to do the honor. Nor was I sufficiently free enough to choose Glen because he would not embarrass anyone because he had never lived in Wichita. But Bill landed the dubious honor and very nervously gave me a nice congratulatory talk.

The weekend should have been wonderfully beautiful and a huge flower for me, but it really was a bit of a wilted flower. I just had too many doubts about the value of the traditional role of a priest. It was sad to me that the only two flowers were the presence of the lumberyard crew at the ordination and Mom saying that I had raised myself. So, a joyless weekend capped my nineteen-year journey to the priesthood.

I volunteered to celebrate the daily Mass on Monday morning for the assistant pastor who had taken a few days off. In those days, a priest went into the confessional a few minutes before Mass to hear confessions of anyone who wished to confess. So, I had my first experience of hearing confessions. Two people came in. The first was an elderly woman who had a few venial sins to confess, and the second was a middle-aged man.

After the initial words, he said, "And Father, I committed adultery one time. And, Father . . ." he went on in a pleading sort of voice, "it was also an act of charity and kindness. The woman, an office associate, was having an especially heavy period and thought that having sex would be helpful for her."

Without a moment's hesitation I, very unpriestly like, moaned, "Oh, give me a break." And so began my priestly sacramental duties.

Years later, the tragedy of Jonestown in South America happened. Several hundred people committed suicide by drinking poisoned Kool-Aid, as they were ordered to do by a maniacal cult leader. Looking back, in my own way, by being ordained and promising to follow the orders of a bishop, I was drinking the Kool-Aid of a softer kind.

Forty-Two

ENTERING THE CLERICAL WORLD

—ೞಂ—

As I drove west to my first assignment as assistant pastor at St. Patrick's in Kingman, Kansas, I thought of my post-ordination family visits. First, it was to California where brother Bill felt the need to spill his guts to me about what a horrible Catholic he had been because he had a vasectomy after Helen almost died giving birth to their fifth child. I tried to tell him I was sure that God would forgive him because I could easily forgive him, and God was far more loving and forgiving than I was. The next morning, he said he drank too much and didn't remember telling me anything about that. Then I went to Phoenix where I learned that again, Glen and his second wife, Connie, were at odds because another priest told him that because they were not married in the Church, he would be committing a mortal sin if they had sex, so they must live as brother and sister. They were barely speaking to each other. I made an oath to myself never to talk to anyone with that so-called moral precept, and I'd work to convey a God with a bigger heart—as J. D. Phillips presented in his book *Your God is Too Small*.

My reverie was interrupted as Highway 54 veered southwest and became the main east-west street in the charming town of Kingman. It had a population of 4,000, and the church was on the highway, on the west side of town. I drove slowly through town and then saw on my right a large, red-brick school; a red-brick rectory; and then a red-brick church—the lot of which took up an entire block. The church was about half the size of St. Theresa's church in Hutchinson, where I had just helped out for two weeks and worked with an uptight priest who would probably say the kind of things that unhinged Glen and Bill.

I pulled into a gravel parking area behind the church and rectory near a two-car, door-less garage housing a dusty Rambler. I took a deep breath, told myself to be a loving person, and got out of the car. A pleasant-looking man with a head full of white hair and a warm smile opened the door.

He said, "Father Don Hanley, I presume?"

"Monsignor Quinten Malone, I presume, back?" We both chuckled and shook hands.

"Well, come in, come in. Welcome to St. Patrick's. I'll show you your room and we can go get your luggage." He held the door open, and I entered the air-conditioned living room. The air was cool, but the room felt warm with wall-to-wall carpet, pinkish-hued beige walls covered with pleasant landscape prints, two large reclining chairs, a matching couch, and a large television set. To the left and jutting out from the living room was an office that looked like it was in use, and next to it, as we crossed the room, was an empty looking office. Malone motioned toward it and said, "That'll be your office." We continued on to a short hallway that led to a bedroom on the left, another bedroom in the middle, and, at the end of the hall, a staircase leading up to a third bedroom.

I chose the bedroom with windows on both sides and placed my small suitcase near the full-sized bed. We then went through the side door to my car. He commented on the still-gray primer-painted hood and helped me with the steamer trunk. I was impressed with his warmth and willingness to help me unload the car.

When we were finished, I fished my pipe out of my pocket and asked, "Is smoking permissible in the house?"

"I'd like to say no, but I smoke, so I'll have to say yes, but not in the kitchen. And it's almost noon. I'll lead you there and introduce you to Mrs. Beat." We went back through the living room, through the dining room, and into the kitchen. Malone said, "Barbara, I'd like you to meet our new boarder, Father Don Hanley."

I took her outstretched hand, "Glad to meet you, Mrs. Beat."

"Me too and welcome to our home, Father. And you're just in time for lunch." She led us to the table in the kitchen's breakfast nook and served us plates of hot roast beef sandwiches with mashed potatoes and gravy, then pulled up a chair and sat down with us. Malone was watching me closely as she sat down, and I wondered why. Later I learned that a previous assistant refused to eat with a servant and insisted that he be served in the dining room. Malone told me that he told the fellow that he was welcome to eat in the dining room but would have to serve himself, and he did. I told Malone that I liked that Barbara enjoyed eating with us because it felt very much like a home. She was the widowed mother of a bunch of kids and grandkids and an excellent cook. By the end of summer, I had gained thirty pounds.

Bishop Byrne seemed apologetic about assigning me to the small parish, and I didn't tell him I was happy to be anywhere but the cathedral, where, it seemed to me, the assistants were too often just glorified altar boys. Monsignor Malone and I settled into an easy routine, dividing Masses and hearing confessions between us. He asked me to take charge of the CCD (Confraternity of Christian Doctrine), the religious education for the parish public school kids, and the CYO (Catholic Youth Organization) for the teens. He also asked if I could teach the religion classes at the school four days a week—grades five through eight. I told him my only experience was teaching one class of sophomores at Cathedral High School in Denver. He said that was more than most. So, starting in September, I would be pretty busy.

Before I left Wichita, I stopped by the lumberyard and thanked the Hustons and others for coming to the cathedral for my ordination. Audra said, "All that Latin was very mystifying, but it was quite a spectacle, and they really dolled you up." When I saw any of my classmates, I'd ask them how they felt about getting all dolled up on that day. Audra also told me she had bought a small Oldsmobile as a second car but didn't like it and thought I might like to buy it from her. She would sell it to me for only $800. I told her that I would like to buy it and would find the money and get back to her.

Before the end of July, my brother Bob called, and I told him about the Olds and he said, "Buy it and if you have payments, I'll make them for you." I gave the old Chrysler to the large Miller family who all came to daily Mass crowded into an old, beat-up Chevy that was in far worse shape than my Chrysler. Bob made two monthly payments and then had to stop because his wife, Ann, objected. I really had to stretch my monthly salary of $150 to include the $42 car payment. I had not been required to take the vows of poverty, chastity, and obedience, but I was expected to live them. So I told myself I had no right to complain.

In July, Malone asked me to represent the parish at the dedication of a new church at Harper, Kansas, about forty miles south of Kingman. He didn't particularly like those kinds of gatherings and said that one priest from our parish was quite enough, and it would give me an opportunity to meet some of my fellow priests. So I attended. Bishop Byrne performed the ceremony, which consisted of blessing with incense and holy water the entrance, sanctuary, and especially the altar of the small, attractive church. He then celebrated a pontifical High Mass, which took a bunch of priests to facilitate. The church was packed, and there was standing-room only. I hadn't thought to bring my cassock and surplus, but fortunately, I wasn't the only one.

After it was all over and the bishop left, about twenty priests gathered around five card-tables in the church's basement. The game was poker, and there was plenty of beer and soda available. I sat at one table with one other young priest and two middle-aged ones. The two older ones started telling off-colored jokes, and many of them would have made the truck drivers at the lumberyard blush. It was shocking to hear priests talk that way, especially the sexist tone of many of the so-called jokes. I had often told some mildly off-color jokes when I was in the seminary, and some of my classmates had tagged me as someone who talked like a construction worker. My seminary jokes were trivial compared to what I heard that evening.

I left early and met another disgruntled priest leaving early. He was a stocky fellow, a little shorter than me, and had a friendly smile. He said, "What's the matter, Hanley, you couldn't take the wonderful wit of our fellow clergymen, huh?" He put out his hand and said, "I'm Dan Orth, I'm a neighbor of yours at my first parish—Waterloo, just a few miles east of Kingman on 54."

I shook his hand. "Glad to meet you. How'd you know my name?"

"I attended your ordination back in May. I was curious to see what kind of crop of newbies we'd have, and I was surprised to see that you were it. So, how do you like Monsignor Malone?"

"I like him. He's a very kind man and easy to be around. This summer hasn't been very busy for me—definitely not as busy as my seminary summers."

"Well, come over to Waterloo one of these days, and I'll fix dinner. I like to cook. Just give a call."

Dan climbed into a shiny, new looking Chrysler. I liked him and made a mental plan to get in touch.

Two weeks later, I had dinner at his large, two-story rectory. Waterloo wasn't even a town. It had a church, a post office, a filling station, and a small general store. I asked him why there was such a large church and rectory for such a small place.

He answered, "I understand that back in the horse-and-buggy days, priests would often have dinner and card parties, and priests would stay overnight. There are a lot of these small German-Catholic parishes around here: St. Joe's, St. Mary's, St. Leo's, just to name a few. Most of them have no non-German Catholics in the parish areas at all. Waterloo was one of them, but we have a few heathens around here now." He chuckled. "I also have a so-called mission parish at Mt. Vernon next to Cheney Reservoir. I'm thinking of moving into the small rectory there because now that the reservoir is open, there are more people at Mass there than here. It is also closer to Wichita, and I go there two or three times a week. I've been appointed director of the Missions' Office where I coordinate donations to our parish in

Barquisimeto, Venezuela, as well as arrange foreign missions all over the world. So I keep busy."

Dan introduced me to Scotch whiskey, and I drank two Scotch on the Rocks and nearly staggered to the dinner table. I didn't particularly like the taste, but I enjoyed the buzz I felt after. I had never joined the drinkers at the Abney clan's gatherings. Audra's nephew's story was that a chemist analyzed beer and reported that it should be poured back into the horse, and up until then I tended to agree. Regrettably, I would later like both beer and Scotch too much.

I asked Malone if it was okay with him if I attended the Liturgical Conference in Oklahoma City. He had never heard of it but agreed to let me go, even though I'd have to miss my ordinary weekend duties of hearing confessions and celebrating Masses. The conference was put on by the same organization that produced the one we had attended in Seattle. I couldn't find anyone else who was planning to go to Oklahoma, so I went down by myself. I found a cheap little old hotel only a few blocks from the convention center.

After only a few weeks, I had learned that my Wichita diocese was a very conservative one and that Oklahoma tended to be more liberal. I wondered why. I felt very comfortable being around a bunch of priests, nuns, and laypeople who were enthusiastic about Vatican II and Pope John XXIII and were still mourning his death. Of course, they were looking forward to having the Mass in English and having the priest facing the people. Every afternoon, they demonstrated the new Mass. The biggest challenge, one speaker told us, was to educate the laity, religious, and clergy that the Mass is a celebration of Christian communion, not an ancient drama to edify us by calling down

Christ into our midst. Christ is always with us, and Mass is to celebrate our union with Him and with one another. Oh, and people went to communion to strengthen their love and compassion with other humans—Catholic or not. Going to communion was not a reward for being good, but a sign of our communion. That was revolutionary. I had heard it the summer before, but it hadn't really sunk in until I spent time with the people of Oklahoma City. I wondered what old Father Johnny Vidal at St. Thomas seminary thought of all this.

When I got back to Kingman, I enthusiastically told Monsignor Malone about it. He assured me it was just a passing fad and not to get too excited. The following week, all the priests of the diocese were asked to attend a clergy conference to learn all about the new English liturgy. Malone said that I should just stay in Kingman and mind the store because I had already learned all about it. I didn't argue, but I was disappointed because I wanted to hear what the other priests of the diocese were hearing. When he returned from the conference, he was more than a bit grumpy about the order to prepare the people to have the English Mass beginning January 1, 1965.

He asked me to select a few laypeople who would lead the people in the English responses at Mass that used to be said by altar boys in Latin and to read the two Epistles, or non-gospel, passages at each Mass. He also encouraged me to set up discussion groups for the laity so that they would better understand the teachings of the Vatican II Council that had been foisted on us. When he said he didn't know what we'd do about having an altar facing the people because it was only a fad and would not be needed after a few months, I talked him into letting me build an altar for us. It seemed clear to me that it was more than a fad, so I built what I thought would be a beautiful and fitting piece of furniture out of oak. In his younger years, Malone had a hobby of cabinetmaking, and so the rectory basement had a great many carpentry tools. I built the altar so that it could be easily taken down, even though I was sure it would be needed for a long time.

We were very fortunate to have a new and very enlightened family move in over the summer. Dennis and Jane Dullea and their five children had lived in Oklahoma City before coming to Kansas. Dennis was a civil engineer and supervisor of a large state highway project near Kingman, and Jane was the president of the diocesan association of women. They had been involved in a group called the Christian Family Movement (CFM for short) and encouraged me to start a group in our parish. Dennis was a handsome, white-haired gentleman who volunteered to be one of the Mass lectors and help me train the others. They invited me to come to their home for Sunday brunch after Mass, where they provided me with a delicious meal and a helpful dose of constructive criticism on my sermons. They were thoughtful and generous, and their coaching helped me become a more up-to-date and effective preacher.

In late August, I gave my little Olds its first long test drive and visited Bonnie and Jim and the kids in Smithville. Their car was in the shop, and they asked me to pick them up in Kansas City. By the time we picked up the kids, and by then there were four of them—Terry, Shelly, Tony, and Kelly—it was after 7:00 p.m. I played with the two youngest in the living room while Terry and Shelly helped put away the groceries and fix dinner. Both Bonnie and Jim kept up a constant barrage of criticisms towards both girls as they worked in the kitchen. On Saturday morning, I got up with the kids and we all played in the living room. Sometime after 10:00 a.m., both parents got up and went straight to the fridge for their breakfast beers and immediately started in on the older girls about their not doing this or that chore. I didn't say anything until Sunday morning, but I just couldn't leave it unsaid any longer; I was really bothered by the angry way they treated Terry and Shelly.

Bonnie yelled, "Don't you dare tell us how to raise our children. You don't have children so you can't know anything about it, so until you do, don't say a damn word about us. You got that?"

"Yes, I got that, but I still can't stand it, so I think I will go back home." I picked up my overnight bag and went to the car. All four kids followed me to the car and begged me not to go so early. It was a heartbreaking goodbye for all five of us. I told them I loved them and how much I liked to be around them but couldn't stand the way my sister treated them. I was barreling down the Kansas turnpike going nearly ninety miles an hour when the Olds threw a rod and stopped. I hiked to the next rest stop and called for a tow truck and headed back to Wichita. All in all, it was an especially dismal trip.

Back in Kingman, I made what I considered one of my biggest blunders ever while hearing confessions. The only good thing, maybe, was that I didn't know who the young woman was who was making the confession.

She asked through the confessional grill, "Father, I am in the last month of my pregnancy, and my husband and I don't want to hurt the baby, so we pleasure one another with our fingers. Is that a sin?"

Oh my God! My lack of knowledge about human sexuality left me entirely out of my depth. I had no idea about how women would be pleasured by fingers. All I knew was how males did it.

Unthinkingly, I blurted out, "Yes, it is, that would be mutual masturbation, and that is a sin."

I immediately regretted it because I had become increasingly convinced that masturbation itself was not a sin. For me, it was just a sleeping pill. As she left the confessional crying, I hoped she'd arrive at her own conclusion that this celibate idiot priest was full of shit.

On a more positive note, I found five more couples who were willing to give the CFM a try. On the last Sunday of August, Jane and Dennis hosted the first meeting of the group, and they made plans to meet every Sunday evening. By the time school started the Tuesday after Labor Day, I had lined up five more adult discussion groups with five to ten couples in each.

I still needed a car, so I asked Earl Huston where he would recommend I go. He introduced me to the manager of the Chevrolet dealership where they bought all the trucks for the lumberyard, and he sold me a 1959 Chevrolet.

I was beginning to feel planted in my new environment. I enjoyed the homey atmosphere of my rectory, and I was ready for a busy school year full of fresh flowers.

Forty-Three

AH... BACK TO BEING BUSY

———— ∞ ————

Keeping my cassock on, I headed over to the parish school on the first Tuesday after Labor Day. I was a little anxious about teaching grade-schoolers, but mostly I was excited by the prospect of a new adventure. My day began with the fifth grade and moved up to the sixth through eighth, spending forty minutes with each class, interrupted in the middle by the morning recess. The textbooks were uniformly boring to me. I feared they would be equally boring for the youngsters.

As I entered the fifth-grade classroom. I thought back to my fifth-grade summer school catechism class and how I was dismissed by the elderly nun for saying I didn't learn any of "that dumb stuff." Now I was going to teach a bunch of kids the same dumb stuff. I wish I had the presence of mind to tell them my story, but I was still not mature nor humble enough to do it. I know I liked the teachers best who worked to learn all the kids' names, so I started in the front row, repeated each name, and put the picture of each student in my head as best I could. By the end of the third week, I knew all thirty-one of their first and last names. As I was learning their names, to get to know them better, I asked them to tell me what they thought they needed to do to be a good Christian. The most frequent answer was "Be good." Followed by "Do what you're told," and "Fear God."

Hoping to challenge them, I asked, "So tell me about the God that we're supposed to fear and how He helps you to be good. How do we know what God wants us to do?" Four girls and one boy raised their hands, and I called on one of the girls.

She said, "God sends us his spirit, and the spirit helps us to have the strength to be good." The other hand-raisers nodded in agreement, and I continued the discussion. My goal was to help them realize that a priest could be friendly and kind, whether or not they learned any moral or dogmatic theology. The children seemed to respond well to this discussion, so I repeated the exercise with the sixth-grade class.

Early in the fall semester, I joined the first graders at recess, and several of them were dancing around me, and I was dancing with them. Two older women were watching us, and when the bell rang, the women came over to me and said, "You know, Father, playing with the children will make them lose respect for you and other priests."

I responded, "Oh, I think you are confusing respect with fear. I believe they will *gain* respect for me and lose their fear of priests." The ladies pushed their noses into the air and muttered a "humph" of disapproval as they walked away.

The seventh graders were a more proactive bunch because of the leadership of four bold and brainy girls who loved questioning almost everything. Those four were amazing and woke me up to see how the new theology was resonating among thoughtful young people. Late in the fall semester, one of the quartet, Debbie, asked to use the chalkboard when we were discussing heaven and hell and who went where when we died. She marched up to the board and made two circles on the left side of the chalkboard and said, "Here's two guys who were baptized when they were born, and one is a bad egg—he is mean and cruel to everyone wherever he goes." She drew a line pointing down across the board. "I'll call this guy Jack to stand for jackass because that's what he is. He spends his entire life being mean as a snake." She made marks all down his lifeline. "Now, you're telling us that this Jack guy can get all holy and, at the last minute, go to confession and, presto, gets to go to heaven?" She zipped a long arrow pointing to the top of the chalkboard and drew a big circle with an H in the middle. Then she went back to the left side of the board and pointed to the second circle. "Now, this guy—I'll call him Joe because he's a holy Joe—is a great guy." She drew a line heading upwards towards heaven and says, "Joe, here, is very kind and loving towards his kids, his wife, and everybody, and then one day he commits a single mortal sin." Then she drew a big X on the line just before it gets to heaven, and continues, "So then, bam! He falls into hell." She drew a long arrow downwards to a big box with an X in it.

Debbie glared at me. "Father, if you tell me that's how *your* God acts, then I'm not going to believe anything you say about God, because I would hate that God! So there!" The entire class had followed Debbie throughout her presentation and clapped when she was finished. I did too. Debbie bowed and ran back to her desk and sat down.

I was laughing and clapping with everyone else, and then I said, "Thank you, Debbie. I will *not* say that is my God, but I will say that is the way God is too often depicted in our religion textbooks. For sure, I like your God better, and that is the best presentation I think I've ever heard. Thank you." I clapped again. Debbie was grinning ear to ear. More than ever, I was convinced that we needed to get rid of the legalistic and moralistic teachings about living and loving and being a good Christian Catholic.

I was on a bit of a high that day as I went into the eighth-grade room. They were as lively as the seventh and for the same reason—a few thoughtful girls. I thought that I should have had them with me as I meandered through seminary classes. The outspoken girls informed me that they were glad that I was not like my predecessor, who was a stickler for exact regular catechism questions and answers and did not allow for discussions like we had that morning with Debbie. I considered that to be a nice flower.

I used Debbie's theology in my next Sunday sermon, and it was well received. Even Dennis and Jane were impressed and encouraged me to bring more of that kind of humor into my sermons.

I looked forward to my four mornings a week at the school and often stayed to join the students for a delicious lunch prepared by one very ingenious cook and her helper. The food was far better than that of the seminary. I was supposed to take Wednesdays off, but after spending a few free Wednesdays playing golf with other young priests and ending up with more severe headaches, I gave that up. Instead of loafing around, I organized the public school religion classes for Wednesday evenings. By the middle of October, I had recruited enough teachers for each grade, first through twelfth. I took the twelve high school seniors, seven girls and five boys, myself. They were an enjoyable bunch, and

I recruited three of them to be leaders of the CYO—Catholic Youth Organization.

The diocesan director of the CYO asked me to coordinate the CYO activates in the Kingman deanery. I didn't know there was such an entity as a deanery, but it sounded interesting, and I accepted. He said that it was a position that just needed to be filled in for a diocesan report, and I could do anything I wanted to with it. I picked up the idea from somewhere about having a basketball league among the deanery's parishes in the four counties around Kingman. Also, I learned that the diocese had a teen play contest in the spring and our deanery had never had a parish with an entry. So, I checked around, and three other parish CYO coordinators were interested in both the basketball league and the play contest, so I got busy organizing the two programs.

Early in the basketball season, a parishioner asked if he could help set up a junior high basketball team and perhaps a league among neighboring parochial schools. He wanted to coach that age group, and he and I got to work. St. Patrick's had an almost new gym that had seen little use, and now it was going to have two basketball teams: high school CYO and junior high. Another former jock volunteered to coach the CYO team and help organize the league. Before Christmas, we had two games for each team in our gym. I just told Monsignor Malone what I was doing and didn't give a thought that I should have asked him for permission. He said later that I should have asked him, but he really didn't mind. None of my predecessors had done most of the things I was doing.

My second Christmas letter read:

> *Oh, Lord, your message of love is so simple to understand but so difficult to do. Could it be because it demands of us what it demanded of you?*

Greetings,

Since my last Christmas letter, a great many things have happened, not the least of which has been my own ordination to the priesthood. This tremendous event in my life has opened an entirely new and wonderful world—that world is full of joyful, sad, loving and striving people who know deep in their hearts the why of the first Christmas.

There have been many delightful experiences this past year that have impressed me with the true meaning of Christmas. But I would like to tell about the incident that impressed me most. It occurred in the fifth-grade class. I had given the children the assignment of telling their mothers that they loved them; this was to show how the Holy Spirit helps us to do good things and not just to avoid bad things. The next day, I called on one girl and asked her what her mother said when she told her that she loved her, and with no hesitation or sign of embarrassment and with a smile that would capture any heart, she replied, "Well, Father, she put her arms around me and said, 'I love you too, darling.'" And you could tell by the look on her face that she knew that her mother loved her and that her mother knew she meant it when she said I love you.

Wouldn't it be wonderful if we all could be like children and be able to express our love for others without embarrassment? How often it seems that we let Christ down by failing to express our love for others. After all, this is the reason that Christ was born into this world, and He died on the cross—to show us the way to love and to express it because true Christ-like love seems so foreign to the world today. Perhaps we must first displace false notions

of love with the true concept of love that Christ gives us.
And when we learn to love, let us not be afraid to express
it. May Christ always instill love in our hearts.

May God continue to bless you with His wonderful gift
to love much.

I will remember you in the three Masses I have the
privilege of celebrating on Christmas Day.

Father Don Hanley

I don't remember what kind of responses I received about this Christmas card, but I imagine it was something like, "Oh, that's nice." And I've always disliked the word nice. I realized, years later, that the simple story expressed my yearning for someone to say, "I love you," to me. They were never spoken in our house—by anyone.

In late February, Dan Orth invited me to join him in attending a workshop called Sensitivity Training conducted by psychologists from a firm in Bethel, Maine. It was being held in a Mennonite mental health clinic in Newton, Kansas, north of Wichita. Dan said that it might help us communicate with others better and help me with my adult education groups. It was for three whole days. I told Monsignor Malone about it, as well as the school principal, and drove over to Dan's parish in Mt. Vernon. We would have to stay in a motel in Newton, and the workshop would cost $100. I could not afford that, but Dan said he would pay for both.

The Mennonite clinic was in a new all-white, one-story building that reminded me of the Catholic Social Services building in Wichita, and I guessed this was an equivalent operation. We received a brief orientation, and then we were divided into two mixed-gender groups. Dan and I decided we would not reveal that we were priests. I insisted on the non-revelation because I was already tired of being seen as a role rather than a person, and I was sure that would help. The leader of my group was a handsome, articulate, dark-haired fellow in his forties. Right away, he told us that everything we shared in the group was confidential and encouraged us to be open and honest with our remarks and avoid generalities and judgments—even of ourselves. Honest humor was also welcome. There were five men and three women in my group, all somewhere between thirty and fifty, I guessed. We were encouraged to just be ourselves and not to share what we did for a living, nor our profession, if we had one. I was pleased that fit in with Dan and my earlier decision, and I was glad that I wouldn't know the profession of the participants other than the facilitator—a word I had never heard before. A facilitator, I learned, was one who aided in communication or understanding, but was not a teacher or leader in the formal sense of the words.

We all sat around in semi-comfortable chairs and smiled nervously at one another. The facilitator, Pete, asked us to put our watches in a container for the day and then share what we were feeling and what we would like to learn from the workshop. I wanted to ask about the mental health clinic and about the Mennonite religion but knew that would not be appropriate, so I just said, "I'm just curious about what we'll be doing, and I have no idea what I'll learn, so I'm just a bit anxious, I guess." Most of the others were similarly vague.

Pete invited us to look around and make eye contact with everyone in the group and hold the look for a long moment and pay attention to how we feel as we look at each person. I was surprised at how quickly I started judging each one of my fellow participants—some had an inviting and friendly look on their faces, and others seemed to be a bit put-offish, I thought. I felt myself feeling more relaxed with some of them, though I didn't quite know why. We took about ten minutes doing this, and Pete asked us to share our experiences. I did what I had done in high school and in my years in the seminary and shared first after waiting only a minute. Others followed, and there were no "reluctant dragons"—what I called those who would not share in my classes. Most must have thought like I did: "I paid for this and took time off for it, so I'm going to learn something."

By the end of the first day, I felt a genuine warmth in the group, and Dan said the same about his experience with his group. A few of the comments shared in that group have stuck with me ever since. One man gave his observation to another fellow, who was quite shy and nervous. "You know, Joe, it sounds like you feel the need to apologize for having been born." I realized that I often felt that way and had since early childhood. I wondered if my birth itself had something to do with it. Another was made directly to me, and it was quite a revelation. "Don, you often talk like you just read what you're saying in a book, or like you are writing it in a book. It takes away from the personal impact of what you're saying." I looked around and several others nodded in agreement. I appreciated this insight and said I'd work on it. Given the camaraderie we had built with each other, I even felt comfortable asking for any suggestions they might have for me in the small time we had left. I wondered if feeling like I need to apologize for existing and talking like I was reading a book were connected?

All in all, I was on a real high when we left Newton, and I wasn't sure why—was it simply because I just felt accepted and didn't have to do anything to earn it? The very next Sunday, I left the pulpit and walked around the sanctuary as I gave my sermon. I shared with everyone my experience in the workshop. Jane said I sounded warmer and more personal and was eager to hear more about the workshop.

Sticking with keeping busy, I held meetings every evening, except Saturday. And every other Saturday, I had to hear confessions. I still had the occasional headache but wasn't taking four aspirin every four hours like I had been doing in the seminary. At the end of third theology, my stomach was really starting to bother me, and the seminary doctor recommended I stop the aspirin and take Empirin 3 instead. The Empirin was aspirin and codeine, and I didn't know until years later that codeine was a narcotic. Stupid? Yes, but it helped dampen the headaches, and at least I was taking fewer pills than I was before.

Dennis helped me train four other men to be lectors, and I trained the altar boys to serve the new English Mass. Monsignor grudgingly went along with the whole thing, convinced that it was all just a temporary fad and things would eventually go back to the way he thought things *should* be, with the priest facing the wall of the sanctuary and celebrating the Latin Mass. He gave me a sort of half-hearted "thank you" for taking care of the transition—bit of a wilted flower, but it was something. Despite his resistance, it all went quite smoothly.

One parishioner had been a high school drama teacher at one time and volunteered to direct the CYO one-act play for our deanery contest, and I volunteered our CYO to host the play contest in April.

The seventh and eighth-grade girls wanted to form a glee club, and I volunteered to be their director. I arranged to have them perform during intermission of the play contest. The auditorium was in the older part of the school building and had been neglected for years. For many years, it had served as a storeroom and was filled for an assortment of junk, so I asked Monsignor Malone if I could get it fixed up and painted for the contest and the new glee club. He gave his okay, and I organized the fix-up, clean-up, and paint-up crews from the upper grades, the CYO, and a few others to help on Saturdays. On the day of the big happening, the auditorium still smelled of paint and soap and was filled with about 200 people ready to watch the plays and hear our glee club.

I really enjoyed the busy year and was looking forward to the next year. On the last Friday of the school year, I said goodbye to the three sisters of St. Joseph who taught at St. Patrick's before returning to the rectory. Monsignor was waiting for me at the door, which immediately struck me as unusual. He looked uncomfortable as he motioned me into my office. I took the few steps and saw two lit candles and a purple stole—the kind that priests wear when giving the sacrament for the dying—framing an envelope. I was puzzled, and I'm sure it showed. Malone just shrugged, looked at the little shrine, and said, "Please open it."

My hands shook as I glanced at my name and the return address on the envelope: Office of the Bishop, Diocese of Wichita. I tore it open and began to read. The bishop was pleased to appoint me assistant diocesan director of the Confraternity of Christian Doctrine, or CCD—the religious education for public school children and adults. Very unpriestly like, I said, "Oh, shit."

"My thoughts, exactly," muttered Malone.

I was to be in residence at St. Patrick's parish in Wichita and report to the CCD office and work with their director, Monsignor Leon McNeill, on June 15, 1965. This new assignment came as a real blow. I had enjoyed working with Monsignor Malone and with the free hand he had given me in working with all the parishioners, young and old. The most valuable thing I learned from the good monsignor was in observing the gentle and kind way he was with people, especially at funerals. That inspired me to cultivate that quality in myself. My first year as a priest had been darkened because, for the vast majority of Catholics, the concept of sinning revolved around sex—impure thoughts, touches, masturbation, birth control, etc. I hadn't yet heard a word about various forms of injustice, intolerance, or prejudice, and only very little about anger and abuse. I had observed a great deal of charity and kindness though. Damnit, I was just getting my feet wet, and I wanted to continue with all the projects I had started, and I'd miss Barbara Beat's fantastic cooking—the best food I ever had in my *life*.

Looking back, I often wondered how my life would have been different if I had continued exclusively involved in parish work instead of getting involved in religious education and all that went with it. My very sanctimonious Christmas message had expressed my "Oh look at me and my pietistic presenting self," and I thought the world wanted me to be that way.

Forty-Four

HAVING BREAKFAST WITH GOD AND BECOMING A DIOCESAN OFFICIAL

—∞∞∞—

I did not know what being an assistant director of religious education was going to entail, but I hadn't known what being an assistant pastor meant either, and I thought I had done pretty well at that. Monsignor Malone suggested I take a vacation before embarking on this new assignment, and I agreed. Feeling more than a little apprehensive about the future, I headed to Denver to visit Mom, Patty, and the other relatives.

Mom and Patty were living on the fifth floor of a new seniors-only subsidized apartment building. Patty was allowed to live there as Mom's caretaker. As I entered, I found Mom sitting in front of the TV watching *As the World Turns*, one of her favorite soaps. That seemed to be her preferred pastime ever since we had gotten our first TV in Wichita in 1952. She was only sixty-nine years old but seemed much older than when she moved to Hot

Springs in 1945. I took the time to visit Marie, Jim, and their family, and Jim, Kay, and their kids. Not a single person said a word nor asked a single question about what I was doing or if I did or didn't like being a priest. I asked Jim Abney how he liked his work with Lockheed-Martin compared to Boeing, but he didn't seem interested in what I was up to at all. I took Mom and Patty to see Jim Hanley's completed Catholic retreat house south of Denver. Mom rarely got out of the apartment, so I made a point of taking Patty and her around Denver. I often wondered what Mom felt about things—her life, all her kids, and well about everything. When I asked her about what life was like living in the sod house, she would just say it was difficult, and leave it at that.

I wondered if she thought she should model herself after Mary, Mother of Jesus—to "ponder things in her heart" and just be quiet?

After ten days of headaches and vacation, I headed back to St. Patrick's rectory on the north side of Wichita. As I drove up, I saw that the rectory was on the south side of the parish complex, and the three buildings—rectory, church, and school—all sat on the bank of the Little Arkansas River that drained into the Arkansas River about four miles south. The church was built in the late forties in a then modern type of architecture in a box-like pattern with buff-brick walls and façade. The rectory, built more recently, was a long and narrow rectangle with few windows. I glanced past the church and saw a long one-story building that matched the other buildings, which I assumed was the school. Behind the rectory was a three-car garage with one car parked closest to the back door. I parked in the farthest place and took two of my suitcases from the trunk.

I knocked on the back door, and it was opened quickly by a Black woman with a big smile. "You must be one of our new priests. I'm Della, your cook and housekeeper."

"Hello Della, I'm Don Hanley and so, you're expecting another one?" I took her calloused hand and smiled back.

A gruff voice came from the adjoining large room that looked like a combination dining-living room. A sprightly old fellow, looking to be in his late sixties, rushed across the room and nearly yelled, "Well, I guess it's about time. And what's your name?" Without giving me time to reply, he quickly went on, "I'm Monsignor Cody, and I'm the pastor here." He didn't smile and glanced at the kitchen cabinets but not at me as he extended a limp hand.

"I'm Don Hanley and I'm the designated resident priest." I took his soft hand and gave it a much stronger squeeze then he had given me.

"Oh, yeah, the new diocesan guy for the CCD. Well, you can get some practice here at our parish and take care of our public school kids. I hear we need to have some education for our adults as well, so if they want to know more about this horrible so-called vernacular Mass and the Vatican Council business—you can tackle that nonsense." We heard the sound of a motorcycle arriving near the garage and Monsignor yelled, "What the hell is that?" We glanced out the door window to see a fellow in a black leather jacket climb off a Harley-Davidson, take off his biker's helmet, and head for the door. He knocked on the door, and Cody opened it and practically yelled, "Who in the hell are you?"

With a schoolboy's sheepish grin, our visitor said, "I'm Father Jim Hoagland, Monsignor Cody." He held out his hand, and Cody seemed reluctant to take it.

"And what the hell is this motorcycle business—the new mode of transportation for young priests these days?"

"No, Monsignor, that is my recreational ride. I have a car, and a friend will be taking me back to Hutchinson to get it. In the meantime, may I park the bike in the middle slot in the garage?" Cody muttered a weak, "Yeah." Hoagland then turned to me, and we introduced ourselves. Della, our housekeeper, stood over by the cabinets and was ignored by Hoagland as she just shook her head. We were told to pick out our offices and bedrooms. Before Jim could say anything, I gave him the first choice because he was the assistant, and I was only the resident assistant. The offices and bedrooms were very much alike, and we would share a bathroom between the two bedrooms.

He boasted to me that he was a very lucky dude. This was going to be his fifth parish, and he had been in the others for two years each and had two years' worth of sermons he had collected in the seminary. "I haven't had to write a sermon for eight damn years! Isn't that great?"

I wanted to say that was the dumbest thing I'd ever heard, but just muttered an unenthusiastic, "Yeah." I had the agonizing misfortune of having to listen to one of his posturing and meaningless sermons a few weeks later and almost fell out of the celebrant's chair when I fell asleep. The altar boy sitting next to me saved me by nudging me when he noticed I was nodding off. To stay awake, I scanned the group of parishioners and noticed that many among them were trying their Sunday best to stay awake, while a handful had simply allowed themselves to take a nap.

Della fixed a very delicious dinner for the three of us, and I was fairly certain that she had never been invited to join the "royalty" sitting down in the dining-living room next to the kitchen. I was correct, she did not join us. I got the sense that Monsignor Cody considered himself a part of some unspoken aristocracy, while Hoagland thought himself lucky to have landed such a secure and cushy job. He reminded me of Father Blanpied's assistant at St. Margaret Mary's. Of my three housemates, I considered Della to be the most pleasant and loving one by far. A few weeks after I had arrived, Della asked me to read a letter one of her sons had sent to her. A day or so after that, she asked me to write a letter back, and she dictated to me what she wanted to tell him. She told me that she wasn't comfortable asking the monsignor to help her, and I guessed she hadn't even thought of asking Hoagland. After my comfortable life with Quintin Malone and Barbara Beat in Kingman, the cold and empty living arrangements at St. Patrick's were a real downer. Della seemed the only authentic person in the place, and when she asked me to help with the letters, it made me feel that, at least in her eyes, I too was an authentic person, which was a lovely flower indeed.

The morning after I came to Wichita, I went to the diocesan chancery office and met with Bishop Leo Byrne. He welcomed me aboard his team and said, "I imagine, Don, that you were counting on being with Catholic charities, as I was in St. Louis, but Father Kocour is doing a fine job there, and nothing is being done at the religious education office, and I'm hoping you'll be able to do something about that." He explained to me that the CCD director in New Orleans had been named a bishop just a few months ago, and Monsignor Leon McNeill was going to be the new director, the position he had held several years ago, and he was a veteran educator, having been the diocesan superintendent of schools for many years. Byrne went on to say that he would be my mentor and I would be his spokesman, as he had a tracheotomy many years ago and now found it difficult to speak in public. Our offices were a bit inauspicious, as they were over the garages at the back of the building. That was only temporary; the diocese had purchased and tore down an old two-story house behind the cathedral and would be breaking ground on a new chancery office there next week. He told me all this as if I was an old confidant of his. I thought that my playing chauffer for him in Denver had turned out to be helpful for both of us.

I don't know where he got the notion that I was planning to be the director of Catholic charities, but I never thought to correct him. It wasn't until years later that I realized he was thinking of grooming me to become a bishop. He wished me well, and I headed out the back door to my office.

Monsignor McNeill was already there and greeted me warmly. He was heavy set, nearly bald, and like Cody, looked to be in his late sixties or maybe early seventies. Unlike Cody, he had a warm smile and gave me a firm handshake. The room smelled musty and looked like it had not been used in years. Monsignor McNeill confirmed that suspicion. He also informed me that he had been the one to ask the bishop to bring in help for our office.

He had just finished saying this when a nun in her mid-thirties came up the stairs. She was Sister Eugenia, and she confidently introduced herself to both of us. She had on the habit of the Sisters of the Most Precious Blood, an order that ran Sacred Heart College in Wichita and staffed several schools around the diocese. We quickly learned a bit about her personality when, after McNeill mentioned we would need to do some cleaning and fixing up, Sister Eugenia loudly exclaimed, "Now, I'll have you both know that I was assigned here to be an educator with both of you and *not* to be your cleaning lady or go-fer, okay?"

McNeill smiled broadly, and I frowned at her. "Neither of us said you were, so you can take the chip off your shoulder." I sounded more defensive than I intended, but that was okay. "I was just going to look for cleaning supplies when you came up the stairs, so there." Then I grinned, and Eugenia smiled back. The tension diffused, we set to cleaning.

I had never worked with a woman before, let alone a nun. I had worked *for* Audra, but she was twenty years older, paid me, and would tell me what she wanted, and I'd get to work on it—it wasn't a *with* kind of thing. Also, in Kingman, I'd worked *for* the principal but not *with* her either, so working with Sister Eugenia was going to be a new experience. That first week, I asked her if I could call her Eugenia without the whole "sister" thing and she said, yes, as long as no one other than the monsignor was around. We both asked the monsignor if we could call him Leon, and he looked surprised and didn't offer a response, so we stuck with calling him monsignor. Luckily, McNeill was more like Malone than Cody—he didn't have a cob up his ass.

We found little evidence that Father Zinn, our predecessor, had done anything to promote any kind of new catechetics as recommended by the Vatican Council, or anything else for that matter. Monsignor suggested that Eugenia and I visit the parishes of the diocese to find out how best we could serve them. And the very first thing we needed to do was become familiar with the Confraternity of Christian Doctrine manual and evaluate the new religion textbooks that were coming out.

I wanted to find out what other dioceses were doing and called around to the three other dioceses in Kansas—Kansas City, Salina, and Dodge City. All three of the directors were also pastors of small parishes near the "See" City—where the diocesan offices and the bishops were located, and it seemed to me that they were more interested in their parishes than their diocesan office of religious education. The one in Kansas City said that he had just started a summer master's degree program in religious education at Loyola University in Chicago and that it was very helpful to him and that I should look into it. All three of them told me that they had heard that Father Joe Dillon in Oklahoma City had a very full staff and program, but they had never visited him or looked into his program. I got Father Dillon's phone number and made an appointment with him.

The following week, I drove to Oklahoma City, and I met Joe Dillon. He was a dignified-looking gentleman who came across to me as a strong, silent, and wise kind of guy. He looked tired and apologized for not being as "up" as he would have liked to be. He had just finished taking part in a youth encounter retreat involving over fifty high school students. I asked him about it, and he said that he and three of his religious education staff members, along with a few parish religious educators, worked with the high school students.

"Some were from Catholic high schools, and the rest were from public schools," he told me. "It started with a group meeting at a Boy Scout campground, and in the middle of the first day's discussion, we heard a loud explosion outside the assembly hall, and everyone hit the floor. Being the oldest member of the team, I was near a phone, and I informed everyone that the explosion meant the end of our country, and we were the last ones alive. Of course, everyone caught on right away, and I started getting them into groups of ten and instructed them to come up with ideas about how the new world should be organized. We spent the rest of the weekend working on rethinking a better world. I, personally, didn't get enough sleep, so you'll have to forgive me."

I was fascinated and asked him to tell me about some of the other things he and the staff were doing to educate the people of the diocese of Oklahoma, which consisted of the entire state, which was known as the land of the 3.2 beer and 3.2 Catholics. He said that about half of the parishes took part in the creative experiences that he had described, but some pastors wanted to stay with the old Baltimore catechism. The traditional catechism teachers only needed to know how to read, so his office didn't bother with them at all. It had taken a few years to get half the parishes on board. I left Oklahoma feeling excited about creating experiences for Wichita religion teachers and for their students. I hoped Sister Eugenia would like the ideas too.

Monsignor suggested to Bishop Byrne that he call for a priests' conference to introduce Eugenia, me, and our CCD program to them. My first thought was, "What program?" All we had was the old CCD manual, which Eugenia and I had only just read. Monsignor insisted and Bishop Byrne announced the two conferences—one to be held at Parsons, one of the largest towns in the eastern side of the diocese, and one in the Cathedral High School auditorium. The command performance event—every priest was expected to attend—was scheduled for the middle of August. Sister Eugenia would attend and allow herself to be introduced but would not give any kind of speech. I would be the performance—period. Oh, shit!

The three of us went to Parsons in separate cars, as we wanted to visit others before the conference. As I drove into the facility in Parsons, I saw the sign, Kansas State Center for Mental Health, and I broke out in a sweat—this was the place Dad had lived when we all left for California! Oh, my Lord. The only person I had ever told about Dad's hospital stay was the seminary rector, at the end of the third year of theology. I had told the rector about the hospital and Dad's seizures, in case they would be revealed before my ordination, and I would be rejected as a candidate for the priesthood. Father Danagher told me that would never be a problem. Visiting the place made me feel somehow tainted for having had a dad who had been a resident in a mental hospital. As I walked down the hall to the auditorium, I passed a door with a sign reading, Ronald F. Haggerty, M.D., Director. I wondered if the bookcases my dad built in the early 1940s were still in use.

At 10:30 a.m., Bishop Byrne announced that McNeill would be working on the publishing of small discussion manuals for use by our Catholic laity as they learned about the Vatican Council and the theology behind the liturgical changes. This was the first time I had heard of this, and I was sure that would also be Eugenia's and my responsibility to promote this adult education project. I added that to my presentation of what we would do, although I had no idea how we would do it. I outlined the traditional CCD program for public school children and promised that we, Sister Eugenia and I, would provide information on the new catechetical texts, which were based on the council's recommendations. We would also conduct workshops for the parish religion teachers, and we still had to work out all the details. Both McNeill and the bishop told me that I had done an admirable job, but I was far from pleased with it myself.

The priests were invited to attend a luncheon provided by the hospital. Sister Eugenia was already seated, and we were joined at our table by Dr. Haggerty, the center's director. Haggerty gave a brief welcoming speech and sat down next to me. I asked him how long he had been in his position, and he said, "I was appointed director in 1940 and discovered that I enjoyed being an administrator very much."

Wow, he was here when Dad was transferred from Osawatomie to Parsons. Sister Eugenia and Monsignor McNeill on my left were both engaged in conversation, so I asked the doctor, "My dad was here in the early 1940s, and he said that the hospital director helped him get discharged from the hospital. Dad said that he was building bookcases in your office and that you thought he was an outside contractor and not a patient here. Do you remember him?"

Before I could give him Dad's name, Dr. Haggerty exclaimed, "Dennis Hanley, indeed I do! Father Hanley, ah, you are his son. This is amazing, is it not? Hanley is a fairly common Irish name and I, oh, I didn't give it a thought. I've thought of your dad often over the years—and how we 'good' doctors too often see patients as items rather than persons. Your dad was a person—a carpenter and a father of a bunch of kids, and then, suddenly, I found out he was a patient. And I never was in contact with him again. How is he doing?"

"I sincerely hope he is doing better in heaven. He died in 1947 in Edgemont, South Dakota. He and I lived together his last three years of his life."

After everyone left, he and I went to his office, and he proudly showed me his beautiful bookcases that extended along one wall and half of another. "As you can see, Father, these bookcases are real pieces of fine furniture, and your dad and I had many discussions as he worked on them. I learned a great deal from him. He was a wise man and a sad man. I'm sorry to hear that he died so young."

I just nodded and said, "Well, Doctor, I'm very glad that I've met you and to hear good words about Dad. He and I really bonded, and I think we had a pretty good life the last three years of his life." Realizing that I had never talked with a psychiatrist before, I asked, "Doctor, I'm now the assistant diocesan director of religious education. What recommendations would you make for our religion teachers so we could have emotionally healthier children?"

He thought for a moment and then said, "Stop making children feel ashamed of their human sexuality and feeling guilty about almost every thought or feelings they have. I think that would be helpful. Thanks for asking."

I thanked him for his time and shook his hand. The flower I found in Parsons was my encounter with Haggerty.

The next day back in Wichita, we repeated the conference with a larger group of priests. Father Dan Orth invited me to join him for dinner at his rectory, and I did. Dan was a good cook and also a good critic of my speeches when he heard them. I told him I didn't like what I said at the conference—mainly that I didn't have anything definite to tell my fellow priests. I asked him what he thought of it.

"First, I think you sounded like you had a brain and were a confident fellow and maybe that you just had breakfast with God." I frowned and raised an eyebrow at the last part, as I wondered if I sounded arrogant. Dan added, "Just kidding, sort of. I think you would have done better if you'd been more transparent and said that you were new at this and needed our help—maybe even pleaded for our help. You sounded like you had a spanking new plan that would change the world. Bishop Byrne often talks like that, and I imagine McNeill used to before he lost his voice. So, my boy, my main message is to be humbler and more transparent." I thanked him for his honest feedback and told him that I enjoyed his scotch and fine dinner. When I left, I was still mentally stewing about talking like I just had breakfast with God.

I applied for the summer program at Loyola University in Chicago and was accepted for the 1966 session. Then I asked the bishop for permission, and he said that was fine, but I would have to find the money for tuition myself. For the first time, I thought of Mom's sister, Agnes Forester, as a possible source of funds. She did not have any children of her own, had attended my ordination, and was very enthusiastic about having a nephew who was a priest. Her husband had died a few years ago, and she lived in a very nice house in Paola, Kansas. So, I asked her if she could loan me $600 for the summer program. She said, "No, I won't loan it to you, but I'll make you a gift of $600." Of course, I hoped she would say that because I did not know how I would pay her back if it were a loan. I often wondered where some priests got the money for their expensive cars and vacations, but I never asked.

I had thought of going to Denver at Christmas time, but my back went out the week before Christmas, so I went to St. Francis hospital instead. For the first time in my life, I missed Christmas midnight Mass, but I did see an inspirational film on television on Christmas eve. It was an old British comedy entitled *The Man Who Could Work Miracles*. It was humorous and educational for me. The protagonist was an ordinary and hapless fellow whom the gods had chosen to be gifted with the power to work miracles. He was depicted moving furniture, mending fractures, and such things, but his real desire was for his friend, a pretty young woman, to fall in love with him. She was very impressed with him and his new powers, but still wanted them to just be friends. The gods tried various ways to teach him that all humans were blessed with free will and so even the gods could not force someone to love anyone if they did not desire it. The film ended with the fellow deciding that if he could not have her be in love with him, he wanted to stop the world so he could get off. So, the gods stopped the world, and he and everything on earth went flying off into space. The movie forced me to, once again, see that I and everyone else had the free will to choose faith, love, hope and even to be a good person— over and over again every day.

After a week in the hospital, I could, with only a little pain, get out of traction and walk up and down the hallways. I hated to pay a taxi to take me home and was surprised when Ron Wiloughby, of the Abney class holiday party people, stopped by the hospital to visit me. It had been years since I had seen him, and he wanted to talk a bit about his marriage. I am sure I was not very much help to him, but he was happy to take me back to St. Pat's.

Forty-Five

JUGGLING THE OFFICE AND HELPING THE PARISH

⸻⠶⠶⸻

The diocesan job was challenging, but not very fulfilling. When I was in Kingman, I felt like I was really involved with people and enjoyed it. I met a few couples at St. Pat's who were very warm, and the first couple to invite me to their home for dinner was Doris and Tom Pirotte. They had five children, three boys and two girls. I had never been around a family quite like them, nor a couple like Tom and Doris. The couple talked about all sorts of things—politics, science, education, mental health, religious topics, and they included the children. The children were polite and respectful but had their opinions—especially the older ones. In my siblings' families, there was very little discussion about anything I thought to be of value, and the kids anxiously awaited the moment when they could be excused from the dining table.

After the first two visits, I told Tom and Doris about the CFM movement, the Dulleas, and the group in Kingman. They were interested and thought they knew a few other couples who would also be interested. They'd talk it up. Their first CFM meeting was on a Sunday evening in early August; Tom and Doris hosted five other couples and me to their home. The kids stayed in the back rooms, and I liked all the couples very much—except one husband, whom I thought was very coarse. The others seemed to tolerate him just fine. This was likely for the sake of his long-suffering wife, who was delightful and the loving caretaker of their eight children. Every Sunday evening, I looked forward to meeting with these couples.

Also at St. Patrick's, I spent much of August recruiting new teachers for the weekly religion classes for public school students. Luckily for me, the previous assistant pastor had left behind six who were dedicated and smart. So, I needed five elementary teachers and two high school teachers. I asked Monsignor Cody if I could teach eighth-grade religion at the school in order to keep in touch with that age group while I was working with the teachers. He said it was okay with him, but I'd have to ask Sister Catherine, the nun who was the principal. The Sisters of St. Joseph, the same order as those at Kingman, had five teachers at St. Pat's. Sister Catherine agreed, and I taught the eighth graders four days a week and visited a first and second-grade classroom on Wednesdays.

Father Hoagland, supposedly the real full-time assistant pastor, asked me if I wanted to take on the Catholic Youth Organization that met on Wednesday evenings. He said he didn't really like teenagers. I never learned what he did like about being a priest and doing pastoral work in general. His only love was his damn motorcycle. All the priests of the diocese received a letter stating that if we donated fort-five dollars to a certain missionary society, and we drove twenty-five miles a day in our ministry, we could be exempted from praying the daily breviary. Jim asked me if I thought the little town of Andale, about fourteen miles northwest of Wichita, would be far enough away that if he rode out there every day, he'd qualify. I said it was far enough and asked him what kind of ministry he conducted in Andale. He winked and said he'd find something. I threw my breviary on the bottom shelf of my bookcase. We had been told in the seminary that the breviary was a sacred duty for every priest around the world. I thought if it was so damned sacred, why could I buy my way out of the duty for forty-five bucks?

I had another interesting and difficult experience at St. Pat's that made me again disappointed in the horrible non-education I received at the seminary. A very pretty young woman in her mid-twenties asked to see me about a troubling moral question. She arrived at the rectory at our agreed time, and I ushered her into my office. I had two chairs in front of a desk, and she sat down about five feet from me and asked, "Father, I would like to know if oral sex is a sin? I have a boyfriend whom I love very much and whom I hope to marry someday. We don't want to have intercourse, but we do have oral sex, and well . . ."

I had only a very vague idea what oral sex was, and I guess my face showed my ignorance, so she asked, "Father, you do know what I mean, don't you?"

I'm sure I was red as a beet. "Please tell me what you mean, Loretta."

It was her turn to turn scarlet, and she slowly said, "Well, I, uh, I kiss his penis, and he kisses my vagina, and uh, we sometimes, uh, have orgasms."

Oh, my God, I thought, and I was glad that my legs were crossed. I coughed and after a moment or so, I solemnly and pompously said, "I think it is commendable that you and your boyfriend refrain from having intercourse, but I do think that what you are doing is dangerously close to a mortal sin, so I would recommend that you stop this practice."

I had almost forgotten my six-year-old sinful experience with Sally, and I again condemned the ignorant and inadequate education I had received at St. Thomas. So, here, in front of me was another casualty of the clerical war on human sexuality, but I still wasn't free enough nor spiritually developed enough to tell this young woman that she and her friend were just doing what I guessed young people often did. Of course, I wouldn't ever add, or even admit to myself, that I really envied her boyfriend. I wondered why she chose an office consultation rather than going to the regular confessional box.

In February 1966, I attended the annual priests' retreat. Last year's had been like the seminary retreats, where a priest from outside the seminary or diocese came and gave pious homilies that were similar to the meditations of Thomas à Kempis's *Imitation of Christ*. We were expected to contemplate these holy words and deepen our own spiritual practices and lives. I never found à Kempis to be inspirational, so this time, I brought a spiritual book that I thought would be more helpful. To be honest, I got little out of that retreat, and I was happy that in 1966, we had the option of attending a dialogue retreat conducted by two Paulist priests from Pueblo, Colorado. I was told that it would be like the encounter group that Dan Orth and I had attended. So, I went to the retreat house and was treated with up-to-date talks on the Vatican Council, recent developments in theology, and a great model of learning new ideas and connecting with other priests. I went to confession to one of the Paulist priests and explored my masturbation problem. I was happy to hear him say, "Don, my recommendation is for you to just enjoy masturbating and forget the sin part." That was something I had considered for years, but he helped me drop the last thread of that inhumane moral injunction to the most common sin among teens and other young men.

There were thirty-two priests in attendance, so we had four groups of eight. After each talk, we were asked to meet with our group and discuss our personal thoughts to what was presented. We were asked not to debate the theology but to state our own thoughts and feelings and not get all abstract about the ideas. In my group, I met my Kingman predecessor for the first time, Father LeRoy Linnebur. He was a handsome native of the diocese and three years younger than me. He was every bit as old-fashioned and rigid as the older priests, and I wondered how the parishioners in Kingman reacted to him and if they were confused by the very different approaches he and I took. I guess he was at least better than my successor in Kingman, whom I learned spent most of his time when he was at the parish lying on his back in bed and watching TV. Anyway, I left the retreat feeling a high similar to the one after the Newton workshop.

Dan also attended the retreat and later invited me to join him for a trip to Kansas City to meet with two priests there who were engaged in a volunteer missionary program. I put missionary in quotes because the "missionaries" were graduates from eastern Catholic colleges, and the mission areas were parishes in the Kansas City diocese. It sounded interesting, so I joined him. The two priests were about Dan's age and ordained ten or so years. One was a scholarly fellow who was very much into the new Vatican

Council theology, and the other was more into organizational work and the one who recruited the missionaries. The summer of 1966 was to be their third year for their program. They usually had from eight to twelve male and female college graduates who would work in pairs and do parish work. The two priests and a couple of other people would conduct a week-long orientation and focus on spiritual development and outreach programs for seniors and Catholic youths—especially those who lived in mixed racial neighborhoods. The host parishes would provide room and board and a stipend for the college grads.

Dan said that he would like to have a similar program in the Wichita diocese and would like for me to be involved in the week-long orientation and pretend it was part of our religious education program in case Bishop Byrne asked about it. Dan saw his role at the missionary office as his own rationale. He had already found four pastors who were willing to host the students, and Monsignor Fisher at All Saints' Parish would provide the facility for the orientation. I told him about my going to Loyola in Chicago in June, and he said the orientation would be scheduled before I left in June. He had found two women who had worked as Catholic lay missionaries and were very savvy about volunteer work; they were also Vatican II thinkers. I told Dan that I didn't think I was qualified, but he said that all I needed to do was share my ideas and back off from sounding like I just had breakfast with God. So, I said, "Yes." Monsignor McNeill was a close friend of Dan's and thought my involvement would be a good educational experience for me. Sister Eugenia was more than a bit miffed that she was not included. I explained that I was only assisting, and the program was not really part of the program, just helping make it official. Later, I learned it was a great orientation to the Loyola program, called the Institute for Pastoral Studies.

During this time, I continued reading a novel every night before going to sleep and reading spiritual and theology books, especially as they pertained to religious education. I didn't pay any attention to whether or not I was growing spiritually, still ignorant of what my spiritual life should be. There seemed to be a gulf between day-to-day living and what the spiritual writers wrote about. I hoped my consciousness was evolving a la Teilhard de Chardin. I settled for just doing my best to be a kind and charitable person and hoped that was good enough.

Forty-Six

LOYOLA AND GOING THROUGH ADOLESCENCE

—— ∞∞∞ ——

I said goodbye to the Religious Education Office, Sister Eugenia, and Monsignor McNeill and, although still sleeping at St. Patrick's rectory, I spent the second week of June 1966, at All Saints parish in southeast Wichita. Eight college graduates, six young women and two young men, arrived on Monday morning. Although I was only two years out of seminary college, they seemed to be teenagers to me.

They were mostly from in and around New York City and had attended Catholic colleges there. Only one of them had ever been west of the Mississippi river, or even New Jersey, so Dan's farmer-ish manners and his and my western drawl seemed strange to them. That was the first time I was ever told I had an accent.

Two of them actually thought that Wichita would have boarded sidewalks and hitching posts and were surprised that it looked like small cities in the eastern part of the U.S.—but, of course, not like New York City itself. I was surprised, too, that they were very much up on the spirit and teachings of the Vatican Council—more than most of the priests of the Wichita diocese. Two of my fellow faculty at the orientation were Judy Johnson and Betty Lies, who were associated with a group of laywomen who volunteered in various kinds of missionary projects, mostly in the U.S. and Latin America. If I remember correctly, it was called The Grail Association, and the two women were kind of like nuns who did not wear habits. They were every bit as enthusiastic about Vatican II as Dan, me, and our college graduates. The final team member was Father Jerry Beat, Barbara Beat's nephew, whom I had only met at the dialogue retreat. Jerry was also very enthusiastic about the changes in the church. He had been ordained one year earlier than me but was four years younger.

Both Dan and Jerry considered me some kind of expert on Teilhard de Chardin and his ideas on the evolution of consciousness, as well as Erich Fromm's theories on love and compassion. Both Betty and Judy were very experienced in educating families and minority populations on the church's position on poverty and social justice and the practical application of what they called the social gospel. Three small books that they and, it seemed, all the college students knew about were *The Prophet* by Kahlil Gibran, *The Velveteen Rabbit, and The Little Prince.* These books opened a whole new world for me, and I became a devotee and later found that most of the nuns and young priests at the Loyola's summer program were club members. I thought that the students that week did more to educate me than I did them.

On Friday, we had an ending farewell dinner and celebration. One student had a Tijuana Brass album that included the music for a Greek folk dance, and she taught all of us how to do the Greek dance to that music. It seemed like everyone involved with the missionary program was eager for me to let go of my super-serious self and enjoy life a little. That spirit and the Tijuana Brass album made the trip to Chicago with me.

I arrived in Chicago on Sunday afternoon, and my first shock was realizing as I was heading east on the freeway (expressway in Chicago), I was going to drive right into a humongous building. I drove through what I later learned was the main post office for the city. Following directions to the campus, I found the university and a nearly empty parking lot next to a building that was to be my home for the next six weeks. There I saw several priests and nuns near a sign-in table, and I joined them. They all looked to be as young or younger than me, and they were all quite friendly.

My workaholic drive forced me to volunteer to celebrate Mass at a local parish. After signing in, I drove to the parish near the west side of the city and checked in. It was a huge rectory, and the pastor—a monsignor, of course—was on his two-month summer vacation, as were two of the four assistants. The lead assistant, a fellow who had been ordained for about twelve years, showed me a seminary-like room and told me I could celebrate the 7:00 a.m. Mass the following week. I had thought that the St. Pat's rectory in Wichita was a cold place, but this Chicago rectory was arctic.

Monday morning, I endured, rather than celebrated, a High Mass, with six candles, and I chanted the proper responses as a poor woman in the choir loft cackled the English songs. It was an agonizing experience, and after fighting the crowded morning rush hour traffic getting to Loyola, I called the chief assistant at the parish and told him that I would stay the night and celebrate Mass the next morning and bow out of my volunteering at the parish because of the traffic. I was just beginning to realize that my workaholic drive was a pain in the ass.

The Chicago archdiocesan CCD director, Father Arthur Stone—"Just call me Art"—gave us a brief orientation. I thought he looked nearly as young as myself, and I was sure he had to be some kind of gifted brainiac to be director in so large a diocese, and I was correct. He confessed he had inherited a CCD program that, like Wichita, wasn't a program at all but a kind of bookstore and supply room for the parishes. Holding up a spiral bound booklet entitled "Parish Religious Education," he asked us all to purchase it for our class with him the first week.

The week's morning sessions would be taught by Monsignor Michael Collins, rector of Cardinal Mundelein Seminary. Oh my god, I thought, a rector and a monsignor, that did not bode well—both titles represented pains in the ass to me. But this guy was more like a young McNeill and even had a sense of humor. He had a Ph.D. in clinical psychology and was devoted to the humanistic psychology of Carl Rogers and Abraham Maslow. I had read a bit of Rogers, but not Maslow. At the Monsignor Collins's suggestion, I bought a copy of *Motivation and Personality*, by Maslow, and it opened a whole new world for me—especially his hierarchy of human needs. It seemed so simple that the bottom rung of the hierarchy, the survival need, was the basic need. As Maslow put it, "For the starving person, paradise is a place with food." After survival, a person needs safety to continue to survive, then love and belonging, then self-esteem. Through them all, we humans are motivated by the need for autonomy. Unfortunately, I thought, we can trade autonomy for survival, safety, belonging, and even believe that we can find self-esteem in the trade.

This concept made me realize that most of the world's population, including my own family, was motivated by the survival needs. And Dad had his seizures because he was failing to help our family survive. It made me wonder if people joined churches and other organizations in order to have a feeling of belonging. And self-esteem: what exactly was it?

I thought that I learned more that first week with Stone and Collins than I had in any year or even two years at St. Thomas, and then it was my reading rather than the lectures (other than those of Bruce Vawter). The only similarities with St. Thomas was that I was one of the few students who asked a question or three at every class. It was refreshing to have women in class—all but one of them from various orders of nuns.

I took walks with two or three Sisters of the Blessed Mother, aka BVMs, and they were open and humorous enough to tell me that their students said that the initials stood for Black Veiled Monsters. A German Jesuit, Horst Meiers, joined our walking groups, and two Chicago high school BVM teachers, Sister Nancy and Sister Marceline, became regular walking partners. Horst usually walked next to Marceline, aka Marcy, and me with Nancy. The three of them were way ahead, in theology and education than nearly everyone I knew back in Wichita, except Sister Mary Kevin, whom I had gotten to know a little. After a few days, we celebrated the Fourth of July by having a day at Monsignor Collin's Mundelein Seminary. The seminary was very impressive, and the Chicago priests at the institute derisively called it the Versailles of the West.

Our foursome was walking along the main road by a beautiful lake in the middle of the seminary grounds, and I spotted a rowboat near the bridge we were standing on. There was no one around, and the oars were sitting idle in the boat, so I suggested we take a boat ride. Marcy said, "What if it is against the rules?" I responded that we'd just dock the boat. "I'm sure they won't put us in jail." It was awkward for the full-habit clad women, but they laughingly climbed in the boat. I took the oars first and started singing, "Row, row, row your boat, gently down the stream." And they all joined me, and then we sang another and another. At one point, I yelled, "This is so much fun! It must be sinful." We all laughed so hard we nearly turned the boat over. It was a wonderful day. I was so stoked, and I couldn't ever remember being so happy.

The following Wednesday evening, several of us went over to Mundelein College, a women's college next door to Loyola to view their weekly art film. That week the film was *Zorba the Greek* with Anthony Quinn. The final scene grabbed me. The story was this: An Englishman had inherited a closed gold and silver mine in Greece. He hired a wild-eyed Greek, who knew mining, to help him open the mine, as many had told him it still contained valuable ore. They worked for months but did not find any valuable ore, so they closed down the operation. The last scene showed the Englishman and Zorba standing on the beach and looking forlornly at the mine. They looked at each other, and the Englishman said something like: "Zorba, I've never said this to a man before, but, Zorba, I love you!" Zorba responded, "I love you too, Englishman, and I think you need one thing to make you free." The other man said, "And what's that, Zorba?" Zorba kissed one of his fingers and pointed at the sky, "A touch of madness!" And the man from England looked questioningly at the Greek, "Zorba, teach me to dance." The camera, to the tune of the Greek folk dance, moved into the sky, showing Zorba and the Englishman, arm in arm, dancing on the beach. I thought to myself, "A touch of madness!" Is that what I need? And maybe, just maybe, that was Jesus's message for all of us.

A delightful priest from Canada walked back to the Loyola campus with me and exclaimed how much he liked the folk dance. I told him about my Tijuana Brass album and that I knew how to do the dance. "You find a phonograph, and I'll get the album, and I'll show you how to do the dance." The summer of 1966 was one of the hottest summers on record for Chicago, and our building was not air-conditioned, so some benevolent person had turned a large library room in the sub-ground floor into a makeshift pub, and many of us drank beer until we got sleepy enough to go to sleep in our ninety degree rooms. The Canadian found a record player, and I put on the album and played the Zorba song and began to dance. Canada joined me along with another young priest and then another until we made a circle. The dance got increasingly faster as it went along, and it ended with only me and Canada still standing. Another small group wanted to learn and after I finished another beer, I began a new class of dancers. This went on night after night, and my fellow students started calling me "Zorba!" "Hey, good morning, Zorba." "How are you today, Zorba?" and on and on. And I loved it! Even some of the nuns violated protocol and joined our dances at the pub.

The one laywoman in our class, Jan, invited a group of us to go out to a local pub one Saturday. I was the only one who had a car at the college, so seven of us piled into my car and headed a few miles to drink and dance. I drank enough beer to really let go and get into a rock-n-roll dance with Jan. We ended up dancing on a table with everyone else clapping for us. I'm sure I was inebriated enough to violate the law as I drove us all back to Loyola after midnight. Was it the beer, or was I really getting a touch of madness? Probably a combination of both, and I didn't get even a hint of guilt for my escapade!

One Sunday, I drove over to Notre Dame to visit Sister Mary Kevin from Wichita, who was in a summer master's program in theology and to see the Catholic university whose football team I had cheered ever since I was a kid. I offered to take Mary Kevin to dinner, and she accepted, but with the proviso that she also invite two other nuns from Wichita and that we dine at the Notre Dame cafeteria. The two nuns, both Sisters of St. Joseph, were also in the master's program. One was a solemn, older woman whose name I heard but promptly forgot, and the other was Sister Anne, who was equally quiet but whom I remembered because she had one of the most beautiful faces I had ever seen and radiated a sense of peace and confidence that was unforgettable. Mary Kevin and I did all the talking, and it seemed that their summer school was as up-to-date as ours at Loyola.

I guess the rule of not being alone with a male was not airtight, as Mary Kevin invited us to join her and attend a presentation by a priest who was a leader in the Catholic Pentecostal movement. The two St. Joseph Sisters declined to join us, so Mary Kevin and I said goodbye and headed for an auditorium that was filled with priests and nuns. I had not heard of the movement. Back in Edgemont I had heard of a Protestant Pentecostal church that was tabbed the holy rollers, because, during their services, some worshipers would be so carried away by the holy spirit (they claimed) that they would swoon, fall on the floor, and roll about. I thought it was all rather hokey but was curious about what it was doing in the Catholic church. A tall, skinny, and pious looking priest, who I guessed to be in his mid-fifties, was greeted with enthusiastic applause by those in the front of the large gathering. To me, he sounded like the few preachers I had seen on Sunday morning television. He explained that the holy spirit had blessed some Catholics with a special presence or vision or something. They claimed to have some kind of special faith and fervor that others did not have. There was a brief question-and-answer period that did not really answer any questions I had—and I was sure he would tell me that was because I wasn't filled with the spirit. Mary Kevin and I walked back to her convent at St. Mary's College, and I think she was credulous of the Pentecostal message, but not enough to want to be one of the group. I told her I'd see her back in Wichita.

Back in Chicago, Sister Nancy and I continued to take walks along Lake Michigan after nearly every noon and evening. I was getting quite fond of her and was very disappointed when she told me that she needed to stop taking the walks because, well, she was getting too close. This went on for a few days and then the following Wednesday after the art film, she dropped a note in my lap that said, "I miss you, Funny Face!" That really picked up my spirits, and the next day we went back to taking our walks.

Our group of four and a few others had our own farewell Mass on the last Friday of the six-week summer program. I was designated to celebrate the Mass in a small chapel in our building. We were all in good spirits but reluctant to say goodbye. I was already missing Sister Nancy; I knew she was going to begin her last retreat before taking final vows immediately following the Loyola summer school. As I was taking off my vestments in the sacristy, Nancy peeked around the doorway and whispered, "Bye, Funny Face. I love you!" That was the nickname she gave me early in the summer, and I was quite fond of it. After her simple remark, she vanished.

I threw off my remaining vestments as fast as I could, stumbled out the door, and dashed down the hall and out the door. I saw her sitting in the back of a car as it left the parking area. She had said, "I love you!" No one in the world had ever said that to me before. She loves me! And now she's driving away! Oh my God! I stood there in the doorway, feeling lost in a daze.

That Friday afternoon I stayed in that dazed condition and walked alone around the building and along the lake where the water was in a turmoil from a storm. My emotions were like the water—in a turmoil. I wanted to get away from Loyola, but I had to wait for one of the Wichita volunteers who needed a ride to Leavenworth, Kansas. Saturday was one of the most confusing and emotionally upsetting days of my life, rivaling only the day Dad died. Someone loved me! And I was sure that I loved her back—in a way I had never experienced before. It wasn't lust, and I really did not have any impure thoughts about having sex with her, so it was a simple realization that I had a primordial desire for someone special to love me.

Forty-Seven

A NEW ENTHUSIASM

───✧───

I dropped the volunteer off at her home in Leavenworth and asked for directions to the Catholic parish in Leavenworth. I knew that my classmate Jack McCoy was stationed there and hoped he was home. Unfortunately, he seemed very depressed, but he was glad that I stopped to see him and unloaded his grief on me. I knew, when we were in our last year at the seminary, that he was very hesitant about going through with his ordination. I encouraged him to keep the faith and go through with it. Then, if he didn't like it, he could quit.

I said, "Jack, I never told you how much I envied your many gifts—your athleticism, your singing voice, your ability to play the sax and guitar, your good looks and positive personality."

"Aw, shit, Hanley, I would have given all that away if I had your brains, man."

I told him that compliment blew me away because I didn't

think I was all that smart. So, I left Leavenworth with mixed feelings. Jack ended up leaving the priesthood later that year and moved to California to be with a younger brother. Soon after, he married a flight attendant he met on the plane ride there.

Back in Wichita, I learned on the first day back that I had been appointed the diocesan director of the Confraternity of Christian Doctrine, aka Religious Education for Public School Children and Adults. Monsignor McNeill told me that Bishop Byrne had asked if he thought I was too liberal for the job. He told me that he told Bishop Byrne he thought I was a very thoughtful priest and followed the Vatican Council more closely than any priest in the diocese. I thanked him for that and thought my new title only changed my need to check with McNeill before taking any new actions. Along with Sister Eugenia, our first chore was to move into our offices at the new Chancery building behind the cathedral. It was a beautiful, buff-brick, three-story building.

Sister Eugenia decided, or maybe it was decided for her, to quit working with me, and I was relieved. We hadn't really meshed, and I never found a way to work comfortably with her. I was sure she felt the same way. The Dullea family I had grown close to in Kingman moved back to Wichita, and their second oldest daughter, who was in college, was looking for a part-time job and came to work for me. Her first job was to type up my re-write of the Parish Religious Education Manual that I had borrowed from Chicago's Father Stone—with his permission, of course. It was simpler and more practical than the old CCD manual. I made Stone's manual even simpler, as the Wichita diocese was about 100 times smaller than Chicago's, and I sent a copy to every parish in the diocese and asked them to purchase extras if they needed them. I sold about 200.

I met the new addition to the Diocesan School Office, Father Leon McKenzie, a bright young priest who had just completed his master's in religious education at the Catholic University in Washington, D.C. His title was diocesan director of religious education for Catholic Schools. I continued muddying up the puddle by often calling myself the diocesan director of religious education for public school children and adults rather than diocesan CCD director—this latter, and more official title. No one ever corrected me, and my (false) ego felt better. At first, I hoped that McKenzie and I could jointly put on some workshops for religion teachers, but he did not seem to be interested at all. Bishop Byrne introduced him to the priests of the diocese just as he had for me a year earlier, but McKenzie's clergy conference was far superior to mine, as he truly added something new for our fellow priests. He wished to promote some ideas on the new catechisms and asked a nun from the Sisters of St. Joseph to conduct a demonstration in front of over 100 priests.

I was surprised when I saw Sister Anne, the one and only beautiful and quiet nun I had met at Notre Dame, confidently entering the room leading twenty-five first graders from the Cathedral Parish school. The six-year-olds boys and girls barely glanced at the over one hundred black-clad priests and climbed up on the folding chairs set out for them up front. Sister Anne led them through a twenty-minute lesson from the new Paulist Press' Come to the Father book. This teacher in front of me was a far different and delightful teacher than I ever had, and she held a class far more positive than the sour and simplistic question-and-answer text of the old Baltimore catechism. Sr. Anne was very much in command and came across as loving, articulate, and kind.

Immediately after school was over, I walked to the school and asked the principal if I could speak with Sister Anne. With his permission I went to her classroom. When I introduced myself, she said that she remembered me from our summer encounter. I didn't tell her that I thought she was terribly shy that evening but went straight to my reason for today's visit.

"Sister, I was there for your presentation to the priests this morning and was so impressed with how you were with the children. As you know, I am the diocesan CCD director, and I want to set up some one-day religious education workshops for parishes around the diocese. I need help with them. Would you have any interest in helping with these workshops? You have a very special way about you that religion teachers really need. Teachers of the old catechism only needed to know how to read and ask questions. Now we ask them to be the presence of a loving Christ and not the scolding old grump like I had when I was in the first grade. What do you say?"

I gave her my phone number. She called back the next day and told me that she had received permission. We met that afternoon, and I told her that I would set up six-hour Saturday workshops for CCD teachers in and around the diocese and perhaps she could be a guest speaker at my religious education class at Sacred Heart College on Tuesday evenings. Sister Anne said she couldn't drive, and I told her I would gladly be her taxi driver.

She was far more confident and at home with herself than Sister Eugenia had been but seemed reluctant to talk about herself and her personal history. To say she shied away from idle talk was an understatement, but somehow, her radiant personality was appealing, and I was comfortable with her in a way that I had never been with Eugenia.

I set up two Saturday workshops, one before Thanksgiving and another between Thanksgiving and Christmas. The first one was at All Saints parish in Wichita, where we had the orientation for Dan Orth's summer program. Monsignor Fisher, pastor of All Saints, was always supportive of any program that helped his parishioners understand and give more support to the ideas of Vatican II. He had assembled a group of about forty people—all but two were women, and most were CCD teachers. We started off with what was going to become our theme-song: *Getting to Know You* from the Rogers and Hammerstein musical. Then I told the story about how the German-Jewish philosopher, Martin Buber, had come up with his I and Thou theory of human connections. I told it like this:

> As a young college professor, Dr. Buber was asked to be a counselor for students. One day, a young man came into Buber's office. He was very depressed, and the young professor talked with him for about an hour, and the fellow left. A few hours later, a friend of that student rushed into Buber's office and said the guy had hung himself. Buber was devastated and thought about that hour with the young man for days, trying to figure out what he might have said or done to help the fellow. He thought he had been a good listener, had not been scolding or judgmental, nor asked too many questions, and so he decided he had been an adequate counselor. But he kept thinking about the boy and what he should have done differently. Finally, he realized he had stayed in a professor-counselor mode and left the student in a counselee mode. He thought he had been way too

impersonal. Buber said it was an "I-it" encounter, and it should have been an "I-Thou" moment. It should have been a Martin to Joe (or whatever his name was) moment and not a role-to-role meeting.

Then I asked them all to stand and make a circle and hold hands and just allow themselves to feel whatever they were feeling. One young woman said, "I really don't feel anything." I walked over near her and said, "Hmmm—you definitely are not dead." And I smiled and added, "You are feeling something different right now—different from what you were feeling before you said what you said. Is that right?" She smiled and said, "Um, ah, yes."

Then I asked every other one to take a step forward, starting with one woman standing closest to me.

They quickly made an inner circle. "Now make eye contact with him or her and do your best to see your new partner as a special 'thou' and not just any person who just happens to be standing in front of you. Now make silent contact with him or her." After a moment, I saw that all but one woman had a partner, and I stood in front of her. She was an older woman with a pleasant smile. After I felt like I had made some kind of contact with her, I said, "Now move to your right and make silent contact with the next person and then the next, and let us all make contact with every person in the other circle." When I got back to the person I started with, I said, "Okay, now tell your first partner how you feel and what you think of this exercise."

Then my pleasant partner said, "I feel much warmer than when we started. I like this, so thank you. I'm going to use it with my class of fifth graders next week."

Each week, I visited parishes to encourage the priests to have their catechism teachers attend our classes and workshops when they were available. I had made dates for five more workshops after Christmas. In late December, I visited a parish north of Wichita and talked with the pastor. He was in his fifties and initially quite friendly. When I started talking about the new religion texts and the Vatican Council, he frowned and asked me where I had gotten so many strange ideas. I told him about the Loyola program and as I started talking about several theologians like Carl Reiner, Bernard Cooke, Hans Kung and others, his frown deepened, and he seemed to be getting a bit agitated. I said, "Father, haven't you heard of these fellows?"

"Listen here, young man: I entered the seminary when I was fourteen years old, and I learned to follow only what the Church teaches. I have not had a personal thought since that time." He sat straighter and announced, "I let the Church do my thinking for me!" I got a chill down my spine as I realized he was saying what most of the priests of the diocese were probably thinking. "Now, until I hear that all these things you are saying are truly the teachings of our holy mother church, then I am not interested. So please peddle your papers elsewhere." I was going to tell him to read the Vatican II documents, but I was so angry I just got up and left without even saying goodbye. I just hoped that there were some priests open-minded enough to give me a chance. Sister Anne just smiled and shook her head after I told her about my meeting with the pastor.

I had missed my 1965 Christmas visit to the family in Denver, so after taking the early morning Mass at St. Patrick's, I headed to Denver to visit Mom, Patty, and the rest of the Hanley family. Jim and Marie had a spare bed in their basement, where I stayed for a few nights. We joined Marie, Jim, and their three kids and went to Jim, Kay, and their three for Christmas dinner. After Christmas, I took Mom and Patty to dinner a few times, and each time, I got the impression that Mom did it just to please me and not the other way around. She did seem to really enjoy shopping for a new hat. She always looked good in a hat, and although she rarely left their apartment, nothing picked up her spirits like a new hat.

Mom complained that Marie and Jim didn't visit very often. Neither one of them acted like they had ever learned a thing about the art of conversation. No matter what I brought up to talk about, I would only get a shrug or an "I don't know." Or "What do you mean?" or "How come you're interested in that?"

In February, Sister Anne had found out that the Paulist Press would be having a one-day workshop on the Come to the Father series. I told Dan Orth about it, and he asked if Anne and I would like to go with him to Excelsior Springs, Missouri, near Kansas City. We said we would, and Anne invited two of the nuns she lived with to go with us. We all fit comfortably into Dan's big Chrysler.

In the afternoon session, the presenter asked if there was anyone in the audience who used the Paulist Press texts in their religion class. No one raised their hand, so I put my hand up and pointed a finger down at Anne, who was sitting next to me. She looked daggers at me, but reluctantly stood up when she was asked to give a demonstration. She received an appreciative round of applause. The young presenter had invited a class of third graders from somewhere near the hotel, and they sat quietly on the stage as he interviewed Anne. Then, as she had done in front of the priests, she gently took command of the third graders in front of her and kept their attention on learning the meaning of the Gospel account of the Sermon on the Mount and the Beatitudes. The audience was mesmerized, and she was given a resounding round of applause. I was glad that she was still smiling as she returned to her seat next to me, and I gently took her hand and held it for a moment.

The Paulist Press guy stopped her before we left the auditorium so he could ask her a few more questions, and we told her that we would go on to the dining room and wait for her before ordering dinner.

After dinner, I asked Anne if she would take a walk with me on the hotel grounds. It was February, so we went to our rooms and got our black overcoats first. We were only a dozen yards from the building when I noticed she had her hands in her coat pockets. I put my left hand in her right pocket and held her hand. In a shocked tone, Anne said, "What are you doing?"

"Putting my hand in your pocket. Do you mind?"

I kept my hand with hers for the moment, and she finally responded, "Oh, I, uh, guess not."

We walked on and the path turned left and made a semi-circle back toward the hotel. I was starting to realize that my relationship with Anne was more than just a mere friendship. I was glad that Dan was paying for my hotel bill because I was saving every penny I could so that I would have enough to pay for my summer Loyola program.

In May, I went with Dan to Kansas City to meet with the two priests who were setting up their summer program, and Dan was hoping we could develop another summer volunteer program in

Wichita. The very knowledgeable woman who helped with the previous summer's program was there. When we got a chance to talk privately, she came over to me, gave me a hug, and said, "Don, it's so good to see you! You've changed so much since I saw you last summer. You know, you're like a rosebud that has opened into a beautifully blossoming rose!" She held out her hand and softly closed and made a fist, then slowly opened her hand as she gave me these wonderful words. I thanked her and gave her another hug. I used the rosebud opening often after that encounter.

The entire year would be a wonderful flower in my life. That flower wilted when I learned that an auxiliary bishop of Denver, David Maloney, was replacing Bishop Leo Byrne as bishop of Wichita. Byrne had been appointed archbishop of St. Paul, Minnesota, and I visited him before he left and congratulated him. He looked very happy. "You know Don, I always hoped to become archbishop of St. Louis, but I just learned that the St. Paul diocese is larger. It is quite an honor." I told him I would miss him and that was not a lie. Although he was too conservative for me, he was moderate compared to Maloney, whom I knew from my seminary days.

That 1966-67 school year was definitely a time for spiritual and emotional growth for me, and I was beginning to feel and enjoy it. I often wonder how my life would have changed if Bishop Byrne, a very orthodox fellow, would have stayed in Wichita and tolerated me instead of the ultra-orthodox Bishop Maloney, who put a damper on the spirits of all of us who wanted to keep open the windows and doors of the church as desired by Pope John XXIII and the Vatican Council.

Forty-Eight

GOING THROUGH MY THIRD ADOLESCENCE

—⊗⊗⊗—

I managed to put aside the thought of working with Bishop Maloney and jumped into the spirit of Loyola's summer program by taking Sister Anne and two Dominican nuns to Chicago with me. The two Dominicans wanted to stop in St. Louis because one of them had a sister who was a Sister of Charity in a hospital there. The three nuns were given rooms in the hospital convent, and I was given the room reserved for the archbishop of St. Louis and other dignitaries. It was like staying in a first-class hotel. Anne wanted to visit her aunt in St. Louis, and we all tagged along with her, with me behind the wheel. When we got to Chicago, I dropped Anne off at the bus station, where she would take the bus to Notre Dame. The Dominican Sisters were enrolled in a similar summer program at Mundelein College next door to Loyola.

Nancy had been sure that she would not come back at the end of last summer. Her close friend, Sister Marceline, "Marcy" Nieman, and I began taking walks after lunch and dinner. Marcy was older than me, but had a youthful spirit, and I enjoyed being with her. She wore plain women's clothes and sometimes even wore slacks instead of skirts. Most of the nuns the previous summer anticipated the changes ahead but thought that they wouldn't make any real difference—just different clothes. I had challenged that, and I was right. Marcy had grown very fond of Father Horst Meyer. He did not return to Loyola either, so she needed a summer companion.

Our first morning professor was a Dutch philosopher of human development, Dr. Bernard Boelen. What little I knew about child development came from my discussion group at St. Thomas, and I never really thought of adult development except Teilhard de Chardin's development of consciousness—which I liked very much. For me, Boelen's most important theory was that there are three adolescent periods and not just the one usually thought of—the teen years. The first adolescence is from infancy into childhood, which begins around age two and ends around six. I liked the thought that the beginning and ending years were the believable open dates rather than questionable fixed ones. The second adolescence from childhood to adulthood arrived around thirteen to around twenty-five. I especially liked the idea that we should consider adolescence to last into the twenties and not expect everyone over eighteen to be adults— before they were able. During this class, I finally gave a lot of thought to the fact that I paid the family grocery bill when I was only sixteen, bought a house when I was eighteen, and built a house when I was twenty-one. No wonder I didn't relate well to my peers when I thought I was an adult and thus above them. In reality, I didn't know how to relate to them. I was an old man at sixteen, long before I should have been. I'd sometimes say things like, "All these young people need to settle down and do what's right and responsible."

Dr. Boelen, in his delightful Dutch accent, went to what was, for me, the welcome idea of the third adolescence that should happen, but often doesn't, between forty and fifty. It sometimes happened as early as thirty-five—ah, that could include me, I hoped. This third personal growth movement was from adulthood to maturity. I, only half-jokingly, told Marcy that I had gone through my second adolescence last summer and that now I was really beginning my third adolescence.

One of Boelen's examples:

So here you are, a comfortable thirty-something fellow who owns a hardware store, and every morning you happily put out a display of hammers, rakes, and hoes and stuff. Then, one day, you say to yourself, "What is this? Am I going to spend the rest of my life selling hammers and nails and stuff?" Then you say, "What is the real meaning of life?" And so, you begin your journey into maturity. Then you meet someone who says things like "How old are you?" "What do you do for a living?" "Where do you live?" And so on. You know they are still only an adult. Once you are comfortable in the mature stage of life, you will not ask such questions, you will only say, "Ah, it is good to know you!" As Martin Buber says, you only see the thou, not an "it" or object.

I put myself, not very solidly, right in the middle of the transition from adult to maturity. Marcy, our cohorts, and I spent hours discussing these ideas. I wondered where most of us priests and nuns fit on his spectrum of adult to maturity? How could we be mature if we had turned over our wills with a vow of obedience? Although we diocesan priests didn't formally take a vow of obedience, we were expected to be obedient to the will of our bishop. From what I had heard from Denver, Bishop Maloney was stuck in the lower rank of adulthood on the spectrum and was only interested in following all the church's rules, laws, and teachings in very minute detail. That meant, as far as I could tell, that all of us, clergy and laity and everyone else, needed to just shut up and do as we were told. That could not be maturity, I was sure.

That summer I still taught the Zorba folk dance, but not as much as the first summer. I chose the theory and practice of Maria Montessori as my first elective course at Loyola. It was taught by a delightful Mundelein College BVM nun, professor, and part-time preschool teacher. We visited her preschool and kindergarten with no desks and many educational and experiential tools. I thought the method should extend throughout all elementary and high schools. She told us that some schools went up to the sixth grade.

Marcy missed Horst Meyer more than I missed Nancy. So, we spent a lot of time together. She liked to talk about nearly everything I was interested in, especially education, psychology, theology, scripture, and human relationships. Marcy was as talkative as Anne was quiet. She asked me if I would like to visit a Carmelite convent in Moline, Illinois. Her widowed mother was a nun there, and she wanted to visit her, but Marcy didn't have a car. The Carmelite convent was a closed convent for women, just as the Trappist's monasteries were for men. I didn't tell Marcy that I had never heard of such a thing.

One Sunday, we left Chicago early and drove west across Illinois and arrived in Moline around 10:00 a.m. I could only meet Marcy's mother through a grilled window, as no men were allowed in the convent proper. Her mother was in the full Carmelite Sister's habit, so I could see only her pleasant and smiling face that looked like an older Marcy when she was still in her full BVM habit. I brought a book with me and read and walked around the parking area a few times, enjoying the quiet. At noon, Marcy joined me, and we went to a restaurant for lunch. She apologized for the quick visit. Because I was a priest, she thought that I could have a longer visit. I told her I didn't mind, and that was true because I was glad to learn a little more about my church and religion. Like with the Trappists, I could admire the dedication and spirituality of the people but couldn't image being one of them. On the way back to Chicago, I realized that we'd miss Sunday Mass, and that was the first time in my life I would miss a Sunday Mass without being sick! And I didn't feel even a little guilty—and that felt oh so freeing! I enjoyed the conversations with Marcy about her life as a nun and learning about how her mother became a cloistered nun after her father died.

The following Sunday, I made a trip to visit Sister Anne at St. Mary's College next to Notre Dame. I had asked her to see if she could find bicycles for the two of us so we could ride around Notre Dame's beautiful campus. As I drove up to the parking area near where Anne was staying, I saw her parking one bicycle and talking with another woman with a bike. Out of orneriness, I honked my horn and startled both of them. Anne turned and frowned and when she saw that it was me, she shook her finger at me and laughed. She introduced me to her friend, Sister Jeanne. The pretty red-head held out her hand, and I shook it. Anne said, "I need to change my clothes. I'll only be a minute." She was wearing what she called a modified habit—a dark blue below-the-knees-skirt, a white blouse buttoned up to the neck, a blue jacket, and a blue pill-box type hat and veil. She had started dressing like that during the second semester of the school year.

Anne re-joined us wearing blue slacks, a white, short-sleeved blouse, and tennis shoes. She looked me over and focused on my hands, then said, "Good, you don't have a camera with you, so you can't take a picture of me dressed like this."

I wondered what her elderly sister friend, whom I had met the previous summer, thought of her attire, but I didn't want to spoil her mood so kept that question to myself. We climbed on our bikes and headed across the highway to Notre Dame. It was even more beautiful than the small part I had seen earlier, and we had a delightful afternoon. At one point, we stopped on a small knoll, got off the bikes, and looked around at the buildings. There was a large expanse of recently mowed grass on one side of the knoll, and I laid down on the grass and looked up at Anne and yelled, "I've wanted to do this for years!" I put my arms down at my side and rolled down the hill. Anne was laughing as she ran after me.

On my way back to Chicago that evening, I heard on the radio about the race riots there and around the country and the war that was just beginning in the Near East. I felt a little guilty about having so much fun while there was so much turmoil around the world and very close to us at Loyola. The next morning, I saw a *Chicago Tribune* with a front-page article and map of Israel surrounded by Syria, Jordan, Lebanon, Saudi Arabia, and Egypt. Listed on the map, under the names of each country, was the number of troops and airplanes in each country. *Wow,* I thought, *The Muslim countries have over ten times as many soldiers and airplanes as Israel—they'll be destroyed in a matter of days.* Of course, the opposite happened. The Israeli air force destroyed the air forces of all the surrounding countries within a week in what would be known as the Six-Day War of 1967. Israel captured several miles of land around them and added about a fourth more to the size of their country. I was glad that I was not involved with it and only slightly involved in the unrest in the U.S. over the Vietnam war and civil rights. I was anti-war and applauded the peaceful protests and Martin Luther King Jr., and thought I should be doing more, but I didn't have any idea what that could be. As far as I could tell, my fellow summer school students didn't have any idea either. After one bunch of riots, I drove through the Chicago ghetto in my air-conditioned car and felt ashamed of myself.

On the Saturday after the last Friday of the summer program, I picked up the two nuns at Mundelein, and we stopped at the bus station to pick up Anne. We didn't stop in St. Louis on our way back to Wichita, but we spent a delightful time singing all the songs we knew.

The summer was a delightful and flower-decked experience despite the turmoil in the world, and that prepared me for the struggle to come with Bishop Maloney.

Looking back, I don't think I realized how deep the fissure was getting between my priestly role and my real life as a human being—especially as a male human being. I felt alive when I was at Loyola and when I was teaching, and especially when I was with Anne. Too often, I felt as though I was just going through the motions when I was performing the duties of my priesthood. I enjoyed the groups I was working with, but—and the *but* was getting larger all the time—I continually wondered and worried about whether I was growing in my spiritual life or was I veering off course. Or maybe just becoming more mature, as Bernard Boelen would say.

Forty-Nine

DISCOVERING MORE ABOUT LOVE

———⊷⊶———

I had talked with my friend Dan about needing a place to hold weekend encounters for teens and adults. The diocese did not have a retreat house, and even it if had, it would probably be too expensive for what I had in mind. Over the summer, Dan had moved his residence to Mt. Vernon, his mission parish. Many years earlier, Mt. Vernon had a small parochial school with three rooms and a kitchen. Dan found thirty-six army cots and enough folding chairs and tables so that we could accommodate thirty or more folks over a weekend.

I began to form a faculty for my first weekend. Dan was a superb organizer but declined being any kind of presenter. Jerry Beat was five years younger than me and very good with youth of both genders. He was an enthusiastic promoter of the new liturgy, and I asked him to help me find a lay couple and a nun to help us with our first weekend, which featured Catholic Youth

Organization girls. He drafted a delightful young couple from his home parish, All Saints, and Sister Julietta, a nun of the Sisters of the Sorrowful Mother from St. Francis Hospital.

Julietta wore the full habit and had a smile that would light up any room. Delightfully, she was not sorrowful and glad to get out of the convent. Plus, she played the guitar. I had the role of master of ceremonies and one of the speakers. Dan lined up some of his parishioners to prepare the meals. He also collected the money we needed for the weekend. We called the weekend a Youth Encounter, after Oklahoma's. It went wonderfully well, but I had a number eight headache throughout the entire weekend. I guessed it was because I was afraid that Bishop Maloney would come down on me like a ton of bricks, but I planned to claim I had the authority because I was in charge of religious education for public school children and adults. My worry was unfounded, and all the twenty-nine high schoolers, a mixture of Catholic and public school students, had a great time—and, I hoped, became better humans.

We had a similar weekend for boys a month later with the same team and the addition of Father Jack Tesch. Jack had only been ordained two years and was Father Bob Blanpied's assistant at St. Thomas Aquinas Parish in Wichita. He had a delightful personality like Sister Julietta and fit right in with us.

This weekend went as well as the one for girls, and we began planning for two more for adult men and women after the Christmas holiday.

Dan had a birthday that fall and invited several people—Jerry, Sister Anne, and her friend from the cathedral, Sister Lucille, and a few others. I had been called into Bishop Maloney's office that day because he had heard that I had a problem with the sacred doctrine that Jesus was the one and only son of God. I tried to tell him that I was not denying the doctrine but emphasizing that He had said that we, too, were sons of God. He tried to pound into my "immature little head" that I needed to be careful. So, I arrived early for Dan's party in a foul mood. While he was preparing a lavish meal featuring roast goose, I began drinking Scotch before anyone else arrived. Before everyone sat down to dinner, I was already two sheets to the wind. I was completely soused by the time we finished dinner and Dan opened his presents. I started staggering around the room and, in a sing-songy fashion, teased all the guests with remarks like, "Dan's goose is cooked!"

I was told that I kept going and saying and doing things that were completely inappropriate and somewhat humorous, like, "Lucille is wearing a string of pearls." And I would touch them and count them out loud and then say, "She has nineteen pearls, and they represent nineteen years. Yep, Sister Lucille is nineteen years old, Dan, jess like you." And then I picked on Anne and said, "And here's Anne, and she can't sing a lick, Dan, she can't carry a tune in a bushel basket, so she didn't sing Happy Birthday. Her lips were moving, but she didn't really make a sound. I know." And on and on until I rushed to the door and stumbled out to the lawn. I made it about fifty feet from the house when I fell down on my knees and puked my guts out. Someone held my head so my face wouldn't fall down into my own puke. Eventually I realized it was Anne who was holding my head, and I was so embarrassed and mumbled, "Tanka you, oh, oh, my God." It was the first time in my life I had ever been totally drunk.

I woke up the next morning fully clothed and on a single bed in Dan's tiny guest room. Over coffee, Dan told me that he and Anne had dragged me into the house, poured me into bed, and took my car keys and hid them. It was 9:00 a.m., and I said, "Oh, my God, I got a meeting with the team for the adult encounter in January, and it's at St. Thomas Parish—clear across town. I better get my rear into gear."

Dan gave me a handful of aspirin, and I took four and put four in my pocket. I had asked Anne and Jerry to be part of the team. I really didn't care what Jerry thought. He'd seen many drunken priests, but I hated to face Anne. I managed to make it through the meeting with some kind of semi-leadership. At the break, I apologized to Anne and thanked her for helping me out the night before. Her response surprised me. "Well, I was kind of glad to see that you were really human." Really human? What in the world was she talking about?

"Now you know that I'm a sad specimen of a human. Thank you," I said.

We mapped out our plans for the adult encounter, and I made assignments for all the presentations before we adjourned. Anne's comments took away a lot of my embarrassment, though I still thought she was off base about my being human. Hell, I was that, but wondered if I was still smart and spiritual enough to be leading people in our church? And I wondered if Maloney ever got drunk—and, even if he never did, I didn't think he was smart or spiritual enough to be a bishop.

I had a very busy fall. Besides the parish CYO, CCD, and adult discussion groups, I was teaching two classes at Sacred Heart College. One college class was a repeat of two classes I had taught the year before for religion teachers, and the other was a required religion class for the regular college freshmen and sophomores. The teachers' class went well because the students were older and more interested, but the required class was a disaster from my viewpoint. Most of the young folks, especially those who had gone to Catholic schools, were completely bored. They had heard it all before—or so they thought. Anyway, I was glad it was over and told the dean that I didn't want to teach it again. For the first time, I taught a morning teacher-training at the cathedral school building. An elderly man, probably in his seventies, asked if he could attend the class and, of course, I said yes. He left an impression on me because of something he said after one class session, where I had criticized how solemn and pontifical the old Catholic High Masses were.

He said, "You may be correct, young Father, but, as a kid in a small country parish before movies and television, I remember looking forward to the drama and pageantry of those Masses. They were quite a show and brightened up our lives, believe me."

I thanked him and mentioned that I had sang in a choir for a Wichita song and dance production called, *The Drama of the Mass*.

I found time to make a few parish visits to check with different pastors about how the diocesan office could help them and encourage them to send their CCD teachers to our various workshops. One visit in particular helped me to, again, realize the hierarchal structure of the church and how much it hampered our work of spreading the message of Jesus. At a small parish about a hundred miles northeast of Wichita, I had called to make an appointment to meet with the young Irish pastor. I arrived early and, as I drove up, I noticed he was mowing the lawn between the church and the rectory. I guess he noticed my arrival because when I went to the front door of the rectory, I had to wait a while for him to come to the door. When he did, he had on his black cassock and black pants rather than the work shirt and jeans he was wearing when I drove up. He was being a proper priest for the bishop's delegate from the chancery office. I thought it was sad that he would think I might report him in ordinary attire. He grew up in Ireland, and I recalled Monsignor Cody saying that Americans didn't know how to properly treat a priest. Cody's proper was bullshit as far as I was concerned because it meant that the laity should treat a priest as some kind of royalty.

Our February weekend for adults went very well. Anne, Sister Julietta, Jerry Beat, Dan, Tom and Doris Pirotte, and I were becoming a wonderful team. We planned three more weekends before the end of the school year. A very progressive young attorney and his wife attended our weekend that I called A Theology of Hope and were delightful participants. Afterwards, they invited me to their home for dinner. They had two young children—a boy and a girl. At dinner, I embarrassed myself by trying to eat mini cocktail shrimp for the first time.

The young wife, seeing my struggle with the shrimp, asked, "Father, how do you like the shrimp?" She was grinning from ear to ear.

I responded, "They're a bit crunchy."

They both chuckled and she said, "Father, you're supposed to take the thin outer shell off before you eat them."

I don't remember how I responded, but I was very embarrassed, and we had, what was for them, a very endearing discussion about my low-class upbringing. That was the first time that I realized that I, as a priest, was supposed to be more of an upper class kind of person. My Aunt Agnes was apparently in the right when she corrected our table manners, and I should have listened better. My stubborn inner self really didn't care.

I had managed to steer clear of Bishop Maloney during the year, except for one event. I was told I needed to be one participant in a pontifical High Mass at the cathedral. The ceremony demanded the effort of about seven priests. My duty was to carry around his ornamental miter (his hat) and have it ready when he needed it. Another young priest carried his symbolic shepherd's crook, called a crozier. The two of us walked around, stood around, and knelt side-by-side. At one point, the two of us stood beside the altar steps, and the bishop walked over to us. I held up his hat, and another priest took it from me and put it on Maloney's head. Then he reached out for the crozier, and my fellow server was slow in giving it to him. When he finally handed it to him, the bishop impatiently took it and with his ringed finger hit my companion in the teeth, then turned around. My fellow server was bleeding a little from the mouth and found a handkerchief in his pocket. I wanted to smack Maloney in the mouth myself, but of course I didn't. It definitely lowered my opinion of him even more than before. He was a sorry excuse for an ambassador of Christ, the humble Jesus of Nazareth, that all of us priests were supposed to be.

I was very pleased with my work for the year and ready for a break in Chicago, getting re-charged with the gang at Loyola. Looking at that year of 1967-68, I was definitely moving away from being part of the traditional clerical world. Flowers of a different kind, I suppose.

Fifty

BEING ORDAINED A FREE THINKER

—❧—

Once again, I picked up Anne and our two Dominican friends and headed for Chicago. We stopped in St. Louis, and Anne and I went out to dinner. This time, I dropped the two nuns at Mundelein College and went on to South Bend to drop off Anne at St. Mary's College. Anne had become a powerful magnet in my life, and I wanted to spend as much time with her as I could. In my life there had been no one with whom I wanted to spend that much time with—except maybe my childhood dog, Pal. It wasn't that she wanted to talk with me very much, but that she radiated a warmth and caring that I had never known before.

At Loyola, I noticed that nearly all the nuns were wearing modest women's clothes and that several nuns and priests had dropped out of the Summer Institute. Bernard Boelen was back and continued to lecture on his philosophy of human development. I liked him very much, and he fit well in with the thinking of

Rogers, Maslow, and Teilhard de Chardin. A young Chicago Jesuit was doing a doctoral dissertation on encounter groups and had an elective course that was itself an encounter group. I signed up for it and joined Sister Marcy, Sister Alice, and three priests in one of two groups. We were told to do our best to share with one another what we were thinking and feeling without censoring ourselves. I screwed myself the second two-hour session by sharing some thoughts that I had often had when entering a new class or group but had never shared with anyone.

"I've often been too judgmental when I meet new people. For example, at our first meeting, I thought that I was taller than you, Steve, and maybe a little smarter than you, Alice; and maybe a better speaker than you, Ted; a better singer than you, Marcy, and dumb stuff like that." Even my calling it dumb stuff didn't help. I must have said it in a way that was very offensive and far different than I had intended. It ruined the group for me and probably for everyone else.

All five of them suddenly looked at me like I was from Mars or had just come down with leprosy or something. They didn't seem to know how to respond to me and just ignored me and began to talk among themselves. The Jesuit visited our group before the session was over, and no one said a word about my sharing. Later Marcy told me that I had been completely stupid and should never have shared that kind of stuff. She didn't want to take a walk with me after dinner that evening. I was glad that she was willing to talk to me the next day, but I was ashamed of myself for the rest of the summer session.

I found some solace when I visited Anne at Notre Dame the following Sunday. I told her about my idiocy in the group. She didn't judge me, but said something like, "I think you did your best at the time. You try to be honest all the time, and that is something I admire about you." We went out to dinner and talked until quite late.

As I drove back to Chicago, I heard on the news that Pope Paul VI had issued an encyclical, *Humanae Vitae: Of Human Life*, stating that all Catholics are forbidden to practice artificial birth control, and it was a mortal sin to do so. I knew that over 50 percent of married Catholic couples in the U.S. practiced birth control and did not consider it a sin. I thought of one couple in St. Patrick's parish that I had advised to continue to do so because they already had six children, and the wife and mother had to remain in bed 24/7 for the last six months of her last three pregnancies due to a pre-existing condition. And I thought of my brothers, Glen and Bill, who I was sure had been given poor advice by priests. Fifty years later, over 90 percent of Catholics of child-bearing age practice some form of birth control, and I think that is progress.

That summer I had been assigned to room off campus in an apartment near the university with a roommate. He was a priest from Canada and had been giving retreats around the U.S. and Canada for priests, nuns, and seminarians. We had many conversations about the church's teachings about women and sexuality. He told me about a high school seminary where he conducted a retreat: one resident priest was assigned to walk on a catwalk above the showers while the boys were bathing to make sure they did not commit the sin of masturbation. So, adding to this stupidity was the ban on birth control. I was sure that the church was continuing its war against human sexuality. My roommate was asleep when I got home that night, and he awoke early.

I immediately said, "Dick, as I was coming back from Notre Dame last night, I heard on the radio that Pope Paul had just issued an encyclical forbidding birth control."

He yelled, "That son of a bitch!" My sentiments exactly.

The following Saturday evening, I was invited to join a Chicago priest and classmate to visit a prominent Catholic couple, Pat and Patty Crowley, who had been on the papal commission studying birth control. I believe they were the only lay couple who had been invited, and I felt honored to be in their home and in their company. They told us that there were about thirty members on the commission, and all but three were in favor of changing the church's teachings on the subject. The majority believed God had given us our minds to use for the benefit of all and that we must not join the true believers who contended that if God wanted us to fly, He would have given us wings. The Crowleys had financed their trips to Rome for several months and felt that they, and the majority of Catholics, were betrayed. As far as I could tell, the students in our program at Loyola were liberals, and a pall descended over the university program for the rest of the summer session.

I got back to Wichita in time to find a letter from Bishop Maloney that had to be read at all the Masses the following Sunday. Maloney had excerpted the most severe portions of the pope's encyclical and inserted them into his letter. I was assigned the 11:00 a.m. Mass and began my sermon. "I am about to do what I believe is the most difficult thing I have been ordered to do since I was ordained and that is to read the following letter from our Bishop, David Maloney." I then read the letter in a deliberate monotone. When I finished, I said, "Now, let us pray for those who have the courage to follow their own conscience." I saw Monsignor Cody standing in the back of the church, and I didn't care. The next morning, the bishop's secretary called me to tell me that Maloney wanted to see me. At 10:00 a.m., I went into his office, and he scolded me for my remarks on Sunday. I sat there and did not say a word until he was finished. Then said, "Is that all, Bishop?" He glared at me, and I got up and left.

In August, Bishop Maloney invited a former rector of St. Thomas Seminary to give us poor ignorant boobs a clear understanding of the church's teachings on birth control in general, and Humanae Vitae in particular. I was sure that the rector was not an outstanding church moral theologian, but I knew he was a very conservative thinker and a severe disciplinarian. The clergy conference was one that all the priests of the diocese must attend. Dan invited me and eight other liberals and moderates among us to join him and discuss how we would express our dissent to the teachings. All of us said that we would stand up and express our thoughts. On the day of the gathering, I joined my fellow priests in the chancery's conference room. Our speaker gave an absolutistic exhortation to all of us that indicated that if we did not adhere to the exact teaching expressed by our divinely appointed vicar of Christ on Earth, Pope Paul VI, we would burn in hell for all eternity. He then said that he was open for questions if there were any.

There was total silence for a few minutes, and I looked around. Just like the seminary, no one stood, raised a hand, or said a word. Where were all the brave souls that met at Dan's place? So, shaking a little, I stood up. The rector nodded for me to speak, and I said, "Thank you for coming to speak to us, Father. I believe that Pope Paul is a good and holy man, but the world is already over-crowded, and people are starving and need our enlightened help. The church has changed in many ways over the centuries, and now I understand that the vast majority of the members of the pope's commission on the subject of birth control, after years of study and deliberation, recommended a change in the church's teachings. So please tell us why the Holy Father set up the commission if he was going to ignore them?"

Father Keneally gave what I thought was a lame answer. "The pope is not obliged to listen to anyone except the voice of the Holy Spirit. The church is not a democracy, and the voice of the Holy Father is the voice of almighty God." I was sure that God did not whisper any such thing in anyone's ear.

Father McKenzie, my counterpart for parochial schools, stood and said, "I understand that bishops of Holland, Belgium, and several other countries have decided not to translate Humanae Vitae into their own languages. Are we to understand, then, that the sinfulness of practicing birth control is a matter of geography?" There was a smattering of muffled laughter among the crowd, and I was glad to hear that there was at least one more priest who was willing to say something. McKenzie definitely rose in my estimation. The presenter gave some kind of superficial answer that I don't recall, and I wondered if Maloney would call McKenzie into his office in the morning. Our speaker received tepid applause at the end of the conference.

That fall, I started two other projects. One was a film depicting the sacraments in a relationship between ourselves and God. The second project was eight ongoing teacher-training classes in Wichita that would be taught by eight different nuns who were excellent teachers—one for each of the eight grades.

I had never forgotten the awful slide show from St. John's that pictured divine grace as residing in a golden tank in the sky and priests manning the spigots on the ground, so I wanted to make a short film depicting the sacraments as enhancing our relationship with God, somewhat like the relationship between a man and woman in love and in marriage. I knew that the oldest daughter of the Miller family had married a fellow who wanted to do some kind of film using an eight-millimeter camera, and I asked him to do the filming. Then I asked an attractive young couple I had gotten to know in Kingman if they would be the couple for me. All three were delighted to participate. So, we filmed the couple meeting, looking into one another's eyes, holding hands, and exchanging rings signifying baptism. We then pictured myself baptizing an infant. Then we had the couple really get into a kiss and act like they were getting ready for bed signifying communion or the Eucharist, followed by a celebration of Mass and people receiving communion. The couple then argued, turned away from one another, made up, came back together, and kissed, signifying the sacrament of penance. Then a scene of a person going to confession. The best I could do for confirmation was to depict the couple, who were farmers, doing daily chores—him going into the fields on a tractor and her doing housework. The women who previewed the first showing of the film groaned with this one. And the sacrament of marriage was just a wedding. The final scene was an elderly person receiving the sacrament of the sick, or extreme unction. It took three months to fit it all in, and I was proud of it and showed it to a few groups with some interest, but it was not as educational as I had hoped. Most viewers seemed to think it was too much of a stretch to see the sacraments in this way.

The weekly teacher-training was more successful than I thought it would be. Ten parishes in and around Wichita sent their CCD teachers to each of the eight classes. Monday evening, we would meet, and I would lead the discussion. At the end of our two-hour session, we would conclude with a Mass. After the third week, one of the nuns suggested that I should just simply put on a stole and celebrate Mass at the dining room table. After all, she explained, the Mass is a reenactment of Jesus's last supper. I liked the idea and asked each one if they thought it would be a good idea and said that we'd have to keep it to ourselves. All eight agreed that it was a fine idea and said they would keep silent about it.

On the Tuesday after our first Monday ending our session and celebrating Mass at the table, I got a call from my friend, Father Gene Gerber, the diocesan vice-chancellor, telling me that I was to be in Bishop Maloney's office at 10:00 a.m. I asked him why, and he said that he didn't know. I thought it might have to do with our home Mass, but dismissed it, as all the nuns agreed to keep it to themselves, so I wasn't sure what Maloney had in mind.

I didn't have to wait long as I was ushered into the bishop's office and sat down in front of his large desk. With a frown and a firm voice, Maloney began, "Father Hanley, I understand that you said Mass last evening without having all the proper and required vestments. Is that correct?"

I hesitated a moment as I pictured my eight catechists, trying to identify the snitch. Sister Ellen was the sternest and least humane of the group, so I guessed it to be her. "Yes, I used only the stole as I would for hearing confessions, performing a baptism, or extreme unction."

"And you do know that, when we celebrate Mass, more than the stole is required, do you not?"

"Yes, ordinarily, that is true, but I believed for our small group of teachers, it could be quite appropriate."

Maloney began to shake a little, and his face reddened. He raised his voice and nearly yelled, "Do you think, Father Hanley, that you know more than the Sacred Congregation of Rites in Rome?" He was shaking even more and looking like I had threatened him.

I knew what he wanted me to say, but I straightened up in my chair, pulled my shoulders back, held my head up, and as solemnly as I could, said, "For a small group of nuns in Wichita, Kansas, bishop? Yes, I do."

He shook even more and turned crimson. I was afraid he was going to have a heart attack. He shouted, "Father Hanley, YOU ARE A FREE THINKER! GET OUT OF MY OFFICE NOW!"

I was shaken to the core. Even with everything I had been through, I had never been scolded like that by anyone. You'd think I had just attacked the pope with a knife or something. With as much dignity as I could muster, I got up from the chair and left the office, walked to the other end of the chancery building to my CCD office, and closed the door to think. It would have been nice to talk to Anne, but she was teaching her first graders, so I called Dan, and I was sure he felt my pain as he had a run-in with Maloney and had been transferred to a small, isolated parish in eastern Kansas. We commiserated a bit, and he invited me to come out to his place and get drunk with him. It was 180 miles away, and I declined.

I sat there and thought about whose shoulder I could cry on and thought of Bob Blanpied. He had asked Bishop Byrne to assign him to a parish away from the cathedral, as he just didn't like it there. Byrne had moved him to St. Thomas Parish in an upscale area in east Wichita. I knew he was having his own troubles with Bishop Maloney because his assistant pastor, Jack Tesch, had given a sermon denouncing Humanae Vitae and had refused to comply with Maloney's demand that he retract what he had said at all the Sunday Masses. Jack refused and instead transferred to the Pueblo, Colorado, diocese that had a more tolerant bishop. Bob invited me to join him for dinner. I drank a little too much but did not get drunk. At least I didn't think so because I managed to drive back to St. Patrick's after dinner. Bob had been ordered by the bishop to tell his parishioners that his assistant had been wrong and that we must, as faithful Catholics, follow the pope's teachings on birth control. Bob was still mulling over whether he would comply. Jack had been ordained only two years, but Bob had been ordained for twenty years, so he felt he had more to lose. He helped me a great deal by saying that I should consider Maloney condemning me as a free thinker a compliment.

As I drove home to St. Patrick's that evening, my spirts were picked up by Andy Williams singing "Born Free" on the radio.

Humanae Vitae was rocking the entire church and seemed to be dividing it between the true believers and the radical liberals. I guess I had to accept what I had learned months earlier: that I was considered a radical liberal by many of the older priests and some in the middle and younger ones.

I didn't realize then the encounter with Maloney would be a step toward the next big experience in my life and that it would come from a far more authentic and meaningful source—my star teacher, Anne. It took me a few months to realize that I was at a crossroads in my life as a priest. Jesus, I was certain, did not line up his followers and teach them hundreds of dogmas and moral precepts and then demand that they blindly follow them. To follow, I am convinced, means that we must learn to love ourselves and others even if it means our death—as He did. Bishop Maloney had truly given me a gift with his condemnation. I began to really enjoy being a free thinker.

Fifty-One

SOMEBODY LOVES ME!

—⁓—

In the summer of 1968, it seemed everywhere in the world there was uproar. In the U.S., demonstrations against the Vietnam War and race riots erupted across the country. I had left the mostly peaceful medium-sized city of Wichita and arrived in huge, tumultuous Chicago. I was possibly fortunate to be in a safe and comfortable area of the city on the North Shore. I say possibly fortunate because, as Martin Luther King Jr. said, "We need to comfort the afflicted, and afflict the comfortable," concerning both the war and racial injustice. I greatly admired Dan and Phillip Berrigan and wanted to be like them, but I didn't do anything to make that happen. My excuse to myself was that I was too busy but felt, down deep, that I really didn't have the courage.

At Loyola, we talked about it, and I was asked to celebrate the weekly evening Mass at the university chapel. I gave a sermon scolding myself and all my fellow students for not doing more to help. I immediately regretted the tone, if not the entire content of the sermon, as it seemed everyone avoided me afterwards. I was following a long tradition in the church—scolding but not offering any solace or recommendation of a better course of action.

The courses were enlightening, and I continued to learn. While talking with my increasingly close friend, Sister Marcy, I reflected that I wondered how many of my fellow priests were, what our professor Boelen called mature persons and had gone through third adolescence? And even whether or not she and I were becoming mature? After hours of discussion, we decided it was a continuum. She laughed when I told her I thought I had gone through the second adolescence my first summer here at Loyola. We agreed that everyone goes through different parts of ourselves at different times. I told her about my acting so adult around age twelve, working all through school, and buying a house at eighteen. I had gone through a lot responsibility-wise, but was slow in social ways, like dating and emotional friendships. She had ideas on both-and rather than either-or, which I liked a lot. One thing that I also really appreciated about her was her openness to dialogue about everything. She made my fourth summer far more meaningful than it could have been without her.

One of my most treasured experiences was celebrating the noon Mass for the Mundelein College's summer students. I learned how to have what we called a dialogue sermon, which was an open discussion of topics presented by the day's scripture readings. I definitely learned more than I taught.

A few times over the summer, I went over to Notre Dame to spend time with Anne, usually not returning to Chicago until around midnight. I felt very fortunate to have Anne as a source of warmth and friendship and Marcy for intellectual stimulation. I also thought that having a close relationship with Marcy kept me from falling too much in love with Anne, but I constantly mulled over whether or not I was in love with Anne.

I had told Marcy about Joe Dillon's religious education office and that he had several nuns and priests working with him. She said that she'd like to get out of teaching Catholic high school and wondered if Joe would like to have another person join him. When I got back to Wichita in August, I called Joe, and he said he'd like to meet her. Marcy asked if she could fly to Wichita and then have me take her to Oklahoma City to meet with Joe. She also asked if I could arrange for a place for her to stay. I arranged for her to stay at Anne's convent. When she arrived in Wichita, I took her and Anne to a nice restaurant in downtown Wichita. She knew about my visiting Anne at Notre Dame but did not know how close we were. At lunch, she kept looking at each of us in a knowing kind of way. On our trips to and from Oklahoma City, she asked me about my feelings for Anne.

I said, "We're good friends, that's all." At the time, I knew it was a bit of a lie, but not a big lie. I was fooling myself. While Joe interviewed Marcy, I took a nap in the office lobby. They both liked each other and made arrangements for her to join his office in September.

In September, my work in Wichita went on, and I became very busy teaching a class at the college, doing workshops, continuing with my duties at St. Pat's and working with the CFM, CCD, and CYO. I started planning to have a post-Christmas conference on religious education for all the religion teachers in the diocese. I also planned to have a six-week Lenten series of talks in as many parishes in and around Wichita as were interested. Six parishes and six speakers were interested. Anne was one of the speakers, and the topic she chose to talk on was Love as Jesus taught. I did my best to keep busy, so I would not spend too much time fantasizing about being with Anne.

Anne continued to be a wonderful help in nearly all of my projects. One Saturday in late October, after we had completed an all-day workshop for teachers, we put away our audio-visual equipment in the CCD office, and we started walking across the parking lot to the convent for dinner. In the middle of the empty parking lot, Anne stopped, and I took a couple of steps ahead of her. Noticing that she had stopped, I turned and saw her looking at me. In a very solemn voice, she said, "Don, I have something important to tell you." She sounded even a bit fearful.

I met her gaze and did my best to make serious eye contact. I was afraid she'd tell me that this had to be the last time she could help me with a workshop or something like that. Trying to match her seriousness, I replied, "Uh, okay, what is it?"

Very slowly and in a near whisper, she said, "Don, I love you."

The way she said it was so super serious and meaningful. If I didn't know earlier, I knew it then that she loved me in a very special way. At that moment, in that glorious moment, something exploded inside me, and it seemed like I split into a thousand pieces. I couldn't find the words to describe the depth of my feelings and shock. Part of me wanted to dance down the street like Gene Kelly in *Singing in the Rain* because I felt so excited and happy. Another part felt as scared as I could ever remember being, worrying she can't really mean it, she doesn't know me. Still another part of me said, "She can't love me like that because I'm a priest, and I can't love her back. Oh my God, what am I going to do? This moment is the biggest moment in my entire life!" Sister Nancy said she loved me, but she scampered away. Anne just said it and isn't running away. There she is standing, looking at me! This beautiful, warm, delightful, intelligent, kind, and wonderful woman says she loves me! Oh, my God! What will she think and what will she feel when she finds out what I'm really like? I was sure that there was a part that was still a worthless pile of shit.

All of this went through my head and my heart in a matter of seconds. Like the stupid idiot that I was, I said, "Uh, thank you." And I turned and walked toward the convent—no hugs, no hand holding, no real appropriate response at all. I was so shaken up— no one had ever said I love you like that before—ever. What do I do with that? I was sure that she was probably disappointed that I did not respond better, but she just slowly turned and walked to the convent.

Now, I know that moment, that glorious moment, when she said, "I love you," was the largest, most magnificent flowering rose in my life! On my way home to St. Pat's, I started singing, "It's a Big Wide Wonderful World."

Fifty-Two

LOVE BY ITS FIRST NAME

—⟨∞⟩—

In 1968, I visited Mom at Christmastime like I always did, and I went to Denver on Christmas Day. As was increasingly my preoccupation, I spent a great deal of time wishing Anne was with me. When I got back to Wichita, I finished setting up the needed presenters for the Religious Education Conference to be held in February.

Father Eugene Kennedy, a Jesuit professor at Loyola, Chicago, would be the keynote speaker. His field was psychology, and he had written books on the relationship between religion and humanistic psychology. I supposed he would be considered a free thinker to people like Bishop Maloney, but I doubted that he had read anything by him. So, on a Tuesday morning in January, I went into the bishop's office to inform him of my planned speakers. When I got to Kennedy, the bishop exploded, "I won't have that man in my diocese." He was almost as upset as the day he condemned me as a free thinker.

"Why not, bishop?" I asked as calmly as I could. I worked to be courteous, but I really wanted to yell back at him. Part of my anger was fueled by him saying *my* diocese—it was *our* diocese, and *he* was the visitor!

"I don't have to give reasons for my actions, now get out of my office."

I was furious but knew he saw himself as Gawd's (his pronunciation) representative on Earth. My protest consisted only of slamming the door on my way out and scaring the hell out of the bishop's secretary, whose desk was right outside his door. I stomped up to my office and called Joe in Oklahoma City.

"Hey, Joe," I said. "When I told you I wasn't certain I could get along with Maloney, you said that if things got too tight, I could come on down and join you. Were you joking?"

He assured me that he was not, and I promptly called Bishop Reed of the Oklahoma diocese, which consisted of the entire state. He had time to see me that afternoon, and I got in my car and headed south. During my three-hour trip I thought a great deal about whether or not I would want to leave the priesthood, a role that I had spent twenty years of blood, sweat, and tears getting to and five years being a priest. And if I did leave, would Anne leave her religious order and marry me? Maybe working as a priest in Oklahoma would give me time to think about it.

Bishop Reed was more like Bishop Carroll and a far more cordial man than Maloney. He said that Joe Dillon had called him and recommended me, so he was quite welcoming. I guessed that he probably knew a bit about the bishop of Wichita and what it might be like working for him.

When I got back to Wichita, the first person I told about my decision to go to Oklahoma was Anne.

Monsignor Cody didn't care. Dennis and Jane Dullea invited me to celebrate Mass at their home and told me to invite the people I felt closest to. I invited all the Sunday CFM couples and a few others and told them of my decision and why. As I was sharing my thoughts and feelings, I broke down and started bawling. I was leaving all the people I had grown to love and depend on whenever I felt defeated and down. I knew that I would miss them a lot. Two days later, and before I took my final leave, one husband who had attended the Mass told me that his wife had just had a premature baby, and she was being kept alive artificially. They wanted me to look at the baby and give them and the doctor the okay to pull the plug. I accompanied them to the hospital and took one look at the poor infant in the incubator, whose only working organ was the tiny heart. I didn't hesitate to tell them that the most loving thing to do was pull the plug. My last official priestly duty was to preside at a brief graveside funeral for the baby. I thought it was an ironic ending to my priestly career in the Wichita diocese.

I took another vacation and visited the family in Denver. No one seemed to give a thought about my moving to Oklahoma City, and that was okay with me. I visited my old seminary friend, Art Grant, who lived in Las Cruces, New Mexico. He was an officer in the Air Force and was married with two young children. While I was there, he paid a visit to the nearby air base, and I visited with his wife. She was an attractive brunette and seemed to enjoy being a mother, but not so much a wife. I told her a bit about my situation, but not about Anne nor my thinking about possibly leaving the priesthood. She told me her concern about Art: his habit of putting on his old black cassock and clerical collar and prancing around the house about once or twice a month. She asked if that was normal. I told her I didn't think it was and that if I were to leave the clerical world, I surely would not want to do that. I stayed overnight and drove back to Albuquerque and left my car in the long-term parking area.

I flew to California and visited brother Bill and his family. I borrowed his car and drove to San Diego to visit two priests I knew from the Loyola summer program. They were working on a doctorate in humanistic psychology and also working with Carl Rogers at his Center for the Study of the Person. Rogers was also on the faculty of the university. They both seemed to like what they were doing, and it seemed to be a very attractive option if I ever left the priesthood.

Back in Oklahoma City, Bishop Reed assigned me to be resident assistant at the downtown parish that had been the former cathedral. The rectory was over a hundred years old, but very comfortable. The pastor was older, friendly, and more than a little cynical. He thought priests like Joe were like Don Quixote—always chasing windmills, but basically harmless. I went to the religious education office each weekday and found something to do that I hoped would be helpful. Joe had liked my parish religious education handbook and asked me if I could revise it for the Oklahoma diocese. First, I would need to visit some parishes to familiarize myself with the diocese. So, I got busy and started driving around the diocese. One observation I made was that nearly all the rural parishes (those outside Oklahoma City, Tulsa, and a few smaller cities) were each staffed by one priest, and it seemed to me nearly all were depressed and drank too much—myself included. A few were liberal, more were moderate, and too many were so conservative they had nothing but disdain toward Joe and his damned office. My journeys did not lift my spirits.

In the spring, two associates at the religious education office, a priest and woman volunteer, resigned and got married. No one seemed to be surprised, as they seemed to be an item for some time. Soon after the two left, Joe called a meeting of the staff and announced that he planned to resign as the director and wanted to know who we, the staff, would recommend to replace him. He wanted to give our recommendation to the bishop. There were three priests and three nuns on the staff, and Joe said that he thought that any of us could do a better job than he had done. Of course, we all disagreed. He even recommended me and added that other organizations brought in leaders from outside the home agency to run things—even the church did that when they chose bishops. I was flattered but quickly stated that I did not want the position if it were offered because it would cause a lot of unneeded negative attention to the office, especially from the diocesan priests. I didn't mention that I was quite unsure how long I would stick around. We settled on recommending the two priests as co-directors—one for the Oklahoma City office and one for the Tulsa office—and we had them sitting there at our meeting. The bishop agreed and on June first, Joe was appointed pastor of St. Patrick's in Oklahoma City, and I was stationed with him as resident assistant. Shortly after I moved in, I headed for Loyola in Chicago to continue with my studies. Back at Loyola, I once again floated through the courses and activities.

At Thanksgiving, Anne went with me to visit Mom in the hospital. Mom had lost even more weight, and Patty said she weighed only ninety pounds. We were both worried about her.

A few days later, I was back in Oklahoma, and Patty called to tell me that Mom had died. It was late in the day, and I panicked. I just had to get to Denver. I called to see if there were any flights to

Denver and learned that the only flight would be mid-morning the following day. There was nothing I could do, but I couldn't shake the compulsion to get to Denver as quickly as possible. I quickly packed a small suitcase, jumped in my car, and left—it was 6:00 p.m.

The trip ordinarily took about ten hours, and so I had ten hours to explore my thoughts and feelings toward Mom and her death. I fought back tears the entire time, as I thought about how I had taken her presence in my life for granted. She was always there in my life. Even when I was not living with her, she was a gentle presence. I wished that she would have said "I love you" and "I'm proud of you," but I knew she did love me and was proud of me. As I drove along those nearly 600 miles, I realized that the greatest gift she and Dad had given me was just needing me—really needing me physically, emotionally, and spiritually. They gave my life purpose and kindled compassion in me. I was sure that I had let them down on the emotional help they needed because that didn't seem important to them or the family, but being needed was truly a gift.

I decided to celebrate the funeral Mass at the parish church where they lived. I asked one of my classmates from the seminary, Mike Kerrigan, to give the sermon. Mom's funeral was the third and last time all eight of us children were together at the same time and place. It was 1969. Patty told me that Mom had mentioned that she would like to be buried near our sister, Agnes. The Catholic cemetery had Agnes's burial on record and told us where to find it. We tromped all around the area, but never found it. We asked for a burial plot in the same general area as Agnes.

Mom's death had a very liberating effect on me that seemed to overshadow my feelings of loss. I think one of the unconscious reasons I was hesitant about leaving the priesthood was that it would disappoint Mom too much. Years later, I learned from two of my nieces that Mom would go on and on about her son, the priest, and that she was so proud of me! That was a meaningful flower.

In mid-January 1970, I was driving to the religious education office in Oklahoma City, and I followed a fellow who had a little boy standing in the front seat beside him as he drove (this is before seatbelts were mandatory). At every stoplight, the toddler would put his arm around his dad's neck, bend over, and give him a hug. After three rounds of this, I started crying, and I said to myself, "That's what I want. I want to be a dad."

That evening, when I was sure Anne would be home, I called her in Pueblo. When she answered, I said, "Anne, I have a very important question to ask you."

"Okay, what is it?"

"Will you marry me?"

After a long pause, I heard, "Yes, I will."

"Wonderful, wonderful!" And then we talked a while longer about the where and when and all that. I wanted to do it real soon, and she thought she should fill out her contract to the Pueblo diocese. So, we decided on late May. I announced that I was leaving at the following Sunday's Masses. I made an appointment to tell Bishop Reed. He asked me if I wanted to be laicized, i.e., reduced to the lay state. He seemed a bit upset when I said no and asked why not. I answered, "Because, Bishop, I don't believe that I was ever elevated out of it." He frowned and uttered, "Hurrumph."

I called Audra Huston to ask if I might return to Wichita and work for them for a few months. She said yes and offered that I could stay with them until I got married. I applied to the university I had visited in San Diego and was accepted into the doctorate program in human behavior. A few weeks later, I learned that the original mortgage on the property I had bought in 1951 was paid off, and I received the deed for the property. I sold the property for enough for me to pay for our wedding, living expenses and best of all, it would pay the tuition and all my expenses for my doctoral studies.

From what I could tell, the priests I knew who had left and gotten married just silently left with little notice. One of Anne's friends created a wedding announcement for our friends, relatives, and, most importantly for me, the priests of the Wichita diocese and a few in the Oklahoma diocese. We asked Father Bob Blanpied to officiate at our wedding and celebrated our union at the apartment of Jack Tesch in Colorado Springs, on May 22, 1970.

Epilogue

Of course, my entire life's story does not end with my marriage. I was married in 1970 at thirty-seven and in 2023 I will be ninety years old. In my first thirty-seven years, I lived in thirty-five places, and now I'm more settled and have lived in my present house in California for forty-six years. As I think back on my days as a priest, I believe, as some scholars do, that we are at one with God by our very creation. I like St. Bonaventure's idea, "The Creator's supreme power, wisdom, and benevolence shine forth in created things." By climbing into the mirror, I discovered my connections to all that is.

We true believers were told that we must obediently follow those higher than us in the church hierarchy or risk spending eternity in a place called hell. These administrators followed the Roman Emperors rather than the humble mystic named Jesus. I believe Jesus's message was simple, "Love your neighbor as you love yourself." And "Love one another as I have loved you." And to even be willing to die for those you love. I lost my faith in the church's structure, but not the basic teachings of Jesus.

The worst thing I did when I left Wichita was to take with me a terrible habit—I had become an alcoholic. Because of this,

I later was too often a very poor father and husband for thirty-some years. I am so grateful that Anne has stayed with me these fifty-two years. And I continue to feel ashamed of my drinking. Another shortcoming I brought to our marriage was always trying to be too independent, never learning to be with another person in a creatively close way—a real intimate way.

After that bishop demanded that I stop thinking, I went on to become a psychotherapist, college professor and administrator and, more importantly, a father of two wonderful girls. All the while, I listened to countless presentations on many topics. I have experienced a great deal and obtained information leading to all sorts of meanings. I believe I have learned from experiencing life, and only sidetracked when I just let it go on by, not even noticing all that was going on around me—including Anne and our girls.

I am grateful to all the wonderful, sincere, and hardworking men and women who work to help others to live healthy and meaningful lives. And I hope more of them will listen to their deeper spiritual selves and put aside non-life-giving moral precepts, such as many so-called natural laws on human sexuality such as birth control, masturbation, and such. I love another wonderful myth entitled, "Where Can We Hide the Truth from Humans?"

God's creative angels got worried when they realized that they had created humans that were so creative, intelligent, and wonderful that they (the lowly humans) might replace them near the throne of God. They began to discuss where they could hide this truth from humans. One angel said, "We'll hide it on the tallest mountain." Another said, "No, they'll climb to it." Another, "Let's hide it in the deepest part of an ocean." "No, they'll swim to it." They argued about it for days. Finally, one angel had the best idea. "Let's hide it in their hearts, then they'll doubt it!" And so, they did.

I believe that there is a loving and amazing being who is creating this vast and complex universe. Astronomer Carl Sagan once said, "There are more stars in the heavens than there are grains of sand on all the world's beaches. And the Universe is so vast and so complex that the human mind cannot begin to comprehend it." And I believe that the God that created this magnificent Universe is far more complex than the Universe—and our minds can only touch it.

Michelangelo's Sistine Chapel painting depicting God's finger touching the finger of Adam is the depiction of how we can come only within a finger-touch of knowing God in this lifetime. And that is okay. And even the journey of finding that may often be difficult. I hope you are on your own journey of hope and discovery!

The anthropologist, Angeles Arian, states that in many shamanic societies, if their fellow tribesmen and women came to the shaman suffering from depression, they would ask them these questions: "When did you stop dancing?" "When did you stop singing?" "When did you stop being enchanted with stories, especially your own?" I grow more aware and spiritual as I grow in my enchantment with my story—and yours. I hope you will grow more enchanted as you continue dancing and singing on your journey.

I think that the evolution of consciousness gives hope—for my own life and that of our human species on this evolving planet. After many false starts, detours, and roadblocks, I hope I have become a loving person. And I still have my doubts, and that, too, has to be okay because I must own my history. By writing these pages, I have found many flowers and I would like to end with this one. When one of our daughters was two and a half years old, she took my hand and said, "Daddy come see what I made!" She pulled me into the backyard, pointed, and said, "See!" She was pointing at a little pile of shit she had made. That was another flower, and I did not scold her but said, "Hey, punkin, that's great!" Now, go gently into the world and CREATE!

Acknowledgements

I want to thank many people who have helped and encouraged me on the writing of this memoir. First I want to thank my publisher Teri Rider who has been so very supportive of my work, and Chelsea Robinson who edited the writing and made many helpful corrections and suggestions. A special thanks to Ghada Osman for supporting me and my writing. I would like to thank many now deceased thinkers such as Teilhard de Chardin, Martin Buber, Abraham Maslow, Carl Rogers, Alice Miller and many others whose visions I have relied on for the ideas contained herein. Among the living, I would like to thank Micaela Myers, my daughter, Ed Coonce, Russ Shor, Patty Clark, Mary Boland-Doyle, Valerie Abney, and Marilyn Salisbury for their patience and helpful suggestions over the months of writing. And finally I want to thank Anne, my wife of 52 years, who said the magic words, "I love you," over 50 years ago and opened me to an entirely new and wonderful world.

About the Author

Don Hanley was born in 1933 during the Dust Bowl in Depression-devastated Nebraska. The tired and over-worked small town M.D. handed him to his older sister with the words, "Well, Maggie, here's another mouth to feed." Don's mother was struggling to stay alive after the difficult birth, and his father had already left for Kansas with Don's 6 other siblings. The family was dirt poor and their economic destitution was matched by their emotional depression as they settled in eastern Kansas.

Don's personality was one of immense curiosity which was not always viewed favorably by his parents and Catholic school teachers, especially as he puzzled over the question of God whom the nuns characterized as all-knowing and loving, but who seemed to Don to be mean and cruel. He emerged from his first two years of Catholic schools thinking that he was stupid, sinful, and worthless and, in his own words, "spent my life trying to prove to myself and the world that I was not a worthless human being."

Don is the only one of eight siblings to graduate from college. His four older brothers and many cousins, all from families of the working poor, said they went to the "School of Hard Knocks."

While Don's real life experience of priests and nuns was not a positive one, the depiction of priests in books and movies of the time was so inspiring that Don worked hard to become a priest so he could become SOMEBODY. He was ordained a priest in 1964 but within a few years, he realized that he could no longer support the Catholic Church's positions on condemning so many natural sexual actions as sinful and he longed to be married.

He fell in love with an intelligent young woman, married, and began to study Humanistic Psychology, earning a Ph.D. After years working as a college professor, administrator, and psychotherapist, he turned to writing: four non-fiction books on psychology and education and three novels. He hoped and still hopes that his writings will help many to be more self-accepting, kind, compassionate, and joyful.

www.ingramcontent.com/pod-product-compliance
Lightning Source LLC
Chambersburg PA
CBHW020917140626
46545CB00015B/80

9 781970 107395